Beginning AutoCAD R13 for Windows

Beginning AutoCAD R13 for Windows

Robert McFarlane MSc, BSc, ARCST, CEng, MIMech E, MIEE, MILog, MIED
Senior Lecturer, Department of Integrated Engineering, Motherwell College

A member of the Hodder Headline Group
LONDON • SYDNEY • AUCKLAND

To Linda and Gerry

First published in Great Britain 1996 by Arnold,
a member of the Hodder Headline Group
338 Euston Road, London NW1 3BH

Second impression 1997

British Library Cataloguing in Publication Data
A catalogue record for this book is available from the British Library

ISBN 0 340 64572 5

Produced by Gray Publishing, Tunbridge Wells, Kent
Printed and bound in Great Britain by The Bath Press, Bath

Contents

Preface   ix

1. Why AutoCAD Release 13?   1

2. System requirements and installation   2
   Hardware   Software   Installation   The author's system

3. Using the book   3
   Concepts of the book   Saving drawings

4. The graphics screen and terminology   4
   Starting AutoCAD R13   Terminology

5. Drawing and erasing   14
   Drawing lines   Blips   Oops   Erasing with a window/crossing
   The selection set   The pickbox   Summary

6. Limits and drawing aids   20
   Limits   Drawing aids   Grid spacing – keyboard entry
   Snap spacing – dialogue box   Toggling the grid/snap/ortho
   Summary

7. Save, exit and open   22
   Leaving R13   Saving a drawing   Opening a drawing
   The yes/no message options   Replacing an existing drawing
   Save versus Save As   Summary

8. Standard sheet 1   25

9. Line creation and co-ordinate input   27
   Absolute co-ordinate input   Relative co-ordinate input
   Polar co-ordinate input   Using all three inputs
   Grid-snap method   Rectangles   Saving the rectangles
   The co-ordinate system   Angle convention   Summary

10. Circle creation   33
    Centre–radius   Two points (on circle diameter)
    Three points (on circle circumference)   TTR: tangent–tangent–radius
    TTT: tangent–tangent–tangent   Saving the drawing   Summary

11. Object snap   37
    Opening the drawing   Using object snap from the keyboard
    Using object snap from the toolbar   Object snap from the menu bar
    Mixing the object snap selection methods   Running object snap
    Cancelling a running snap mode   Summary

12. User exercise 1   42
    What we did   What actually happened

13. Arc, donut and ellipse creation   45
    Arcs   Ellipses   True ellipses   Donuts   Solid fill   Summary

14. Fillet and chamfer   49
    Fillet   Chamfer   Saving   Some fillet/chamfer options
    Error messages   Summary

15. Offset, extend and trim   53
    Offset   Extend   Trim   Summary

16. Layers and standard sheet 2   59
    Getting started   The layer control dialogue box
    Linetypes   Linetype scale   Colour   Creating new layers
    The current layer   Saving the created layers   Layer icons
    Renaming and purging layers   Summary

17. User exercise 2   67
    Taking stock

18. Text   69
    Single line text   Dynamic text   Editing existing screen text
    Text justification   The TEXT selection option   Text style
    Summary

19. **Dimensioning** 75
*Dimension exercise   Linear dimensioning
Baseline dimensioning   Continuous dimensioning
Diameter dimensioning   Radius dimensioning
Aligned dimensioning   Angular dimensioning
Leader dimensioning   Dimension options
Dimension terminology   Summary*

20. **Dimension styles 1** 82
*Setting dimension style STDA3
Using the STDA3 dimension style   Ordinate dimensioning
Dimensioning small entities   Summary*

21. **Construct and modify** 87
*Getting ready for the exercise   Copy   Move   Transparency
Rotate   Scale   Multiple copy   Mirror   Summary*

22. **The selection set** 99

23. **Grips** 102
What do grips do?   How grips work   Types of grip   Summary

24. **Drawing assistance** 107
Point filters   Construction lines   Rays   Summary

25. **Viewing a drawing** 113
Pan   Zoom   Aerial view   Summary

26. **Hatching** 119
*User-defined hatch patterns – Select Objects option
User-defined hatch patterns – Pick Points option   Hatch style
R13's predefined hatch patterns   Associative hatching
Editing hatching   Hatching with text   Summary*

27. **Point, polygon and solid** 134
Point   Polygon   2D solid   Summary

28. **Polylines and splines** 138
*Polyline options   Line and arc segments   Spline curve
Summary*

29. **Modifying polylines and splines** 146
*The join option   Edit vertex option   Editing a polygon
Editing spline curves   Summary*

30. **Divide, measure and break** 153
Divide   Measure   Break   Summary

31. **Lengthen, align and Stretch** 156
*Lengthen   Dynamic lengthen   Align   Stretch
Keyboard dimensions   Summary*

32. **Enquiring into a drawing** 161
*Point identification   Distance   Area   Mass properties   List
Time   Status   Calculator   Transparent calculator   Summary*

33. **Text font and styles** 169
*Getting started   Creating text styles   Using created text styles
Text control codes   Paragraph text   Spellcheck
Editing paragraph text   Summary*

34. **The array command** 179
*Rectangular array   Polar array with rotation
Polar array without rotation   Polar array with partial fill angle
Using polar arrays   Angular rectangular array   User exercise 3
Summary*

35. **Changing properties** 185
*Several entities   Using properties   Single entity selection
Changing text   Summary*

36. **Dimension styles 2** 191
*Creating new dimension styles   Modifying the new styles
Using the customised dimension styles
Comparing dimension styles   Dimension variables
Problems with dimension styles   Tolerances and limits
Dimension families   Diameter family   Angular family
Geometric tolerancing   Tolerance frames   Applying tolerances
Adding user text to dimensions   Summary*

37. **Drawing to different sizes** 202
*Drawing in inches   Large-scale drawing   Small-scale drawing
Summary*

38. **Groups and filters** 207
Grouped objects   Object filters   Summary

39. **Multilines** 213
Using the default multiline   Editing multilines

40. Blocks   218
    Creating a block   Inserting a block   Exploding a block
    Block options   Using blocks   Layer 0 and blocks   Summary

41. WBLOCKS   228
    Creating WBLOCKS   Inserting WBLOCKS
    About WBLOCKS   Summary

42. Attributes   234
    Getting started   Defining the attributes
    Creating the attribute block   Testing the block with attributes
    Attribute information   Attribute example 2   Summary

43. Tool customisation   243
    Displaying a new toolbar   Summary

Tutorials   245

Index   273

Preface

So this is Release 13! So what?

This was my initial reaction when I installed the package onto my system. I soon found out that R13 is everything AutoDESK claimed it would be – it is fast and very user-friendly.

This book is intended for:

(a) new users to AutoCAD
(b) experienced AutoCAD users wanting to upgrade their skills to R13.

The objective of the book is to introduce the reader to the essential basic 2D draughting skills required by every Auto-CAD user, whether beginner or advanced. The book will prove invaluable to casual AutoCAD users, as well as the student studying any of the City and Guild CAD schemes. BTEC and SCOTVEC students will also be able to use the book in their courses. It will also be useful to undergraduates and post-graduates at higher institutions who require draughting skills. Industrial CAD users will be able to use this book both as a text book and a reference source.

As with all my AutoCAD books, the reader will learn by worked example and I have included some of my old tutorials (with some new twists in them) as back up material. All the drawings, figures and tutorials have been completed using R13 and have been checked to ensure there are no errors. If there are any mistakes in the text or the drawings, then I can assure you they are completely unintentional and I hope they do not spoil your CAD learning process. Any comments you would care to make would be more than welcome.

Good luck with 13, and remember – the more time you spend at AutoCAD, the better you will become.

1. Why AutoCAD Release 13?

AutoCAD Release 13 (R13) is a new draughting package and *not* an upgrade as previous releases. AutoDESK claim that R13 is 'the most powerful AutoCAD ever'. The package has many new concepts, some of which are:

❑ **Usability**
- user interface – organised for Microsoft Windows
- toolbars – multiple floating toolbars with flyouts and pop-up explanatory text to identify icons
- menus – extensive use of pull-down menus, dialogue boxes and toolboxes
- drawing preview – when opening a drawing.

❑ **Interoperability**
- object linking and embedding (OLE) – link and embed files from Windows software into AutoCAD R13 drawings and vice-versa
- external database links with an SQL interface
- file compatibility – upward and downward **.DWG** and **.DXF** file compatibility between AutoCAD R11, R12, R13 and LT.

❑ **Design and draughting**
- advanced 2D and 3D features for design, draughting and detail
- multiple parallel lines with text editing
- NURBS – non-uniform rational B-spline curves, true ellipses.

❑ **Construction and editing**
- UCS flexibility – less restrictive
- enhanced TRIM and EXTEND – greater flexibility
- new FILLET and CHAMFER enhancements
- object snap additions
- linetypes – addition of shapes and text to linetypes
- explode unequal scaled BLOCKS
- PURGE at any time.

❑ **Dimensioning**
- dimensioning standards – support for national standards
- geometric tolerancing – support for national symbol standards
- flexible styles and properties
- usability – automatic vertical or horizontal dimensions.

❑ **Hatching**
- associative hatching – automatic update as boundaries change
- editing of existing hatch patterns
- hatch enhancements – automatic island and text detection
- block hatching – areas with BLOCKS can be hatched.

❑ **Text editing**
- text formatting – effective support for multiline objects
- word processor – text control with dialogue-based word processing
- spellchecker – specific text or entire drawings can be checked
- font support – improved display quality.

❑ **Solid modelling**
- extrusions generated along a path
- conversion of some AME models into ACIS R13 geometry.

❑ **Rendering and visualisation**
- faster performance and enhanced image quality – improved efficiency and reduced rendering time
- materials library and editor – control of colour, ambient light and reflectivity with user-defined materials
- 3D studio compatibility – import and export .3DS files.

AutoCAD users will benefit from R13 with:
- increased productivity and creativity
- higher quality drawings and designs
- complete Windows integration.

2. System requirements and installation

The system requirements for AutoCAD R13 are given below.

Hardware

- 386/486/Pentium-based IBM or fully compatible PC – a 486 or Pentium is recommended
- maths coprocessor
- minimum 16 MB RAM – 24 MB is recommended
- minimum 35 MB RAM hard disk space
- permanent swap file of 64 MB
- Windows supported video display (VGA or better)
- Windows supported pointing device (e.g. mouse)
- Windows compatible printer/plotter.

Software

- Windows 3.1 or higher in enhanced mode
- MS DOS 5.0 or later.

Installation

Installing AutoCAD R13 is dependent on company/institution policy. The installation manual supplied by AutoDESK should be read and followed. When the package has been installed and Windows 'is run', AutoCAD R13 will be displayed on the screen in its own dialogue box with the following icons available for selection:

1. The AutoCAD R13 compass – the draughting package.
2. Quick tour.
3. What's new.
4. AutoCAD help.
5. AutoCAD release notes.
6. ADI release notes.
7. Network release notes.
8. Render release notes.
9. ASE/ASI release notes.

Before AutoCAD R13 is started, it is *highly recommended* that icons 2, 3 and 4 be investigated by all users. They contain useful information about using AutoCAD R13, as well as details about the new additions. An icon is 'activated' with a double-click on the mouse left-hand button.

The author's system

The system used by the author in the preparation of all drawing material was as follows:

- Elonex PC-466 with 16 MB RAM and 200 MB hard drive
- Elonex colour low-radiation SVGA monitor
- Microsoft two-button mouse
- Calcomp Designmate A1 plotter
- Brother A4 laser printer
- MS-DOS version 6.2 and Windows version 3.11
- The named directory for the AutoCAD R13 package was **ACADR13**.

3. Using the book

This book is intended to teach the reader how to use AutoCAD R13 by a series of interactive exercises. The exercises will be backed up by tutorials, allowing the reader to 'practice the new skills'. While no previous CAD knowledge is required, it would be useful if the reader knew how to use:

- the mouse to select screen items
- Windows packages:
  (a) maximise screens
  (b) exit windows packages.

Concepts for using the book

There are several simple concepts with which the reader should become familiar. These are:

1. Menu select will be in bold type, e.g. **Draw**.
2. A menu sequence will be in bold type and be either:
   (a) **Draw**   or (b) **Draw–Dimensioning–Linear.**
       Dimensioning
       Linear
3. User keyboard entry will also be highlighted in bold type, e.g.
   (a) co-ordinate input – **125,36; @100,20; @220<56**
   (b) command entry – **LINE; ZOOM; COPY**
   (c) response to a prompt – **15**.
4. Icon selection will be displayed as a small drawing of the icon where appropriate – usually the first time the icon is used.
5. The AutoCAD R13 prompts will be in typewriter face, e.g.
   (a) prompt `from point`
   (b) prompt `second point of displacement`
6. The symbol **<R>** or **<RETURN>** will be used to signify pressing the RETURN, ENTER or ↵ key. Pressing the mouse right-button will also give the **<RETURN>** effect – called right-click.
7. The term **pick** is continuously used with AutoCAD, and refers to selecting a line, circle, text item, etc. The mouse left-button is used to **pick an object** – called left-click.

Saving drawings

All drawings should be saved for recall at some later time should this be necessary. Drawings can be saved either:

- on a formatted floppy disk
- in a directory on the hard drive.

It is the user's preference as to which method is used, but it will be assumed that a floppy disk is being used. Thus when a drawing is saved or opened, the symbol **A:** will be used:

(a) save drawing as **A:WORKDRG**
(b) open drawing **A:EXER_1**.

If a directory is to be used, this can be made within the Auto-CAD R13 directory structure, or simply in the C: root directory. The directory name should be as simple as possible, e.g. **BOBR13**. The procedure for saving/opening drawings from a named directory is the same as from a floppy with the exception that both the *directory* and the *drawing name* must be specified:

(a) save drawing as **C:\BOBR13\WORKDRG**
(b) open drawing **C:\BOBR13\EXER_1**.

4. The graphics screen and terminology

Starting AutoCAD R13

AutoCAD R13 is started from Windows with a double-click on the AutoCAD R13 icon (a compass) with the mouse left-hand button. This results in the **INITIAL** graphics screen (Fig. 4.1) which displays the following:

1. The title bar.
2. The menu bar.
3. The standard toolbar.
4. The object properties toolbar.
5. The command window area.
6. The status bar.
7. Scroll bars.
8. The drawing area.
9. The co-ordinate system icon.
10. The on-screen cursor (cross-hairs).
11. The grip box at the cross-hair intersection.

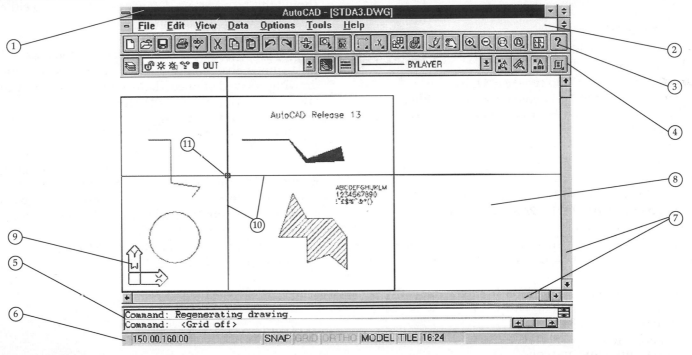

Fig. 4.1. Initial graphics screen.

Title bar

At the top of the screen between the left and right window icons. The title bar will display the current drawing name, or [UNNAMED] if no drawing file has been opened.

Menu bar

The first time that AutoCAD R13 is started, the menu bar displays the options shown in Fig. 4.1. By moving the mouse into the menu bar area, the cross-hair changes to a **pick arrow**. With a left-click on any option, a pull-down menu will be obtained offering further option selections to the user. Any pull-down menu can be cancelled by moving the pick arrow to the blank area at the right of the menu bar and left-clicking.

AutoCAD Release 13 has two pull-down menu options:
(a) a short menu – initial screen as Fig. 4.1
(b) a full menu – with additional pull-down menu options.

Generally most users will want the full menu, and all work in the book will be with this full menu. To 'load' the full menu, enter at the command prompt line **MENU <R>**
prompt   Select Menu File dialogue box with:
      1. File names
        (a) acad.mnu – the short menu
        (b) acadfull.mnu – the full (long) menu.
      2. Directory name
        c:\acadr13\win\support (or similar).
      3. Drive
        c:
respond 1. **Pick (left click) acadfull.mnu** and
        (a) it turns blue
        (b) it appears in the File Name box as Fig. 4.2.
      2. **Pick OK.**

The drawing screen is restored with the menu bar displayed the full menu options of:

File Edit View Draw Construct Modify Data Options Tools Help.

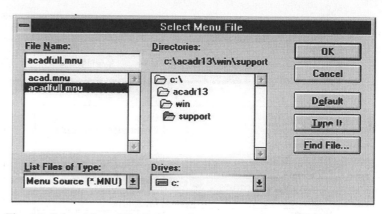

Fig. 4.2. Select Menu File dialogue box.

Figure 4.3 displays the full pull-down menu selection for four of the menu bar items, i.e. File, Draw, Modify and Options.

Your system may already have the full menu loaded, in which case the MENU sequence is not required. Once the full menu has been loaded, it will automatically be displayed until the short menu (acad.mnu) is loaded.

Notes

1. Pull-down menu items which display '...' result in a screen dialogue box when the item is selected.
2. Pull-down menu items displaying ▶ result in a further menu (cascade) when selected.
3. Menu items can be selected using the **Alt** key with the letter underlined, e.g.
    (a) Alt with C – the Construct pull-down menu
    (b) C – the Copy command
    (c) Esc key to cancel.

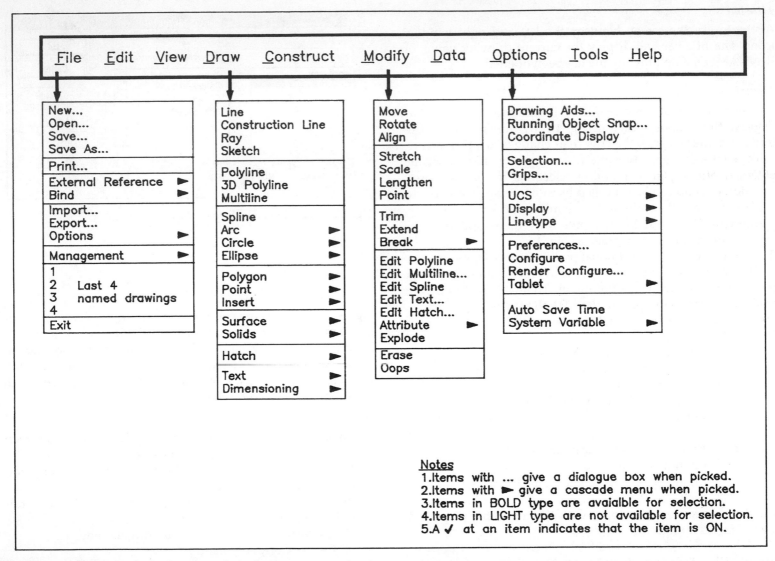

| File | Edit | View | Draw | Construct | Modify | Data | Options | Tools | Help |

File menu:
- New...
- Open...
- Save...
- Save As...
- Print...
- External Reference ►
- Bind ►
- Import...
- Export...
- Options ►
- Management ►
- 1
- 2   Last 4
- 3   named drawings
- 4
- Exit

Draw menu:
- Line
- Construction Line
- Ray
- Sketch
- Polyline
- 3D Polyline
- Multiline
- Spline
- Arc ►
- Circle ►
- Ellipse ►
- Polygon ►
- Point ►
- Insert ►
- Surface ►
- Solids ►
- Hatch ►
- Text ►
- Dimensioning ►

Modify menu:
- Move
- Rotate
- Align
- Stretch
- Scale
- Lengthen
- Point
- Trim
- Extend
- Break ►
- Edit Polyline
- Edit Multiline...
- Edit Spline
- Edit Text...
- Edit Hatch...
- Attribute ►
- Explode
- Erase
- Oops

Options menu:
- Drawing Aids...
- Running Object Snap...
- Coordinate Display
- Selection...
- Grips...
- UCS ►
- Display ►
- Linetype ►
- Preferences...
- Configure
- Render Configure...
- Tablet ►
- Auto Save Time
- System Variable ►

Notes
1. Items with ... give a dialogue box when picked.
2. Items with ► give a cascade menu when picked.
3. Items in BOLD type are avaialble for selection.
4. Items in LIGHT type are not available for selection.
5. A ✓ at an item indicates that the item is ON.

Fig. 4.3. Pull-down menus for four menu bar selections.

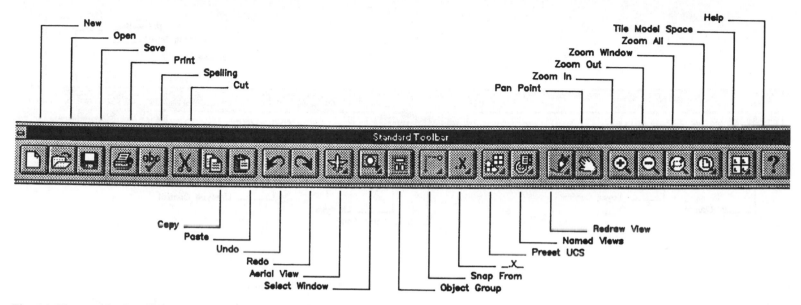

Fig. 4.4. The standard toolbar.

Standard toolbar

The standard toolbar is positioned just below the menu bar and allows the user access to 25 icon selections including open, save, redraw, zoom and help. Figure 4.4 identifies the 25 icons. By moving the cursor pick arrow to an icon and 'leaving it for about a second', the icon name will be displayed in yellow. The standard toolbar can be positioned anywhere on the screen or 'turned off' if required by the user.

Object properties toolbar

Positioned below the standard toolbar on the initial graphics screen. Figure 4.5 identifies the nine icon options. Again this toolbar can be moved to a screen position of the user's choice, or 'turned off'.

Command window area

The command area is where the user 'communicates' with R13 to enter:

(a) a command, e.g. LINE, ERASE, COPY, etc.
(b) co-ordinate data, e.g. 120,100; 50<30
(c) values, e.g. a radius of 23.

The area is also used by R13 to give information to the user, which could be:

(a) a prompt, e.g. from point
(b) a message, e.g. object does not intersect an edge.

The 'two line' command area can be increased in size using Windows techniques and it can also be moved to any position on the screen. My recommendation is to leave the command area at the bottom of the screen with its two line default.

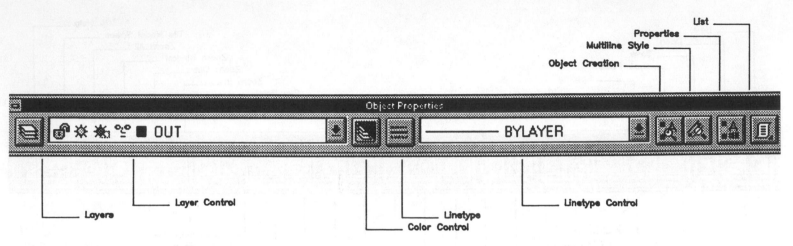

Fig. 4.5. The Object Properties toolbar.

Status line

Positioned at the bottom of the screen and gives the user information about drawing aids, e.g.

(a) on-screen cursor X and Y co-ordinates
(b) SNAP, GRID and ORTHO – ON or OFF
(c) Model or Paper Space
(d) the time.

Aids are active if in BLACK type, and inactive if in GREY type.

Scroll bars

Positioned at the left and bottom of the drawing area and used to scroll the drawing area. They are useful for larger sized drawings and can be 'turned-off' if they are not required.

The drawing area

This is the user's sheet of paper and can be 'sized' as required. The default paper size is usually A3.

Co-ordinate system icon

This is the X–Y icon at the lower left of the drawing area. This icon gives information about the co-ordinate system in use. The default system is the traditional Cartesian system with the origin (0,0) at the lower left-hand corner of the drawing screen. The icon (and origin) can be positioned anywhere on the drawing screen, and can also be 'turned-off' by selecting from the menu bar the sequence **Options-UCS-Icon** which removes the ON tick.

Cursor cross-hairs

Used to indicate the on-screen position and movement of the mouse will result in the co-ordinates in the status bar changing. The cross-hairs are also used to pick entities for editing.

Grip box

The small box attached to the cross-hairs is the grip box, used for grip selection. The box can cause confusion to new Auto-CAD users, and it is my experience that this box should be 'turned off'. This can be achieved with:

Enter	Prompt	Enter
PICKADD\<R>	New value for PICKADD\<1>	0\<R>
PICKFIRST\<R>	New value for PICKFIRST\<1>	0\<R>

Terminology

R13 terminology is basically the same as previous releases although there are a few new ideas. The following gives a brief description of the items commonly encountered when using R13.

Menu

A menu is a list of options from which the user selects (**picks**) that required for a particular task. Picking a menu item is achieved by moving the mouse over the required item and left-clicking. AutoCAD R13 has different types of menu including pull-down, dialogue box, cascade and screen.

Command

A command is an AutoCAD function used to perform some task. This may be to draw a line, rotate a shape or edit text. Commands can be activated by:
(a) selection from a menu
(b) selecting the appropriate icon from a toolbar
(c) entering the command at the prompt line
(d) entering the command abbreviation at the command line
(e) using the Alt key as described earlier.
Options (a) and (b) will be the main selection methods and option (c) will also be used. Options (d) and (e) will not be considered.

Entities

Everything drawn with R13 is an entity, e.g. lines, circles, text, dimensions, hatching, etc. Entities are also referred to as 'objects' and the user picks (left-click) the appropriate entity when prompted.

Default setting

AutoCAD R13 has certain values and settings which have been preset by AutoDESK and are essential for certain operations. These default settings are contained within < > brackets, but can be altered by the user as and when required. For example:
1. From the menu bar select **Draw**

               Polygon

               Polygon – yes two polygon picks

prompt   `_polygon Number of sides<4>`
respond   **Press the Esc key** to cancel the command.
Note: 1. <4> is the default value for the number of sides.
        2. _polygon is the activated command.
2. From the menu bar select **Options**

               Linetypes

               Global linetype scale

prompt   `ltscale New scale factor<1.0000>`
enter   **0.5\<R>**.
Note: 1. <1.0000> is the default value for the scale.
        2. We have altered the linetype scale to 0.5.
        3. _ltscale is the activated command.

The escape (Esc) key

This is used to cancel any command at any time, and is equivalent to the CTRL+C in other releases. It is a very useful option for the user, especially if they are 'lost in a command'. Pressing the Esc key will return the command prompt line.

Icon

An icon is a menu item in the form of a picture contained in a toolbar. Icons will be used extensively in this book.

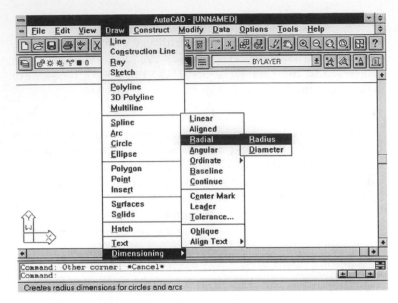

Fig. 4.6. Cascade menu.

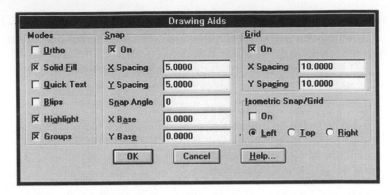

Fig. 4.7. Drawing Aids dialogue box showing: (a) grid ON and set to 10, (b) snap ON and set to 5, (c) blips, quick text, ortho OFF.

Cascade menu

A cascade menu is obtained when an item in a pull-down menu with ▶ after its name is selected, e.g. by selecting the sequence

Draw
Dimensioning
Radial

the cascade effect shown in Fig. 4.6. will be displayed. Cascade menus can be cancelled by:

1. Moving the mouse to the right of Help in the menu bar and left-clicking – the complete cascade menu is cancelled.
2. Pressing the Esc key – cancels the last cascade menu.
3. Clicking in the drawing area, if the grip pickbox is DEACTIVATED.

Dialogue boxes

A dialogue box (originally called a pop-up menu) is displayed when an item with '...' after its name is selected from a pull-down menu. By selecting from the menu bar **Options**

Drawing Aids...

the Drawing Aids dialogue box (Fig. 4.7) will be displayed. All dialogue boxes allow the user to alter parameter values, or 'toggle' an aid ON/OFF. Aids are toggled using the small box adjacent to their name and:

(a) an X in the box means that the aid is ON
(b) a blank box means that the aid is OFF.

Thus in Fig. 4.7, the drawing aids Snap and Grid are ON with the grid spacing set to 10 and the snap set to 5. The modes Ortho, Blips and Quick Text are OFF, while Solid Fill, Highlight and Groups are all ON.

This **X – on, blank – off** concept is common in dialogue boxes. Note the OK, Cancel, Help options at the bottom of the dialogue box. These are available in *all* dialogue boxes and are used as follows:

OK – accept the values in the current dialogue box

Cancel – cancel the dialogue box without altering the 'set' values

Help – gives information about the dialogue box displayed in a 'Windows screen' and usually allows access to other help information. The help screen can be cancelled with File-exit or Close.

Toolbars

Toolbars are aids for the user. They allow the R13 commands to be displayed on the screen in the form of icons. The required command is activated by picking the appropriate icon. There are 17 toolbars available to the user and two are already displayed in the drawing area, these being the Standard toolbar and the Object Properties toolbar. Toolbars can be:

(a) displayed and positioned anywhere in the drawing area
(b) customised to the user preferences.

To activate a toolbar select from the menu bar **Tools–Toolbar–Draw.** The Draw toolbar with ten icons will be displayed on the screen. The icon commands will be displayed in yellow by moving the pick arrow onto an icon. Figure 4.8 shows the drawing screen with the toolbars for Draw, Modify and Dimensioning. When toolbars are positioned in the drawing area as shown they are called **FLOATING** toolbars.

Toolbars can be:

(a) moved to a suitable position on the screen by the user. This is achieved by moving the pick arrow into the blue title area of the toolbar and holding down the mouse left button. Move the mouse to the required position and release the left button.
(b) altered in shape by 'dragging' the toolbar edges
(c) cancelled by picking the 'Cancel box' to the left of the title bar.

Generally only toolbars should be displayed which will be used in the drawing, i.e. if the drawing is not being dimension-

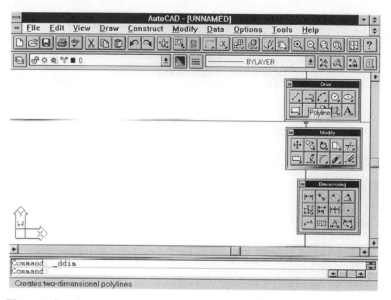

Fig. 4.8. Graphics screen with three floating toolbars.

ed, why have the dimensioning toolbar displayed? It can easily to displayed when required, and stops the drawing area becoming 'cluttered with toolbars'.

Toolbars can be **DOCKED** to the edges of the drawing area by moving them to these edges. The toolbar is automatically docked when the edge is reached. Figure 4.9 shows the Draw, Modify and Dimensioning toolbars with:

(a) Draw toolbar docked at the left of the drawing area.
(b) Modify toolbar docked at the right of the drawing area.
(c) Dimensioning toolbar docked at the top of the drawing area.

Toolbars *do not have to be used* – they are a user aid. All commands are available from the menu bar. It is recommended that toolbars are used, as they greatly increase draughting

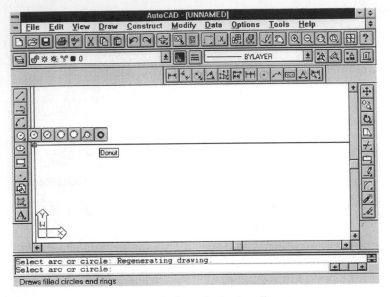

Fig. 4.9. Graphics screen with three docked toolbars.

speed and efficiency. If they are used, it is user preference if they are left floating or are docked.

Fly-out menu

When a toolbar icon is picked (left-click), a command is executed. If an icon is picked which has a ◢ at the lower right corner of the icon box, and the left button on the mouse held down, a **FLY-OUT** menu is obtained. Fly-out menus contain further icon selection options. By moving the pick arrow (while still holding down the left button) to another icon then releasing the button:

(a) the selected icon command is activated
(b) the selected icon is positioned in the toolbar
(c) the fly-out disappears.

Figure 4.10 shows a fly-out menu from the Circle icon (a) as a Floating toolbar (b) as a Docked toolbar.

Screen menu

The initial R13 drawing screen does not display an on-screen menu. R13 has the ability to display an on-screen menu and this can be obtained by selecting from the menu bar **Options –Preferences...**

prompt   Preferences dialogue box
respond 1. Click at screen menu (i.e. X in box).
         2. Remove X at scroll bars.
         3. Pick OK.

The on-screen menu will be displayed at the right of the screen and there will be no scroll bars – Fig. 4.11. Note that the screen menu items are the same as the menu bar items, and different from other Releases. On-screen items are activated by moving the mouse over the required item and left clicking. It is user preference as to whether the on-screen menu will be used but no on-screen menu will be used in the book.

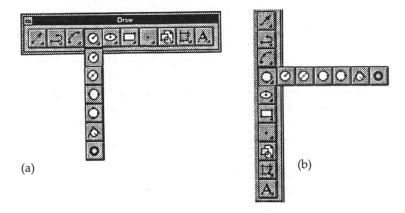

(a)　　　　　　　　　　　　　　　　(b)

Fig. 4.10. Fly-out Circle menu from the Draw toolbar. (a) Floating. (b) Docked.

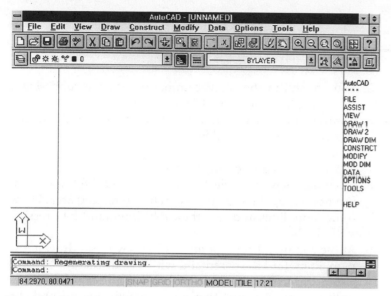

Fig. 4.11. Graphics screen with on-screen menu and no scroll bars.

Function keys

Several of the keyboard function keys can be used as aids while drawing, these keys being:
  F1: Calls the Help menu
  F2: Flips between the Text and Graphics windows (screens)
  F4: Tablet calibration
  F5: Isoplane toggle (top/right/left) – for isometric drawings
  F6: Co-ordinate toggle
  F7: Grid toggle
  F8: Ortho toggle
  F9: Snap toggle
  F10: Status bar toggle.

Toggle

The phrase for an aid being turned ON/OFF, and usually refers to pressing a key, e.g. the grid aid is toggled ON by pressing the F7 key, and turned OFF by pressing the F7 key again. It can also refer to the X – ON, BLANK – OFF effect in a dialogue box.

Drawing files

When a drawing has been completed it should be saved for future recall and all drawings in R13 are called *files*. They must be given a name when they are saved, and there is a simple protocol to remember when naming files:
(a) maximum name is eight characters long
(b) spaces and full stops (.) cannot be used
(c) avoid AutoCAD words
(d) names should be allocated which are meaningful.
  Consider the following drawing file names:

DRG_1	acceptable
DRG.1	unacceptable due to (.)
dRg1	acceptable
drg 1	unacceptable due to space
DRAwing1	acceptable
DRAWING-1	unacceptable due to too many characters
**1	acceptable.

All users should keep a note of their drawing file names, with a brief description of each drawing.

5. Drawing and erasing

In this chapter we will investigate how to draw and erase lines with an exercise given as a sequence of steps. We will use different methods to activate commands, and then investigate the Selection Set, which is a powerful aid when editing screen entities.

Drawing lines

1. Start R13 with a double left-click on the compass icon.
2. Customise the graphics screen to your preference. The following is a recommendation only:
   (a) no screen menu and no scroll bars
   (b) full menu in the menu bar
   (c) Draw, Modify and Select Objects toolbars, floating at the right of the drawing area (**Tools–Toolbars–Draw**, etc. to display).
3. Activate the LINE icon from the Draw toolbar and observe the prompt line.
   The prompt is `_Line From point`
   You now have to pick a **start** point for the line to be drawn, so move the mouse and pick (left-click) any point on the screen. Several things should happen:
   (a) a small cross *may* appear at the start point of the line – if it does not, don't panic
   (b) as you move the mouse away from the start point a line is dragged from this point to the on-screen cursor position. This drag effect is called the **RUBBERBAND**.
   (c) the prompt is: `To point`.
4. Move the mouse to any point on the screen and left-click. Another cross may appear at the picked point and a line will be drawn between the two picked points on the screen **This is your first R13 entity.**

5. You are still in the LINE command with the rubberband effect and still being asked for the line endpoint.
6. Continue moving the mouse and pick points on the screen to give a series of 'joined lines'.
7. Finish the LINE command with a right-click on the mouse and the Command prompt will be returned.
8. From the menu bar select **Draw–Line** and the From point prompt will again be displayed in the command area. Draw some more lines and end the LINE command by pressing <RETURN>.
9. At the command prompt enter **LINE**<R> and draw a few more lines. End the command with a right-click.
10. Using the icon, menu bar or keyboard entry draw lines until you are satisfied that you can activate and end the command.

Blips

Several users may have small crosses at the end of the lines drawn on the screen. These crosses are called **BLIPS** and are used by R13 to identify the start and end points of lines, circle centres, etc. They are *not entities* and will not be plotted on the final drawing. Personally I find them a nuisance and always turn them off. This can be achieved by selecting from the menu bar **Options**
   Drawing Aids...
   Blips box no cross, i.e. OFF
   OK
If you do not want to turn the blips off, then by selecting the REDRAW icon from the Standard toolbar, the drawing screen is regenerated and the blips are removed.

Erasing lines

Now that we have drawn some lines on the screen, we will investigate how they can be erased (seems daft!). The erase command will be used to demonstrate different options available to us when editing a drawing. The actual command can be activated by the following three methods:

(a) picking the Erase icon from the Modify toolbar

(b) selecting from the menu bar **Modify**

Erase

(c) entering **ERASE**<R> at the command line.

Before continuing with the exercise, select from the menu bar **Options–Selection...** to display the Object Selection Setting dialogue box. Ensure that the following are set:

Noun/verb setting   OFF, i.e. blank box
Use shift to add   OFF
Press and drag   OFF
Implied windowing   ON, i.e. X in box
Object groups   ON
Set box size to suit
Pick OK when altered.

We will now continue with the erase exercise.

1. Ensure you still have several lines drawn on the screen – Fig. 5.1.

2. Pick the ERASE icon from the Modify toolbar and the prompt displays `Select objects`. The cursor cross-hairs will be replaced by a 'pickbox', which moves as you move the mouse.

3. Position the pickbox over one of the drawn lines and left-click. Two things will have happened:
    (a) the selected line 'changes appearance'
    (b) the prompt displays `select objects: 1 found` then `Select objects`.

4. Continue picking other lines to be erased (about six) and each line picked will change appearance.

5. When enough lines have been picked, right-click the mouse.

6. The selected lines will be erased and the Command prompt is returned (Fig. 5.1b).

Oops

Suppose that you had erased the wrong lines. Before you do anything else, select from the menu bar **Modify**

Oops.

The erased lines will be returned to the screen. Consider this in comparison to a traditional draughtsman who has rubbed out the wrong lines.

OOPS can also be entered directly from the keyboard. The command will only work if it is used immediately after the erase command (or any other editing type command).

Erasing with a window/crossing

Individual selection of entities is satisfactory if only a few lines have to be removed. When a large number of entities require to be edited, the individual selection method is very tedious. AutoCAD R13 overcomes this by allowing the user to position a 'window' over an area of the screen which will select several entities 'at the one pick'.

To demonstrate the window effect, ensure that you have about 20 lines on the screen then:

1. Refer to Fig. 5.1(c) and select the ERASE icon from the Modify toolbar and

prompt   `Select objects`
respond   **Select the Window icon from the Select Objects toolbar**
prompt   `First corner`
respond   **position the cursor at a suitable point and left-click**
prompt   `Other corner`
respond   **Move the cursor to drag out a window (rectangle) and left-click**
prompt   `???  found` and certain lines highlighted

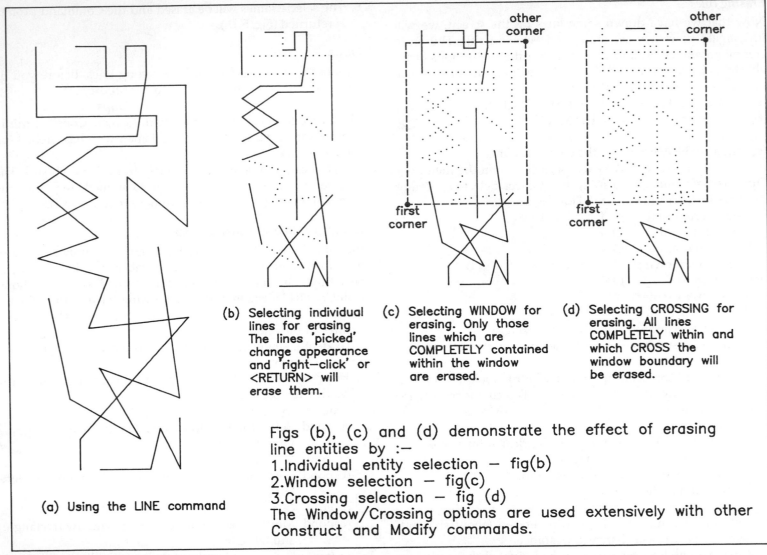

(b) Selecting individual lines for erasing The lines 'picked' change appearance and 'right-click' or <RETURN> will erase them.

(c) Selecting WINDOW for erasing. Only those lines which are COMPLETELY contained within the window are erased.

(d) Selecting CROSSING for erasing. All lines COMPLETELY within and which CROSS the window boundary will be erased.

(a) Using the LINE command

Figs (b), (c) and (d) demonstrate the effect of erasing line entities by :-
1. Individual entity selection - fig(b)
2. Window selection - fig(c)
3. Crossing selection - fig (d)
The Window/Crossing options are used extensively with other Construct and Modify commands.

Fig. 5.1. Drawing and erasing line entities.

then   `Select objects`

respond **Right-click or <RETURN>**

The highlighted entities will be erased.

2. From the menu bar select **Modify–Oops** to restore the erased lines then select from the menu bar **Modify**

                              Erase

prompt   `Select objects`

respond From the menu bar select **Edit**

                       Select Objects

                       Crossing

prompt   `First corner`

respond **pick a point on the screen**

prompt   `Other corner`

respond **drag out a window and pick the other corner**

prompt   `??? found` and highlighted lines

then   `Select objects`

respond **Right-click** to erase the highlighted entities – Fig. 5.1(d).

3. The window/crossing concept of selecting a large number of entities will be used frequently with other editing type commands, e.g. erase, copy, move, rotate, etc. The entities are selected as follows:

window – all entities *completely* within the window are selected

crossing – all entities completely within and *also which cross* the window boundary are selected.

4. The window/crossing option can be activated by:
   (a) picking the icon from the Select Objects toolbar
   (b) selecting Select Objects from the menu bar
   (c) entering **W** or **C** at the command line at the prompt.

5. Figures 5.1(c) and (d) demonstrate the window/crossing effect with the erase command.

The selection set

Window and crossing are only two options contained within the selection set. The complete set can be obtained from the Select Objects toolbar or from menu bar with **Edit–Select Objects**. At this stage we will investigate three further selection set options.

1. Erase all entities from the screen.
2. Draw some lines similar to Fig. 5.2(a) – size is unimportant.
3. Refer to Fig. 5.2(b), select the ERASE icon from the Modify toolbar and:

prompt   `Select objects`

respond **Select the Fence icon from the Select**
              Objects toolbar

prompt   `First fence point`

respond **pick a point** (point 1)

prompt   `Undo/<Endpoint of line>`

respond **pick a suitable point** (point 2)

prompt   `Undo/<Endpoint of line>`

respond **pick points 3, then 4, then 5, then right-click**

prompt   `??? found` and certain lines highlighted

then   `Select objects`

respond **Right-click** and highlighted lines are erased.

4. Select **Modify–Oops** to restore the previous erased lines.
5. Refer to Fig. 5.2(c) and from the menu bar select **Modify– Erase** and

prompt   `Select objects`

respond from the menu bar select **Edit–Select Objects– Window Polygon**

prompt   `First polygon point`

respond **pick point 1**

prompt   `Undo/<Endpoint of line>`

respond **pick points 2,3,4,5 then right-click**

prompt   `??? found` and highlighted lines

then   `Select objects`

respond **Right-click** to erase the highlighted entities.

6. Enter **OOPS**<R> at the command line.

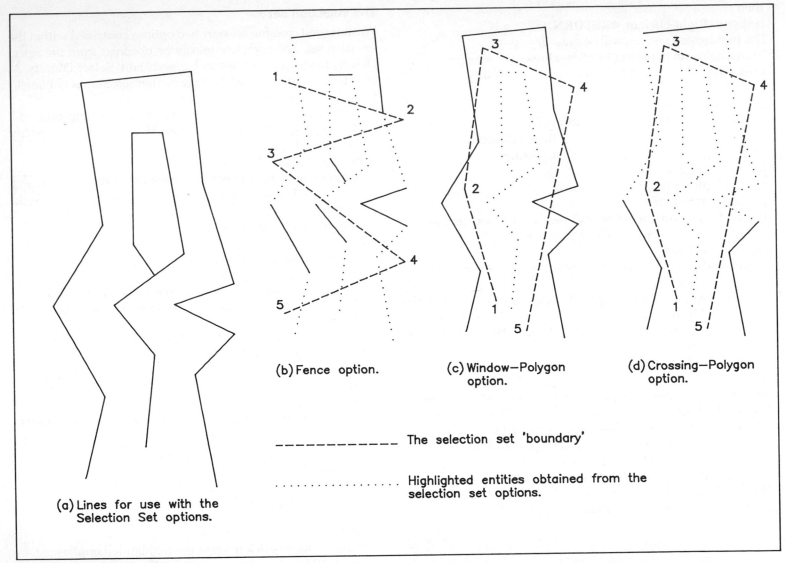

(a) Lines for use with the Selection Set options.

(b) Fence option.

(c) Window—Polygon option.

(d) Crossing—Polygon option.

— — — — — — — — The selection set 'boundary'

. . . . Highlighted entities obtained from the selection set options.

Fig. 5.2. Further Selection Set options.

7. Select the icons:
   (a) ERASE from the Modify toolbar
   (b) Crossing Polygon from the Select Objects toolbar and repeat step 5. Pick points similar to before to give the effect as Fig. 5.2(d).
8. The Fence/Window Polygon/Crossing Polygon options are very useful when the 'shape' to be edited does not permit the use of the normal rectangular window. With these three options, the user can 'make their own shape' for editing.

The pickbox

When using the ERASE command, the user positions a PICK-BOX over the entities to be selected. The 'size' of this box may be 'too big' and can be altered by:

(a) at the command line entering **PICKBOX**<R>
   prompt   New value of PICKBOX<?>
   enter   **3**<R>
(b) selecting from the menu bar **Options–Selection...**
   prompt   Object Selection Settings dialogue box
   respond   alter Pickbox Size to suit using the Min/Max arrows
   then   pick OK.

It is the user's preference as to the size of the pickbox, but I usually prefer to set it to 3 or 5.

Activity

Spend some time using the LINE and ERASE commands and become proficient with the various selection set options for erasing. Investigate both the toolbar and menu bar methods for activating the two commands as well as the selection set options. It is in your own interest to be able to use the selection set options, as they will be used extensively in later chapters.

❏ *Summary*

1. The LINE command can be activated:
   (a) using the LINE icon from the Draw toolbar
   (b) from the menu bar with **Draw–Line**
   (c) by entering **LINE**<R> at the command line.
2. The ERASE command can be activated:
   (a) using the ERASE icon from the Modify–Erase toolbar
   (b) from the menu bar with **Modify–Erase**
   (c) by entering **ERASE**<R> at the command line.
3. The ERASE command allows the user access to a **SELECTION SET**.
4. The selection set has several options, which include fence, window, crossing, window polygon, crossing polygon, last.
5. The selection set options can be activated:
   (a) using the appropriate icon from the Select Objects toolbar
   (b) from the menu bar with **Edit–Select Objects**
   (c) by entering the letter(s) at the command line, e.g. F, W, C, WP, WC, L.
6. The term WINDOW, refers to all entities completely contained within the window boundary.
7. CROSSING includes all entities which cross the window boundary and are also completely within the window.
8. The selection set options are available with all editing type commands.
9. **OOPS** is a useful command which 'restores' the previous command.
10. **BLIPS** display the start and end points of lines to the user. They are *not* entities and can be 'turned off' using the Drawing Aids dialogue box.
11. **REDRAW** is a command which will 'refresh' the screen and remove both BLIPS and any 'ghost image' from the screen. The REDRAW command is best activated using the icon from the Standard toolbar.
12. The editing PICKBOX size can be altered at any time by the user to suit the screen size which is current.

6. Limits and drawing aids

Now that we know how to draw and erase lines, we will investigate how to set our drawing limits, and how drawing aids can be activated to assist the user. Hopefully you are still in AutoCAD R13, but if you are not, start it with a double left-click on the icon from the Windows menu.

Limits

1. Erase all entities from the screen – easy?
2. Move the mouse to the lower left-hand corner of the drawing area to the upper right-hand corner and observe the screen co-ordinates displayed in the status bar at the bottom of the screen. Did the co-ordinate values alter? If they did not, press the F6 function key to toggle the co-ordinates ON.
3. My co-ordinate values changed from (0.0000,0.0000) at the lower left, to about (595.0000,295.0000) at the upper right. If your co-ordinate values are different from mine, don't worry.
4. From the menu bar select **Data**
                                Limits
   prompt   `Reset Model space limits`
   then   `ON/OFF/<lower left corner><??????>`
   enter   **0,0**<R>
   prompt   `Upper right corner<??????>`
   enter   **420,297**<R>.
5. From the menu bar select **View–Zoom–All.**
6. The drawing screen has been set to A3-size paper, and as you move your mouse, you should now get co-ordinate values similar to those in step three. It may be that your screen was already set to A3 paper, in which case the steps entered were really unnecessary.
7. We will investigate smaller/larger paper in a later chapter.

Drawing aids

R13 has three useful drawing aids which are:

Grid   allows the user to put a series of imaginary dots over the drawing area. The grid spacing can be altered by the user at any time while the drawing is being created. As the grid is imaginary, it does *not* appear on the final plot.

Snap   allows the user to set the on-screen cursor to a predetermined point on the screen, this usually being one of the grid points. The snap spacing can also be altered by the user at any time.

Ortho an aid which allows only horizontal and vertical movement.

   The grid and snap spacing can be set:
1. From the Drawing Aids dialogue box.
2. Using keyboard entry.

Grid spacing – keyboard entry

At the command line enter **GRID**<R>
prompt   `Grid spacing(X) or ON/OFF/Snap/Aspect<?>`
enter   **10**<R>.

   A series of dots will appear over on area of the screen, these dots being 10 mm apart and covering the 420 × 297 area set with the LIMITS command.

Snap spacing – dialogue box

From the menu bar select **Options–Drawing Aids** and:

prompt   Drawing Aids dialogue box

with   (a) X at grid: ON

          (b) Grid spacing: 10

respond 1. No X at Blips: OFF.

         2. X at Snap: ON.

         3. Snap spacing: 5.

         4. OK.

If you now move your mouse, you will find that the on-screen cursor 'snaps' to:

(a) a grid point

(b) a point midway between any two grid points.

Toggling the grid/snap/ortho

The three drawing aids can be toggled ON/OFF with:

1. The function keys: F7 – grid; F8 – ortho; F9 – snap.
2. The Drawing Aids dialogue box: X – ON; blank – OFF.
3. Double-left click on the aid name in the Status bar.

Note

1. My preference is to set the grid and snap values from the dialogue box, then use the function keys to toggle ON/OFF.
2. Take care with the ORTHO drawing aid. As it only allows horizontal and vertical movement, line drawing may not be as expected. I tend to work with ortho off.

Activity

You are now in the position to try a drawing for yourself, so:

1. Erase any entities from the screen and refer to Tutorial 1.
2. Set a grid to ten and a snap to five.
3. Use the LINE (and perhaps ERASE?) command to draw some simple shapes as shown. The size and layout does not matter, the object of the exercise being to let you practice with the drawing aids.
4. When you have had enough, proceed to Chapter 7.

❏ *Summary*

1. Drawing limits can be set for any paper size, including A3, A2, A1 and A0.
2. The three drawing aids (grid, snap, ortho) can be toggled ON/OFF using the function keys or the Drawing Aids dialogue box.
3. The grid and snap spacing value can be set from the Drawing Aids dialogue box or by keyboard entry.

7. Save, exit and open

It is essential that *all* users know how to save and open a drawing, and how to exit AutoCAD R13 correctly. In my experience, both in industry and education, these operations cause new users to CAD a great deal of concern. This chapter will explain how the three operations can be achieved quite easily. Make sure that you have:
1. A formatted floppy disk in the A: drive.
2. The Tutorial 1 drawing on the screen.

Leaving R13

Having created our first AutoCAD R13 drawing (Tutorial 1) we now want to leave AutoCAD, so from the menu bar select **File–Exit**. In response to this selection, AutoCAD R13 displays the Message dialogue box as shown in Fig. 7.1 with:
(a) `? Save Changes to UNNAMED?`
(b) `Yes, No, Cancel` options.
This dialogue box will be encountered quite frequently, and it is important that all users understand the replies that are pos-

sible. The dialogue box is informing the user that since starting R13 there have been changes to the drawing screen. It is also asking if these changes have to be saved. The responses are activated with a left-click and are:
1. Yes – saves the current screen drawing using the stated name.
2. No – exits R13, but the drawing changes will not be saved.
3. Cancel – returns the drawing screen – nothing has been changed.
At this stage **left-click on Cancel**.

Saving a drawing

All R13 users should note that: *drawings should be saved before exiting AutoCAD*. This is a very simple statement and if you practice what it says it will stop you losing drawings. At this stage we *have not saved* the Tutorial 1 drawing created in the previous chapter.
1. From the menu bar select **File**
                  Save As...
prompt Save Drawing As dialogue box (Fig. 7.2)
with   the following 'areas':
      1. The file name to be saved box.
      2. The previously saved drawing files column.
      3. The current directory.
      4. Other available directories.
      5. The drives – current and available.
      6. List of file types.
      7. A preview area.
      8. The Type it box.
      9. OK and Cancel options.

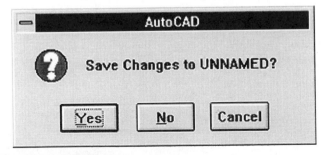

Fig. 7.1. Save Changes message dialogue box.

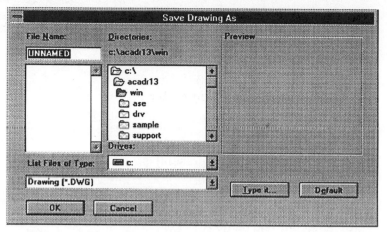

Fig. 7.2. Save Drawing As dialogue box.

respond **pick the Type it ... box**
prompt dialogue box disappears
and `Save Drawing As<UNNAMED>`
enter **A:TUT-1<R>**
prompt `Current drawing name set to A:TUT-1`
and `Command line returned.`
2. Now **File–Exit** from the menu bar to leave R13 – no message box?
3. You should be returned to your Windows program manager.

Note

1. There are other methods of saving a drawing. These will be discussed in later chapters. For now, the Type it option will be used.
2. Readers who are using a hard drive directory to save their work, should enter drive, directory and drawing name at the Save Drawing As prompt, e.g. **C:\BOBR13\TUT-1**.

Opening a drawing

To load a previously saved drawing into R13, it is necessary to 'open a drawing file', so:
1. Start R13 from Windows.
2. Ensure the floppy with the saved drawing is in the A: drive.
3. From the menu bar select **File**
Open...
prompt Select File dialogue box which has a similar layout to the Save Drawing As dialogue box
respond **pick the Type it ... box**
prompt dialogue box disappears
and Enter name of drawing
enter **A:TUT-1<R>**
4. The saved drawing will be displayed, and is available for editing.
5. Readers with a hard drive directory should enter **C:\BOBR13\TUT-1**.

The yes/no message options

Add a few lines to your TUT-1 drawing then select **File–Exit** from the menu bar. The AutoCAD message box will be displayed, but this time if you pick:
(a) Yes – the modified drawing will be saved as A:TUT-1 and will 'overwrite' the original A:TUT-1 drawing
(b) No – the modified drawing will not be saved, and the original A:TUT-1 drawing will be 'untouched'.
Cancel the Message box.

Replacing an existing drawing

1. From the menu bar select **File–Save As...–Type it...** and:

   prompt   `Save Drawing As<A:\TUT-1>`

   enter   **A:TUT-1**<R>

   prompt   `A drawing with this name already exists`
            `Do you want to replace it?<N>`

   enter   **N**<R>.

2. This means that we do not want to save the modifications as A:TUT-1 and allows us to enter another drawing name if required.

Save versus Save As

The menu bar selection of **File** allows the user to select either Save or Save As. The reader should be aware of the difference between these two options:

Save – will save the current screen drawing with the name with which it was opened. It automatically overwrites the original drawing of the same name.

Save As – allows the user to enter a drawing name. If a drawing exists with the entered name, a warning is displayed on the screen.

Task

Exit AutoCAD R13. Decide for yourself if any alterations to the A:TUT-1 drawing have to be saved.

❏ *Summary*

1. The recommended procedure for exiting AutoCAD is:
   (a) complete the drawing
   (b) save the drawing
   (c) File–Exit AutoCAD R13.
2. The SAVE procedure (at present) is:
   (a) select File–Save As...
   (b) pick Type it...
   (c) enter drawing name A:????????
3. The OPEN procedure (at present) is:
   (a) start R13
   (b) select File–Open ...
   (c) pick Type it...
   (d) enter drawing name A:????????
4. Other SAVE/OPEN methods will be discussed later.

8. Standard sheet 1

Traditionally the first thing that a draughtsperson does when starting a new drawing is to get the correct size sheet of drawing paper. This paper will probably have borders, a company logo and other details already printed on it. The drawing is completed to fit 'into' the preprinted material. CAD draughting is no different from this, with the exception that the user does not 'get a sheet of paper'. Companies who use AutoCAD R13 will want their drawings to conform to their standards in terms of name box, text size, linetypes, dimension styles, etc. Parameters which govern these factors can be set every time a drawings is started, but this is tedious and is against CAD philosophy. It is desirable to have all standard requirements set automatically, and this is achieved by making a drawing called a *standard sheet* or *prototype drawing* – you may have other names for it. Standard sheets can be made to suit all sizes of paper, e.g. A3, A2, A1, A0 as well as any other size required, and will contain the company/customer requirement/individual settings. It is this standard sheet which is the CAD draughtspersons 'sheet of paper'.

We will create an A3 standard sheet, save it, and use it for future work. At this stage, the standard sheet will not have many 'settings', but we will continue to refine it and add to it as we progress through the book.

As with all our work, the procedure is given as a sequence of easy steps.

1. Start AutoCAD R13.
2. Standard and Object Properties toolbars, docked at top.
3. From the menu bar select **Data–Drawing Limits** and set:
   (a) lower left corner: 0,0
   (b) upper right corner: 420,297.
4. Select **View–Zoom–All** from the menu bar.

5. Using the **Options–Drawing Aids...** dialogue box set:
   (a) blips: OFF, i.e. No X in box
   (b) snap: ON with 5 spacing
   (c) grid: ON with 10 spacing
   (d) ortho: OFF
   (e) highlight: ON.
6. Enter **PICKBOX** at the command line, and set it to 3.
7. Disable the grips box from the command line with:
   enter   **GRIPS**<R>
   prompt   New value for GRIPS<?>
   enter   **0**<R>
   enter   **PICKFIRST**<R>
   prompt   New value for PICKFIRST<?>
   enter   **0** <R>
   Grips will be discussed in a later chapter.
8. Select from the menu bar **Options–Preferences...** and use the dialogue box and:
   (a) pick System – Screen Menu: OFF
       Scroll Bars: OFF
       Automatic Save: 30 mins
   (b) pick International – Measurement: Metric
       Drawing Type: Metric/ISO Size A3
   (c) pick OK.
9. From the menu bar select **Data–Units...**
   prompt   Unit Control dialogue box (Fig. 8.1)
   respond (a) decimal units to 0.00 precision, i.e. two decimal
             places
         (b) decimal degrees for angles to 0.0 precision
         (c) direction: East 0.0
         (d) counter-clockwise positive (Fig. 8.2)
         (e) remember OK.

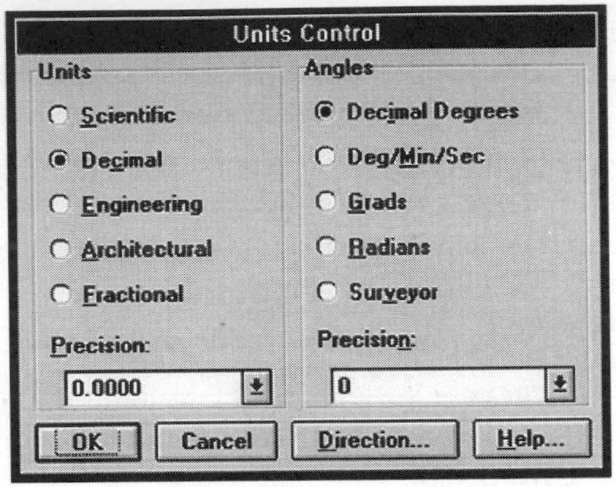

Fig. 8.1. Units Control dialogue box.

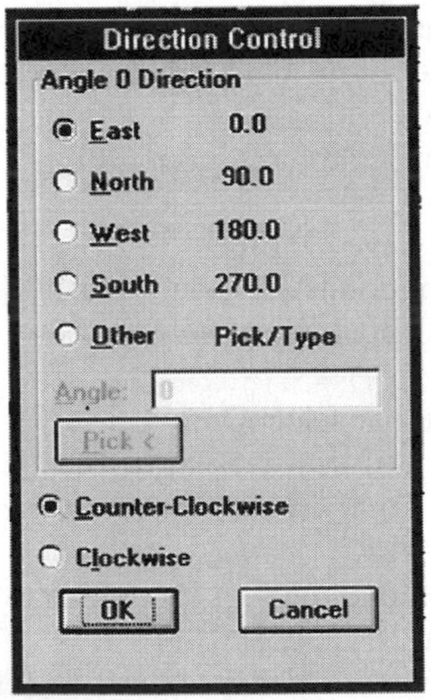

Fig. 8.2. Direction Control dialogue box.

10. Using **Tools–Toolbars** position the Draw, Modify and Select Objects toolbars floating towards the right of the screen grid.
11. Select **Options–UCS–Icon** (no tick) to remove the icon at the lower left of the screen.
12. Use the LINE command with:
    prompt   From point and enter **0,0**<R>
    prompt   To point and enter **380,0**<R>
    prompt   To point and enter **380,270**<R>
    prompt   To point and enter **0,270**<R>
    prompt   To point and enter **c**<R>.
    These lines give a 'border effect' on the A3-size paper. All drawings will be created within this border. The border is not drawn to the 'limits' due to plotting restrictions.
13. From the menu bar select **File**
                            Save As...
                            Type it...
    prompt   Save Drawing As<UNNAMED>
    enter   **A:STDA3**<R>
    prompt Current drawing name set to A:STDA3
14. We have created an A3 standard sheet with units, grid, snap, screen layout set to our own preference. This standard sheet will be used for all future drawing work, although it will be updated as we progress through the book.

9. Line creation and co-ordinate input

The lines created in Chapter 5 were drawn at random on the screen without any attempt being made to specify position or line length. To draw lines (and any other entity) accurately, co-ordinate input is used and there are three 'types' available:

1. Absolute input.
2. Relative (incremental) input.
3. Polar (incremental) input.

In this chapter we will use our standard sheet to create several rectangles (size 75 × 50) using the different co-ordinate methods. To start the exercise:

1. Load AutoCAD R13.
2. Ensure a floppy disk is in the drive.
3. From the menu bar select **File–Open...**
   prompt   Select File dialogue box
   respond **pick Type it...**
   prompt   Enter drawing name
   enter   **A:STDA3**<R>
4. This will display our previously saved standard sheet.
5. Toolbars as required.
6. Now refer to Fig. 9.1.

Absolute co-ordinate input

This is the traditional Cartesian system, the origin being positioned at the lower left-hand corner of the drawing area with the co-ordinates (0,0). This origin point can be moved by the user, but this will be investigated in a later chapter.

Select the **LINE** icon from the Draw toolbar and in response to the prompts, enter the following X–Y co-ordinate pairs, pressing <RETURN> or right-click after each entry: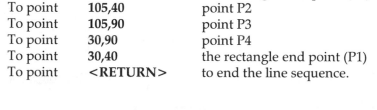

From point	**30,40**	the rectangle start point (P1)
To point	**105,40**	point P2
To point	**105,90**	point P3
To point	**30,90**	point P4
To point	**30,40**	the rectangle end point (P1)
To point	**<RETURN>**	to end the line sequence.

Relative co-ordinate input

Takes co-ordinates from the **last point** entered, and uses the @ symbol for incremental sizes. From the menu bar select **Draw–Line** and enter the following X–Y co-ordinate pairs in response to the prompts, remembering right-click/<RETURN>:

From point	**150,30**	rectangle start point
To point	**@75,0**	
To point	**@0,50**	
To point	**@–75,0**	
To point	**@0,–50**	rectangle end point
To point	**right-click**	to end line sequence.

The @ symbol has the following effect:

(a) @75,0 is 75 units in the positive X direction and 0 units in the Y direction from the last point, which is 150,30
(b) @0,–50 is 0 units in the X direction and –50 units in the negative Y direction (i.e. downwards) from the last point on the screen.

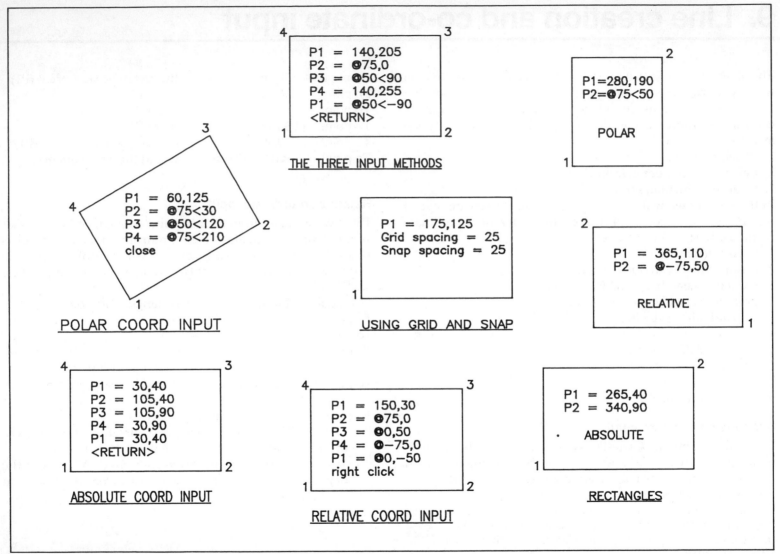

Fig. 9.1. Line creation using different methods

Polar co-ordinate input

Also allows co-ordinates to be specified relative to the last point entered and uses the @ symbol, but also introduces angular input using the < symbol.

Activate the LINE command (icon or menu bar?), then enter the following co-ordinates:

From point	60,125	rectangle start point
To point	@75<30	(note: no comma)
To point	@50<120	
To point	@75<210	
To point	enter C<R> to close the rectangle and end the line sequence.	

These entries can be read as follows:
(a) @75<30 is 75 units at an angle of 30° from the last point, which is 60,125
(b) @50<120 is 50 units at an angle of 120° from the last point. Note the entry C<R> is the **CLOSE** option which:
1. Closes the rectangle, i.e. a line is drawn from the current screen position to the start point of the shape. This will work for all straight sided shapes.
2. Ends the line sequence.

Using all three inputs

The three co-ordinate input methods (absolute, relative, polar) can be used in the one line sequence. Select the LINE command, then enter the following (remembering <RETURN>/right-click):

From point	140,205	absolute
To point	@75,0	relative
To point	@50<90	polar
To point	140,255	absolute
To point	@50<−90	polar
To point	right-click	ends sequence.

Grid-snap method

The grid and snap are drawings aids, and can be 'set' by the user to any value suitable to the current drawing. From the menu bar select **Options–Drawing Aids...** and:
(a) set the grid spacing to 25
(b) set the snap spacing to 25
(c) use the LINE command with a start point of **175,125**, and visually draw a 75 × 50 rectangle.
(d) set the grid spacing back to 10, and the snap spacing back to 5.

Rectangles

This is a useful command which allows the user to create rectangular shapes by specifying two points on a diagonal of the rectangle. It can be used with absolute and relative co-ordinate input.

Absolute input

From the menu bar select **Draw**
                          Polygon
                          Rectangle

prompt	First corner	
enter	265,40<R>	
prompt	Other corner	
enter	340,90<R>	to give a 75 × 50 rectangle.

Relative input

Select the rectangle icon from the Draw toolbar and:
prompt First corner and enter **365,110**<R>
prompt Other corner and enter **@−75,50**<R>

Polar input

Activate the rectangle command and enter **280,190** as the first corner. In response to the other corner prompt, enter @**75<50**<R>. This will give a shape which is not a 75 × 50 rectangle, i.e. the polar input for the 'other corner' is not correct.

Task

Can you work out the correct entry for a perfect 75 × 50 rectangle using polar co-ordinates for the 'other corner' using 280,190 as the first corner? Some trig is needed!

Saving the rectangles

Your drawing should now have eight rectangle shapes positioned as Fig. 9.1 (but with no text). This drawing must now be saved as it will be used in other chapters, and it will be given the name **DEMODRG**.

From the menu bar select **File–Save As...** and:
prompt Save Drawing As dialogue box
respond **pick Type it...**
prompt `Save current drawing as <A:STDA3>`
enter   **A:DEMODRG**<R>
prompt `Current drawing name set to A:\DEMODRG`
The above procedure is only one method of saving a drawing, and others will be discussed as we progress through the book. The following points are worth noting:

1. We opened a drawing as **A:STDA3** – our standard sheet.
2. We created several rectangles.
3. The **Save As...** option displayed the dialogue box with the default file name as <A:STDA3>, i.e. the name of the 'opened drawing'.
4. The **A:DEMODRG** entry as the file name to be saved, means that the created entities will be saved with this drawing name. The original A:STDA3 standard sheet will thus be 'untouched'.

The co-ordinate system

The terms 'co-ordinates' and 'angles' have been used in the construction of the rectangles without any explanation of their meaning. The X–Y axis convention used in AutoCAD R13 is shown in Fig. 9.2 and displays four plotted points with their co-ordinate values.

As an added exercise, erase all entities from the screen (making sure you have saved the rectangles) and then use the LINE command with:

From point	20,30
To point	–40,50
To point	–60,–70
To point	50,–60
To point	C.

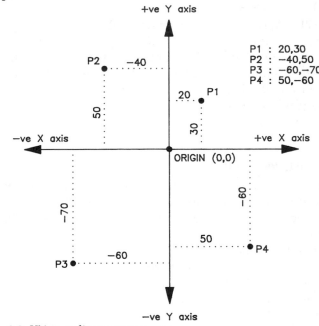

Fig. 9.2. *XY* co-ordinate system.

This will result in two line segments being drawn near the origin point (lower left of screen). By selecting **View–Zoom–All** from the menu bar, the four lines will be 'seen'.

When using the normal X–Y co-ordinate system:

(a) a positive X direction is to the right and a positive Y direction is upwards

(b) a negative X direction is to the left, a negative Y direction is downwards.

Angle convention

When using polar co-ordinates, the < symbol is used to signify angular input and

(a) positive angles are anti-clockwise

(b) negative angles are clockwise.

Figure 9.3 shows four lines drawn from the origin using polar entry. Using the LINE command, enter the following:

1. From point 0,0   To point 30<30.
2. From point 0,0   To point 50<130.
3. From point 0,0   To point 60<–130.
4. From point 0,0   To point 70<–60.

These four lines should be drawn in the 'zoomed all' screen from the previous exercise.

Task

Exit AutoCAD R13, thinking carefully about the response to the message box prompts. Do you want to save the changes made since the drawing was last saved? The answer is *no*! Why *no* and not *yes*?

Activity

This activity will be completed with the LINE command only (and possibly ERASE?), so:

1. Start AutoCAD R13.
2. Open your A:STDA3 standard sheet using the Type it option.

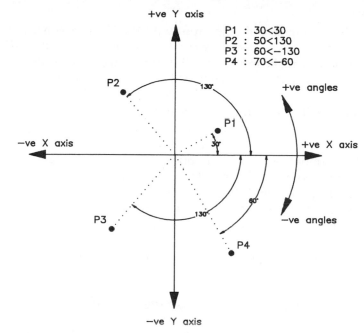

P1 : 30<30
P2 : 50<130
P3 : 60<–130
P4 : 70<–60

Fig. 9.3. Angle convention.

3. Refer to Tutorial 2 and draw the three template shapes using co-ordinate input. Any entry method can be used but my recommendations are:
   (a) position the start point with absolute entry
   (b) use relative entry as much as possible.
4. When the drawing is complete, save it using:
   (a) File–Save As...
   (b) Type it...
   (c) enter A:TUT-2 as drawing name.
5. Exit AutoCAD, read the summary and proceed to the next chapter.

Note

1. When using co-ordinate input with the LINE command, it has been my experience that new users to AutoCAD frequently make mistakes with their entries. If you enter co-ordinates, and the drawn line 'does not go in the direction it should', then simply enter **U<R>** at the keyboard or pick the **UNDO** icon from the Standard toolbar. This will remove the last line drawn on the screen. You can then enter the correct co-ordinates.

2. The symbol @ is useful if you want to 'get to the last point referenced on the screen'. Try the following:
   (a) draw any single line on the screen
   (b) end the line sequence with a right-click
   (c) reactivate the line command
   (d) enter @<R> at the keyboard
   (e) cursor 'snapped' to the end of the last line drawn?

❏ *Summary*

1. Co-ordinate input can be **absolute**, **relative** or **polar**.
2. ABSOLUTE entry is from the origin – the point (0,0). Positive directions are UP and to the RIGHT, negative directions are DOWN and to the LEFT. The entry format is always x,y, e.g. 30,–40, i.e. 30 units in the positive x direction and –40 units in the negative y direction.
3. RELATIVE entry refers to co-ordinates to the *last point entered,* and uses the @ symbol to achieve this. The entry format is @x,y, e.g. @–50,60, i.e. 50 units in the negative x direction and 60 units in the positive y direction from the last point entered.
4. POLAR entry also refers co-ordinates to the last point entered, and uses the @ symbol as well as the < symbol for angular entry. The format is @$x<a$, e.g. @50<60, i.e. 50 units at an angle of 60° from the last point.
   Note that there is *no comma* with polar entry.
5. An angle of –45° is the same as an angle of +315°.

6. The following polar entries are the same:
   (a) @–50<30
   (b) @50<210
   (c) @50<–150.
7. All three co-ordinate input methods can be used in the same line sequence.
8. A line sequence can be terminated (stopped) by:
   (a) using the <RETURN> key
   (b) right-clicking on the mouse
   (c) 'closing' the shape.
9. The rectangular command is useful, but care must be taken with the second set of co-ordinates.
10. The LINE command can be activated by:
    (a) ICON selection
    (b) menu bar selection
    (c) command entry.
    It is the user's preference as to what method is used.

10. Circle creation

In this chapter we will investigate how circles can be created by adding several to the rectangles created in the previous chapter.

1. Start AutoCAD R13 and from the menu bar select **File–Open...** then from the Open File dialogue box:
   (a) pick Type it...
   (b) enter **A:DEMODRG**<R> at the prompt
2. The drawing of the rectangles should be displayed with toolbars? It may be however, that your drawing will *not* display the toolbars which were active when the drawing was saved. This would mean that someone else had used AutoCAD R13 and altered the drawing screen from when you last used it. This is common and there is no need to worry – you simply reactivate the required toolbars.
3. Refer to Fig. 10.1 and:
   (a) activate the Draw and Modify toolbars
   (b) erase the 'smallest' rectangle.

AutoCAD R13 allows circles to be created by six different methods, the user specifying:
   (a) the circle centre point and radius
   (b) the circle centre point and the diameter
   (c) two endpoints on a diameter of the circle
   (d) any three points on the circle circumference
   (e) two tangent points and a radius
   (f) three tangent points.

The circle command can be activated by:
   (a) menu bar selection
   (b) icon selection
   (c) command line entry.

When drawing circles, absolute co-ordinates are usually used to specify the circle centre, although the next chapter will introduce the user to the Object Snap modes. This allows greater flexibility in selecting existing entities.

Centre–radius

1. From the menu bar select **Draw**
   Circle
   Center,Radius
   prompt `3P/2P/TTR<Center point>`
   enter **65,65**<R>
   prompt `Diameter/<Radius>`
   enter **20**<R>
2. Select the Circle Center, Radius icon from the Draw toolbar and:
   prompt `3P/2P/TTR<Center point>`
   enter **200,55**<R>
   prompt `Diameter/<Radius>`
   enter **25**<R>

Two points (on circle diameter)

From the menu bar select **Draw–Circle–2 Points** and:
   prompt `First point on diameter`
   enter **215,205**<R>
   prompt `Second point on diameter`
   enter **215,255**<R>

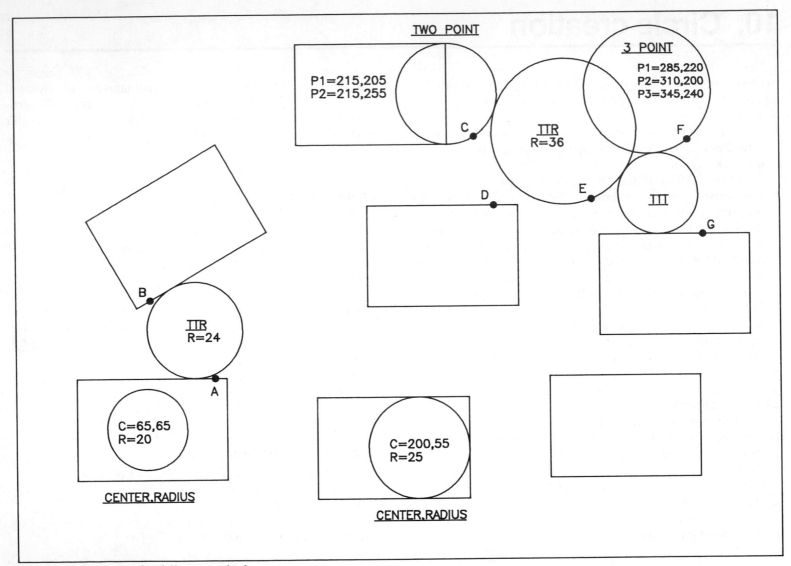

Fig. 10.1. Circle creation by different methods.

Three points (on circle circumference)

From the Draw toolbar:
1. Pick the circle icon and hold down the left button.
2. Move the cursor to the Circle 3 Point icon.
3. Release the left button and:
   (a) the Circle 3 Point icon is in the Draw toolbar
   (b) the 3 point command is activated

   prompt First point and enter **285,220<R>**
   prompt Second point and enter **310,200<R>**
   prompt Third point and enter **345,240<R>**

TTR: tangent–tangent–radius

This method allows the user to select two entities (lines, circles, arcs, etc.) which will be tangent to the circle to be created, and then specify the radius of the circle.

1. From the menu bar select **Draw**

   Circle

   Tan,Tan,Radius

   prompt Enter Tangent spec
   respond **pick line A**
   prompt Enter Tangent spec
   respond **pick line B**
   prompt Radius<?>
   enter **24<R>**

2. From the Draw toolbar select the Circle fly-out and pick Circle,TanTanRad icon: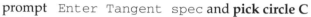

   prompt Enter Tangent spec and **pick circle C**
   prompt Enter Tangent spec and **pick line D**
   prompt Radius and enter **36<R>**

This circle is interesting as it is tangent to the circle but not the line. AutoCAD R13 assumes that the tangent spec line is extended, and draws the circle tangent to this extended line.

TTT: tangent–tangent–tangent

Allows a circle to be drawn which is tangent to three entities specified by the user.

From the menu bar select **Draw-Circle-Tan,Tan,Tan** and:
prompt First point: tan to
respond **pick circle E**
prompt Second point: tan to and **pick circle F**
prompt Third point: tan to and **pick line G.**

Saving the drawing

At this stage your drawing should resemble Fig. 10.1 (without the text) and is ready to be saved for future modification. From the menu bar select **File–Save As...** and:
prompt Save Drawing As dialogue box with File name DEMODRG
respond **pick OK**
prompt Replace existing file message box – Fig. 10.2
respond **pick Yes.**
The DEMODRG is saved and the command prompt is returned.

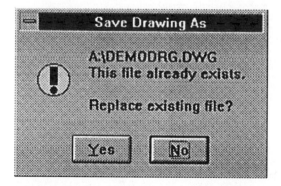

Fig. 10.2. Replace drawing message.

Activity

Open your A:STDA3 standard sheet and attempt Tutorial 3. It can be completed with only the LINE and CIRCLE commands (and ERASE?). The method of construction is at your discretion, but remember that absolute co-ordinates are best suited for the start point and then relative co-ordinate entry should be used to complete the shape. You may require some 'sums' for certain circle centres, although most are created with TTR or TTT. When the tutorial is complete, save it as A:TUT-3.

❑ *Summary*

1. Circles can be drawn by six different methods, the user specifying:
   (a) the centre point and radius
   (b) the centre point and diameter
   (c) two endpoints on a diameter
   (d) any three points on the circle circumference
   (e) two tangent points and a radius
   (f) three tangent points.
2. The tangent–tangent options can be used with lines, circles and arcs.
3. The centre point can be obtained by:
   (a) co-ordinate input
   (b) picking a point on the screen
   (c) referencing existing entities – see the next chapter.
4. The radius can be obtained by:
   (a) keyboard entry
   (b) pick any point on the screen
   (c) referencing existing entities.

11. Object snap

The lines and circles drawn so far have been created by co-ordinate input. While this is the basic method of creating entities, it is often desirable to reference entities already drawn on the screen, e.g. we may want to draw a circle with its centre at the midpoint of an existing line, or draw a line from the centre of a circle perpendicular to another line. These types of operations are achieved using the **object snap modes** – often referred to as OSNAP – and they are one of the most useful draughting aid.

Object snap modes are used **transparently**, i.e. while in another command, and they can be activated:
(a) from the Object Snap toolbar
(b) from the menu bar
(c) by direct keyboard entry.
While the toolbar icon selection method is the quickest to use, we will investigate the other two methods.

Opening the drawing

To demonstrate the use of the object snap modes, we will use our DEMODRG of the rectangles and circles, so:
1. Start AutoCAD R13
2. From the Standard toolbar select the OPEN icon and:
    prompt   Select File dialogue box
    respond (a) select the drive arrow
             (b) pick the **a:** drive
             (c) pick **demodrg.dwg** from the list and:
                  (i)   it turns blue
                  (ii) it appears in the File Name box
                  (iii) a preview of the drawing is displayed as Fig. 11.1.
             (d) pick OK.

3. The A:DEMODRG of the rectangles and squares will be loaded.
4. Activate the Draw, Modify and Object Snap toolbars using Options–Toolbars from the menu bar. Position these toolbars towards the right of the drawing screen.
5. The Object snap toolbar icons are detailed in Fig. 11.2, while Fig. 11.3 displays the menu bar selection method.
6. I suggest that you toggle the SNAP OFF during these exercises.
7. Refer to Fig. 11.4

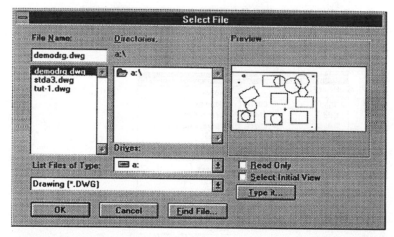

Fig. 11.1. Select File dialogue box.

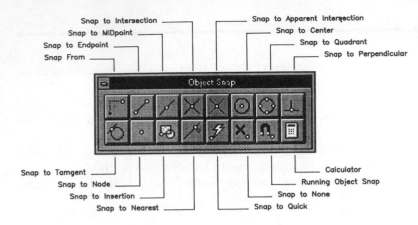

Fig. 11.2. The Object Snap Toolbar and icon description.

Labels around the toolbar:
Snap to Intersection
Snap to MIDpoint
Snap to Endpoint
Snap From
Snap to Apparent Intersection
Snap to Center
Snap to Quadrant
Snap to Perpendicular
Object Snap
Snap to Tamgent
Snap to Node
Snap to Insertion
Snap to Nearest
Calculator
Running Object Snap
Snap to None
Snap to Quick

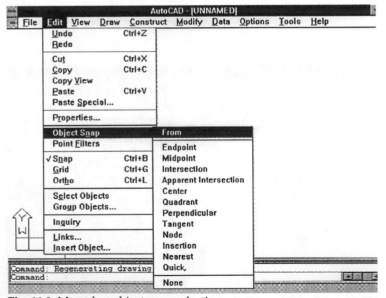

Fig. 11.3. Menu bar object snap selection.

38 *Beginning AutoCAD R13 for Windows*

Using object snap from the keyboard

The first example will draw two line segments using keyboard entry, so activate the LINE command and:

prompt   From point
enter   **MID\<R>**
prompt   of
respond   **pick line d1**
prompt   To point
enter   **CEN\<R>**
prompt   of
respond   **pick circle d2**
prompt   To point
enter   **PER\<R>**
prompt   to
respond   **pick line d3**
prompt   To point
respond   **right-click** to end LINE sequence.

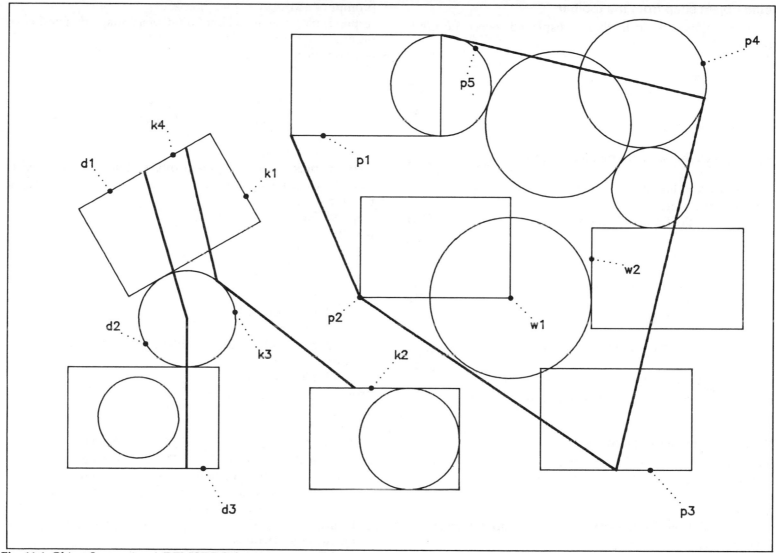

Fig. 11.4. Object Snap using A:DEMODRG drawing.

Using object snap from the toolbar

Ensure the Object Snap toolbar is displayed, select the LINE icon and:

prompt   From point
respond **pick the Snap to Endpoint icon**
prompt   endp of
respond **pick line p1**
prompt   To point
respond **pick the Snap to Intersection icon**
prompt   int of
respond **pick point p2**
prompt   To point
respond **pick the Snap to Midpoint icon**
prompt   mid of
respond **pick line p3**
prompt   To point
respond **pick the Snap to Tangent icon**
prompt   tan to
respond **pick circle p4**
prompt   To point
respond **pick the Snap to Quadrant icon**
prompt   qua of
respond **pick the circle p5**
prompt   To point and right-click to end sequence.

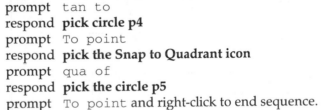

Object snap from the menu bar

This time we will create a circle using the object snap modes, so activate the circle (cen,rad) command and:

prompt   Circle centre
respond pick from menu bar **Edit–Object Snap–Intersection**
prompt   int of
respond **pick point w1**

prompt   Radius
respond pick from menu bar **Edit–Object Snap– Perpendicular**
prompt   per to
respond **pick line w2.**

Mixing the object snap selection methods

The three selection methods can be used in the one sequence, so select the LINE command and:

prompt   From point
respond **pick Snap to Apparent Intersection icon** from the Object Snap toolbar
prompt   appint of
respond **pick line k1**
prompt   and
respond **pick line k2**
prompt   To point
enter   **TAN<R>**
prompt   to
respond **pick circle k3**
prompt   To point
respond pick from menu bar **Edit–Object Snap–Nearest**
prompt   nea to
respond **pick line k4**
prompt   To point and right-click.

Notes
1. At this stage your drawing should resemble Fig. 11.4.
2. Save the drawing as **A:DEMODRG** – it will be used again.
3. The endpoint snapped to depends on the point 'picked'.
4. As a circle has four quadrants, the quadrant snapped to depends on the circle pick point.
5. Figure 11.5 displays the pick points using the ENDpoint and QUAdrant selections.
6. With keyboard entry – END, end, eNd are permissible.

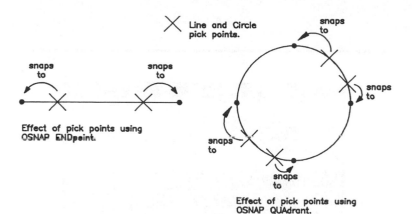

Line and Circle pick points.

snaps to

snaps to

Effect of pick points using OSNAP ENDpoint.

snaps to

snaps to

snaps to

snaps to

snaps to

Effect of pick points using OSNAP QUAdrant.

Fig. 11.5. Effect of pick points with OSNAP.

Running object snap

Using the object snap icons from the toolbar will increase the speed of the draughting process, but it can be 'tedious' to have to pick the icon every time an ENDpoint (for example) is required. AutoCAD R13 allows the user to 'preset' the object snap mode to ENDpoint, INTersection, CENter, etc., and this is called a **running object snap**. Presetting the object snap does not preclude the user from selecting another mode, i.e. if you have to set an ENDpoint running mode, you can still pick the CENter icon to snap to a circle/arc centre. The running snap mode can be set:

1. From the menu bar with **Options**

> **Running Object Snap**

This will display a dialogue box and by picking the desired box, that mode will be preset – Fig. 11.6.

2. By selecting the running snap icon from the Object Snap toolbar, which will also display the dialogue box.

3. By entering **OSNAP**<R> at the command line:
   prompt   Object snap mode
   enter   **END**<R>.

Fig. 11.6. Running Object Snap dialogue box.

Cancelling a running snap mode

A running snap mode can be left 'active' once it has been preset, but this can cause problems if you do not want to snap to the preset mode. The running object snap can be cancelled:

1. From the menu bar (Options–Running Object Snap) and removing the X from the mode.
2. Picking the None icon from the toolbar.
3. Entering OSNAP<R> then <RETURN> to the prompt.

Activity

Using your A:STDA3 drawing sheet, attempt Tutorial 4. It can be completed using lines and circles, and Object Snap should be used as much as possible. I've given you some hints! When complete, save the drawing as A:TUT-4.

❏ *Summary*

1. Object snap (OSNAP) is used to reference existing entities.
2. OSNAP is an invaluable aid to draughting.
3. The user can preset a running object snap.
4. Object snap is an example of a transparent command, as it is used while another command is active.
5. The snap modes can be activated by toolbar, menu bar or keyboard entry.

12. User exercise 1

By now you should have the confidence and ability to create line and circle entities by various methods, e.g. freehand, co-ordinate input and by referencing existing entities with OSNAP.

Before proceeding to investigate other draw and edit commands, we will create a working drawing which will be used to introduce several new concepts, as well as reinforcing your existing skills. The exercise will also be used to demonstrate how a 'new' drawing is created from our existing A:STDA3 standard sheet.

1. Start AutoCAD R13 and ensure the floppy used to save the drawings is in the drive.
2. Either select **File–New...** from the menu bar or pick the **New** icon from the Standard toolbar.
3. The Create New Drawing dialogue box will be displayed.
4. Note the existing name in the Prototype box is **acadiso.dwg**. This is AutoCAD R13's default drawing name.
5. Using the pointing device:
   (a) left-click to the left of the dot, i.e. acadiso|.dwg
   (b) backspace to erase the acadiso name, i.e. |.dwg
   (c) enter a:stda3, i.e. a:stda3|.dwg
   (d) left-click at the New Drawing Name... box
   (e) enter A:WORKDRG to give Fig. 12.1
   (f) pick OK.
6. Your A:STDA3 standard sheet will be displayed on the screen.

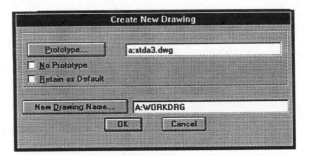

Fig. 12.1. Create New Drawing dialogue box.

7. Refer to Fig. 12.2 and draw full size the given shape:
   (a) *do not attempt to add* dimensions
   (b) the start point is given – *use it as it is!*
   (c) use absolute co-ordinate input for the start point, then use your discretion for the other inputs (recommend relative)
   (d) the only commands are LINE and CIRCLE (Center,Radius)
   (e) hopefully you will not need to use ERASE?
   (f) you may need some simple 'sums' for the circle centres.
8. When the drawing is complete, pick the SAVE icon from the Standard toolbar.
9. The command line will display **_qsave**, then be returned 'blank'.
10. Read the rest of this chapter, exit AutoCAD or proceed to the next chapter.

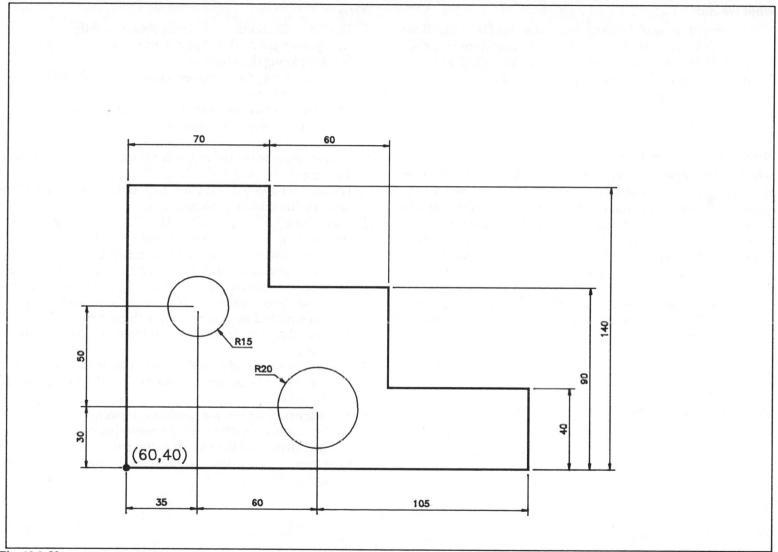

Fig. 12.2. User exercise 1. (1) Draw to the sizes given. (2) Do not dimension. (3) Use the SAVE icon when complete.

What we did

1. We created a new drawing from our A:STDA3 standard sheet – referred to by AutoCAD R13 as a Prototype drawing.
2. The new drawing name was entered as A:WORKDRG.
3. The drawing was saved with the SAVE icon.
4. Why was A: entered?

What actually happened

Selecting the New... option (icon or menu bar) allows the user to enter their own prototype drawing name as well as the drawing to be saved name. We entered A:STDA3 as the prototype drawing name and A:WORKDRG as the new drawing name. When OK was picked, AutoCAD loads the prototype drawing (A:STDA3) with all its default settings, and the user can complete the required drawing as normal. Selecting the SAVE option (icon or menu bar) *automatically* saves the drawing on the screen using the new drawing name (A:WORKDRG). This saved drawing has all the prototype drawing settings.

Notes

1. The same effect could have been obtained with:
   (a) opening the A:STDA3 standard sheet
   (b) completing the drawing
   (c) using Save As... and entering A:WORKDRG as the drawing name.
2. The user now has two methods of starting a new drawing:
   (a) using the New–Save options
   (b) using the Open–Save As options.
3. Both methods make use of the A:STDA3 standard/prototype drawing.
4. The method selected is at your discretion, but the New–Save option is 'theoretically' more correct.
5. Take note of the AutoCAD R13 prototype name **acadiso.dwg** – you may need it later.
6. There are two options for saving a drawing:
   (a) **Save**: saves the current screen drawing using the name that was 'started' – the user having no control over this name. This option will 'overwrite' the existing named drawing and should be used with **caution**
   (b) **Save As**: gives the user control to enter the name to be saved.
7. I would recommend that the **Save As** option is used until the user becomes proficient with AutoCAD R13. I generally use **Save As**.
8. There are two options for starting a drawing:
   (a) **New**: opens a drawing, the user specifying the prototype name and the new drawing name
   (b) **Open**: usually used to display a previously saved drawing.

13. Arc, donut and ellipse creation

These three drawing commands will be discussed in turn. Each command can be activated from the Draw toolbar, the menu bar or by direct command entry, and both co-ordinate input and referencing existing entities are permissible. We will use our rectangle/circle drawing so:

1. Start AutoCAD R13 and open drawing **A:DEMODRG**.
2. Refer to Fig. 13.1 and erase:
   (a) all lines created during the OSNAP (Chapter 11)
   (b) the top rectangle and the top four circles
   (c) the bottom two circles.
3. Activate the Draw, Modify and Object Snap toolbars.

Arcs

There are ten different arc creation methods and they are basically all the same. Arcs are drawn with combinations of the arc start point, end point, centre point, radius, included angle, length of arc, etc. We will investigate five different arc creation methods, and you can try the others at your leisure.

1. Start,Center,End

From the menu bar select **Draw**
  Arc
  Start,Center,End
prompt   `Center/<Start point>`
respond **Snap to MIDpoint icon and pick line d1**
prompt   `Center`
respond **Snap to Center icon and pick circle d2**
prompt   `Angle/Length of chord/<End point>`
respond **Snap to Nearest icon and pick line d3.**

2. Start,Center,Angle

From the menu bar select **Draw–Arc–Start,Center,Angle** and:
prompt   `Center/<Start point>`
respond **Snap to Intersection icon and pick point d4**
prompt   `Center`
respond **Snap to Midpoint icon and pick line d5**
prompt   `Included angle`
enter   −80<R>

3. Start,End,Radius

From the Draw toolbar, activate the arc fly-out menu and pick the Start,End,Radius icon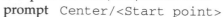
prompt   `Center/<Start point>`
respond **Snap to Endpoint icon and pick arc d6**
prompt   `End point`
respond **Snap to Endpoint icon and pick line d7**
prompt   `Radius`
enter   80<R>

4. Three point

Activate the arc 3 point option (Draw toolbar or menu bar) and:
(a) start point and **pick Snap to Midpoint of line d8**
(b) second point and **pick Snap to Center of circle d9**
(c) end point and **pick Snap to Midpoint of line d10.**

5. Continuous arcs

R13 allows continuous arcs to be created from the end point of the last arc drawn. Repeat the three point arc command and:
(a) start point   enter **20,15**<R>
    second point **Snap to Midpoint icon and pick line d1**
    end point   enter **160,40**<R>

(b) select from the menu bar **Draw–Arc–Continue** and:

    prompt   `End point`

    respond   **Snap to Endpoint icon and pick line d10**
               (leftside)

(c) select the Arc-continue icon from the Arc fly-out and

    prompt   `End point`

    respond   enter **@0,–25<R>**

(d) Finally repeat the arc continue selection (menu bar or toolbar) and at the end point prompt, enter **@–245,0<R>** which should draw the arc back to the start point.

Ellipses

To draw an ellipse, the user specifies:

(a) the ellipse centre and axes endpoints

(b) three points on the axes endpoints.

1. Activate the ELLIPSE icon from the Draw toolbar

    prompt   `Center of ellipse`

    enter   **170,220<R>**

    prompt   `Axis endpoint`

    enter   **220,220<R>**

    prompt   `<Other axis distance>/Rotation`

    enter   **170,245<R>**

2. From the menu bar select **Draw–Ellipse–Center** and

    prompt   `Center of ellipse`

    respond   **Snap to Center icon and pick ellipse just drawn**

    prompt   `Axis endpoint`

    enter   **@0,40<R>**

    prompt   `<Other axis distance>/Rotation`

    enter   **R<R>**

    prompt   `Rotation about major axis`

    enter   **30<R>.**

3. Select **Draw–Ellipse–Axis,End** and:

    prompt   `Arc/Center/<axis endpoint 1>`

    enter   **30,200<R>**

    prompt   `Axis endpoint 2`

    enter   **70,260<R>**

    prompt   `<Other axis distance>/Rotation`

    enter   **60,220<R>**

4. AutoCAD R13 allows partial elliptical arcs to be created. From the Draw toolbar, activate the Ellipse fly-out menu, and select the Ellipse Arc icon:

    prompt   `<Axis endpoint 1>/Center`

    enter   **250,230<R>**

    prompt   `Axis endpoint 2`

    enter   **360,230<R>**

    prompt   `<Other axis distance>/Rotation`

    enter   **305,260<R>**

    prompt   `Parameter/<Start angle>`

    enter   **210<R>**

    prompt   `Parameter/Included<end angle>`

    enter   **0<R>**

True ellipses

The ellipses drawn with R13 are 'true ellipses', i.e. they have a 'real centre point'. Pre-R13 users will know that ellipses were created from a series of arcs, each arc having its own centre. This made it impossible to 'snap to an ellipse centre'.

    Activate the LINE command and:

prompt `From point`

respond **Snap to Centre icon and pick ellipse d11**

prompt `To point`

respond **Snap to Quadrant icon and pick ellipse d12**

prompt `To point`

respond **Snap to Center icon and pick ellipse d13**

prompt `To point`

respond **Snap to Center icon and pick ellipse d14**

prompt `To point`

respond **Snap to Quadrant icon and pick ellipse d14**

prompt `To point` and right click to end line sequence.

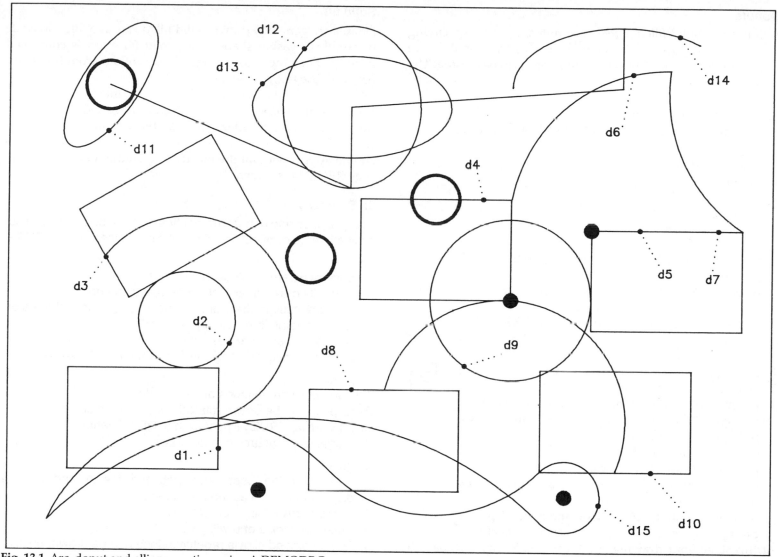

Fig. 13.1. Arc, donut and ellipse creation using A:DEMODRG.

Donuts

A donut is a 'solid filled' circle or annulus, the user specifying the inside and outside diameters as well as the donut centre point. The command allows repeated donuts to be created. The centre point can be:

(a) entered as co-ordinates

(b) referenced to existing entities.

1. From the menu bar select **Draw–Circle–Donut** and:

prompt	Inside diameter
enter	**0**<R>
prompt	Outside diameter
enter	**7**<R>
prompt	Center of donut
enter	**125,30**<R>
prompt	Center of donut
respond	**Snap to Endpoint icon and pick line d5**
prompt	Center of donut
respond	**Snap to Center icon and pick circle d9**
prompt	Center of donut
respond	**Snap to Center icon and pick arc d15**
prompt	Center of donut and right-click to end sequence.

2. From the Draw toolbar, select the Circle fly-out and pick the Donut icon and:

prompt	Inside diameter and enter **23**<R>
prompt	Outside diameter and enter **25**<R>
prompt	Center of donut
enter	**150,145**<R>
prompt	Center of donut
respond	**Snap to Midpoint icon and pick line d4**
prompt	Center of donut
respond	**Snap to Center icon and pick ellipse d11**
prompt	Center of donut and right-click.

At this stage your drawing should resemble Fig. 13.1. Save it, although we will probably not use it again.

Solid fill

Donuts are generally drawn 'solid filled', i.e. as a filled-in circle or annulus (washer shape). This solid fill effect is controlled from the Drawing Aids dialogue box (Options from the menu bar) with the toggle effect, i.e.

(a) X at Solid Fill – ON, i.e. donuts drawn 'filled'

(b) blank at Solid Fill – OFF, i.e. donuts 'not filled'.

Toggle the solid fill OFF, then at the command line enter **REGEN**<R>. This will regenerate the screen, and the donuts should appear without the fill effect. Turn the solid fill back on, then REGEN the screen.

❑ *Summary*

Arcs, ellipses and donuts are entities and can be created by co-ordinate input or by referencing existing entities using OSNAP.

Arcs

1. Several different selection methods.
2. Normally drawn in an anti-clockwise direction.
3. It is very easy to draw arcs in the 'wrong sense', if the start and end points are wrongly selected.
4. Continuous arcs are possible.
5. Entering a negative angle will draw the arc clockwise.

Ellipses

1. Two selection methods are available.
2. Ellipses can be drawn rotated about the major axis.
3. R13 draws TRUE ellipses with a 'REAL' centre.
4. Partial elliptical arcs can be drawn.

Donuts

1. Drawn by the user specifying the inside and outside diameters as well as the donut centre.
2. Can be drawn 'filled' or 'unfilled'.
3. An inside radius of 0 will give a 'filled circle'.
4. The command allows repetitive donuts to be drawn, until cancelled by the user.

14. Fillet and chamfer

Once a drawing has been completed and saved, it may be necessary to alter/modify it to meet the customer's requirements. AutoCAD R13 is equipped with several commands which allow the user to 'edit' an existing drawing, and we will begin by investigating the fillet and chamfer commands. Both commands can be activated from the menu bar, the Draw toolbar, or by command line entry.

1. Start AutoCAD R13.
2. Open the **A:WORKDRG** created and saved (I hope) in Chapter 12.
3. Activate the Draw and Modify toolbars.
4. Refer to Fig. 14.1.

Fillet

A fillet is a radius added to existing line/arc/circle entities, but before it can be used the required radius must be 'set' to the required value.

1. From the menu bar select **Construct**
   Fillet

prompt	(TRIM mode) Current fillet radius = ? Polyline/Radius/Trim/<Select first object>
enter	**R**<R> – the radius option
prompt	Enter fillet radius <?>
enter	**20**<R>.

2. Repeat the **Construct–Fillet** selection and:

prompt	(TRIM mode) Current fillet radius = 20.00 Polyline/Radius/Trim/<Select first object>
respond	**pick line d1**
prompt	Select second object
respond	**pick line d2.**

3. The corner selected will be filleted to a radius of 20, and the two 'unwanted line portions' will be erased.
4. From the Modify toolbar, activate the CHAMFER fly-out, pick the FILLET icon and at the prompt: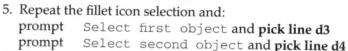
   enter **R**<R> – the radius option
   prompt   Enter fillet radius<20.00>
   enter **12.5** <R>.
5. Repeat the fillet icon selection and:

prompt	Select first object and **pick line d3**
prompt	Select second object and **pick line d4**

6. Using the fillet command (menu bar or toolbar) set the fillet radius to (a) 18; (b) 7; and fillet the two additional corners indicated in Fig. 14.1.

Chamfer

A chamfer is a straight 'cut corner' added to existing line entities. Like the fillet command, the chamfer distances (2) must be 'set' before the command can be used.

1. From the menu bar select **Construct–Chamfer** and:

prompt	(TRIM mode) Current chamfer Dist1 = ? Dist2 = ? Polyline/Distance/Angle/Trim/<Select first object>
enter	**D**<R> – the distance option
prompt	Enter first chamfer distance<?>
enter	**25**<R>
prompt	Enter second chamfer distance<25.00>
enter	**25**<R>.

2. Repeat the **Construct–Chamfer** selection and:

prompt	Select first object and **pick line d1**
prompt	Select second object and **pick line d5.**

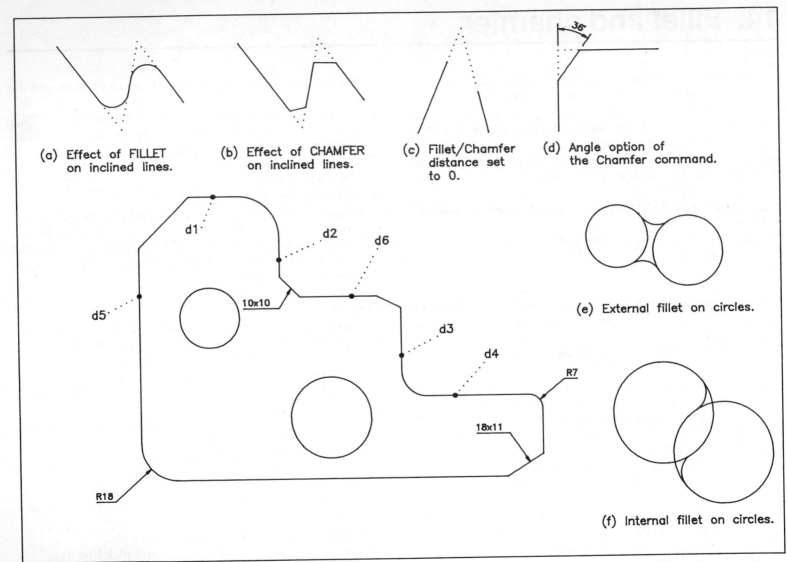

(a) Effect of FILLET on inclined lines.

(b) Effect of CHAMFER on inclined lines.

(c) Fillet/Chamfer distance set to 0.

(d) Angle option of the Chamfer command.

(e) External fillet on circles.

(f) Internal fillet on circles.

Fig. 14.1. A:WORKDRG after using the fillet and chamfer commands.

3. The selected corner will be chamfered and the unwanted line portions erased.
4. Select the chamfer icon from the Modify toolbar and at the prompt:

   enter   **D<R>** – the distance option

   prompt   Enter first chamfer distance and enter **12<R>**

   prompt   Enter second chamfer distance and enter **6 <R>**.
5. Repeat the chamfer icon selection and:

   prompt   Select first object and **pick line d6**

   prompt   Select second object and **pick line d3.**
6. Using the chamfer command, set the chamfer distances to (a) 10 × 10; (b) 18 × 11; and chamfer the two corners indicated in Fig. 14.1.

Saving

When the four fillets and chamfers have been added, make sure you save your work as **A:WORKDRG** for future chapters. Remember:

(a) Save – will automatically update the drawing which was opened

(b) Save As allows the user to enter the drawing name, and a message box will result if the same drawing name is used. In our case – Yes should be picked.

Some fillet/chamfer options

Although simple to use, the fillet and chamfer commands are very powerful with several options available. We will investigate some of these options using the 'space' around the drawing on the screen, so refer again to Fig. 14.1.

1. Fillet/Chamfer with inclined lines.

   Our working drawing demonstrated that fillets and chamfers can be added to lines which are perpendicular to each other, but they also work with inclined lines – Figs 14.11(a) and (b). Draw a few inclined lines (three or four) then use the fillet/chamfer commands on each set. You only have to be careful with the size of the fillet radius and chamfer distances used. Why are these important?

2. Fillet/Chamfer with a value set to zero.

   If the fillet radius/chamfer distances are set to zero, the two commands can be used to extend two lines to a point – Fig. 14.1(c). This is a useful option to know. Try it by drawing two lines, then set the fillet radius to zero.

3. The Chamfer Angle option.

   A variation on entering two distances. Draw any two lines and activate the Chamfer command:

   prompt   Polyline/Distance/Angle...

   enter   **A<R>** – the angle option

   prompt   Enter chamfer length on the first line

   enter   **15<R>**

   prompt   Enter chamfer angle from the first line

   enter   **36 <R>**

   Now fillet the two lines as before – Fig. 14.1(d).

4. Circles can be filleted, externally – Fig. 14.1(e) or internally – Fig. 14.1(f). These are very useful options. Circles cannot be chamfered.

Task

Try the fillet and chamfer options above then exit the drawing, *but do not save these changes!*

Error messages

Generally the fillet and chamfer commands are used without any problems, but two error messages which may occur are:

1. No valid fillet with radius of ...
2. Chamfer requires 2 lines ... .

These messages should be self-explanatory to the user. The first is the most common, and probably means that the radius value you are using is too small for the lines/circles selected.

❏ **Summary**

1. FILLET and CHAMFER are construct commands.
2. Both commands can be activated from the menu bar, the Modify toolbar or from the command line.
3. Both commands require the radius/distances to be set before they can be used.
4. When values are entered they remain the defaults until altered by the user.
5. Lines, arc, circles can be filleted.
6. Lines can be chamfered with the same/different distances.
7. A fillet radius of zero is useful in extending two inclined lines to a point.
8. Chamfer distances of zero will also extend two inclined lines to a point.
9. The second chamfer distance is assumed to have the same value as the first distance, unless a different value is entered by the user.
10. The first chamfer line picked 'takes' the first chamfer distance.
11. The chamfer Angle option allows the user to specify the chamfer line at an angle to the first distance entered.

15. Offset, extend and trim

In this chapter we will investigate three of the most commonly used draughting commands, and will demonstrate them by adding centre lines (of a sort) to our working drawing from the previous chapter, so:
1. Start AutoCAD R13 and open **A:WORKDRG** – easy by now?
2. Activate the Draw and Modify toolbars.

Offset

This command allows the user to draw parallel entities, i.e. lines, circles and arcs. The user can specify:
(a) the offset distance
(b) a point the entity to be offset has to pass through.
1. Refer to Fig. 15.1 and from the menu bar select **Construct**
                                                         Offset

prompt	`Offset distance or Through<Through>`
enter	**35<R>** – the offset distance
prompt	`Select object to offset`
respond	**pick line d1**
prompt	`Side to offset`
respond	**pick any point d2 to the right of line d1**
and	line d1 will be offset by 35 units to the right
prompt	`Select object to offset`
	(i.e. any more 35 offsets)
respond	**right-click** to end sequence.

2. Activate the Copy fly-out menu from the Modify toolbar and select the OFFSET icon and

prompt	`Offset distance or Through <35.00>`
enter	**80<R>**
prompt	`Select object to offset`
respond	**pick line d3**
prompt	`Side to offset`

respond	**pick any point d4 above line d3**
prompt	`Select object to offset`
respond	**right-click**

3. We have now offset a vertical and horizontal line which gives 'centre lines' – I did say 'of a sort' – through one of the circles.
4. Using the same procedure (menu bar or icon selection), offset the same two lines by the distances given in Fig. 15.1 to give 'centre lines' through the other circle.
5. We will now see how these 'centre lines' can be 'tidied up'.

Extend

The extend command will extend an entity 'to a boundary', the user specifying:
(a) The actual boundary (an entity).
(b) The entity to be extended.
1. Refer to Fig. 15.2(a) and from the menu bar select **Modify**
                                                          Extend

prompt	`Select boundary edges (...)`
	`Select objects`
respond	**pick line d1**
prompt	`1 found`
then	`Select objects`, i.e. more boundary edges
respond	**pick line d2**
prompt	`1 found`
then	`Select objects`
respond	**right-click** to end boundary edge selection
prompt	`<Select object to extend>/Project/ Edge/Undo`
respond	**pick lines d3, d4 and d5 then right-click.**

2. The three lines will be extended to the boundary edges selected.

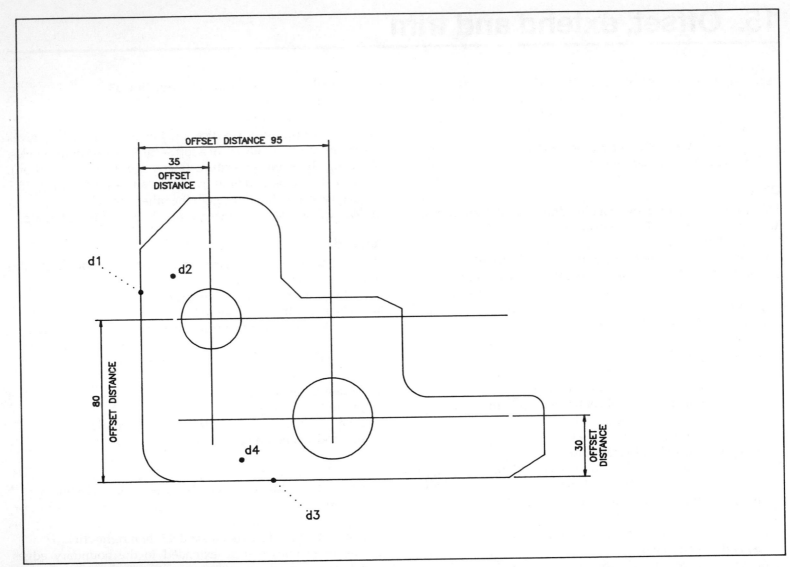

Fig. 15.1. A:WORKDRG after the OFFSET command.

3. Use the EXTEND icon (Modify toolbar–TRIM fly-out) and extend the other three lines (two vertical and one horizontal) to give Fig. 15.2(b).

Offset (again)

Use the OFFSET command and:
(a) enter an offset distance of 5
(b) pick one of the circles at any point on its circumference
(c) pick a point 'outside' this circle
(d) pick the other circle and offset it 'outwards'
(e) right-click to end the OFFSET command.

Trim

The trim command is used to erase an entity at a boundary edge, the user specifying:
(a) The boundary edge (an entity).
(b) The entity to be trimmed.
1. Refer to Fig. 15.2(c) and select from the menu bar **Modify–Trim** and:

    prompt   Select cutting edges (...)
              Select objects
    respond   **pick circle d6 then right-click**
    prompt   <Select objects to trim>/Project/
              Edge/Undo
    respond   **pick lines d7, d8, d9 and d10 then right-click.**

2. The four 'centre lines' will have been trimmed to the offset circle, which can now be erased.
3. Using the other offset circle as the cutting edge, TRIM (using the icon) the other four circle centre lines then erase the offset circle to give Fig. 15.2(d).
    Note, one of these trim lines may be difficult to pick at this stage, so just leave it for the present time.
4. You have now added 'neat centre lines' to your work drawing.

Saving

At this stage save your work as **A:WORKDRG** – we will be using this modified drawing shortly.

Further exercises

Before leaving this chapter, we will investigate the offset, extend and trim commands with some further examples. I would recommend that you try these examples, so erase your A:WORKDRG (after saving) and refer to Fig. 15.3 which displays:
(a) using the OFFSET command to find the centre point of a circle. This is one of the most common uses for the command, and the example shows the horizontal line offset by 18.6 and the vertical line offset by 23.4. The intersection of the two offset lines can be used as a circle centre point
(b) the OFFSET command has an option which is very useful. Suppose that you want to offset a line through a certain point (say the centre of a circle), then activate the OFFSET command and:

    prompt   Offset distance or Through
    enter   **T<R>** – the Through option
    prompt   Select object to offset
    respond   **pick the required line**
    prompt   Through point
    respond   **Snap to center icon and pick circle**

  The line will then be offset through the circle centre
(c) lines and arcs can be extended to other lines, arcs and circles
(d) lines, arcs and circles can be trimmed to each other
(e) circles can be trimmed to other circles. The selected cutting edge and entities to be trimmed can give different results. Can you obtain the three options shown?
(f) lines, arcs and circles can be offset 'outwards and inwards'. The result can be interesting?

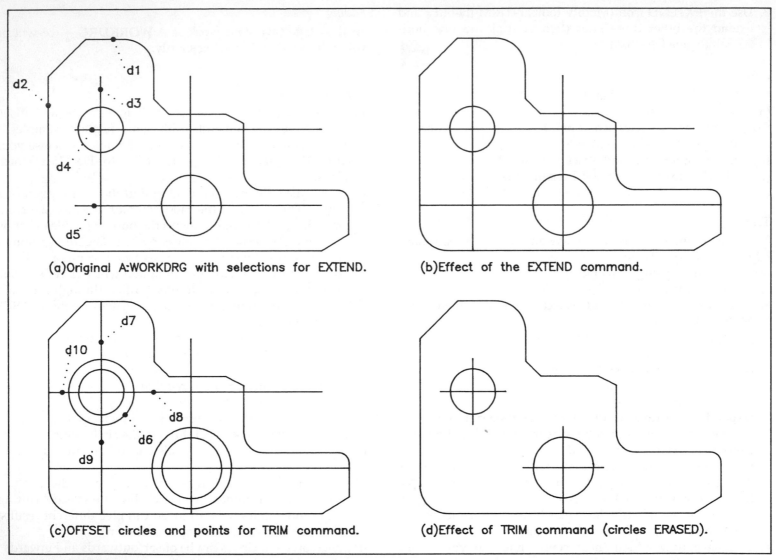

(a)Original A:WORKDRG with selections for EXTEND.

(b)Effect of the EXTEND command.

(c)OFFSET circles and points for TRIM command.

(d)Effect of TRIM command (circles ERASED).

Fig. 15.2. A:WORKDRG after the EXTEND and TRIM commands.

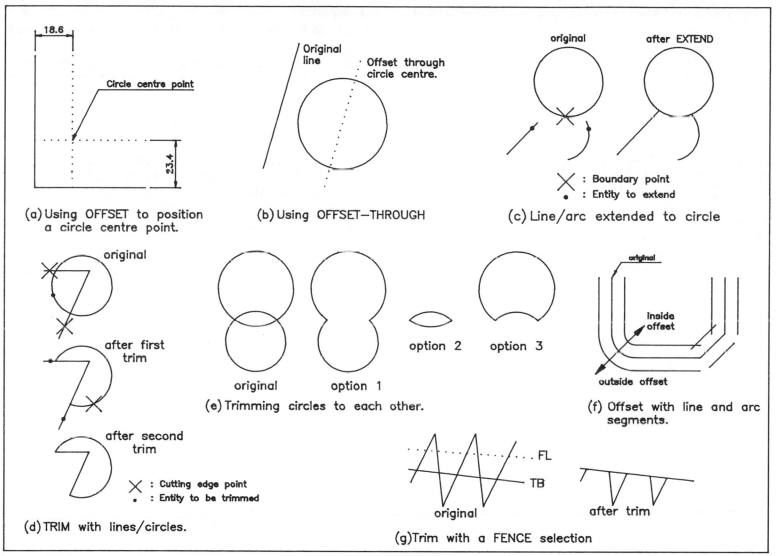

18.6

Circle centre point

23.4

(a) Using OFFSET to position a circle centre point.

Original line

Offset through circle centre.

(b) Using OFFSET—THROUGH

original

after EXTEND

✕ : Boundary point
• : Entity to extend

(c) Line/arc extended to circle

original

after first trim

after second trim

✕ : Cutting edge point
• : Entity to be trimmed

(d) TRIM with lines/circles.

original

option 1

option 2

option 3

(e) Trimming circles to each other.

original

inside offset

outside offset

(f) Offset with line and arc segments.

FL

TB

original

after trim

(g) Trim with a FENCE selection

Fig. 15.3. OFFSET, TRIM and EXTEND examples.

(g) trim with the fence option is useful. The effect is achieved by:
1. Selecting the TRIM command.
2. Picking the trim boundary (TB) then <R>.
3. Selecting from the menu bar Edit–Select Objects–Fence.
4. Draw in the fence line (FL).
5. Right-click.

Figure 15.3 may appear rather cluttered, but it is useful. I would recommend that the user spends some time with the three commands by drawing lines, circles and arc entities and then trying OFFSET, TRIM and EXTEND.

Activity

Tutorial 5 displays two components. These can both be drawn using LINE, CIRCLE, FILLET, OFFSET, TRIM, etc. As before use your standard A:STDA3 sheet and save your work as A:TUT-5.

❏ *Summary*
1. OFFSET, TRIM and EXTEND are three very useful commands.
2. All three commands can be activated from the menu bar or by icons. Offset is a Construct command, while Trim and Extend are Modify commands.
3. Lines, arcs and circles can be offset by:
   (a) entering the offset distance
   (b) selecting an entity to be offset through.
4. Extend and trim have the same command 'format':
   (a) select the extend/trim boundary (cutting edge)
   (b) select the entity to be extended/trimmed.
5. Lines and arcs can be extended
6. Lines, circles and arcs can be trimmed.

16. Layers and standard sheet 2

All the entities which have been drawn so far have had a continuous linetype, and no attempt has been made to introduce the idea of centre or hidden lines. All AutoCAD releases have a facility called **LAYERS** which allows the user to assign different linetypes and colours to named layers. For example, a layer may be for red continuous lines, another may be for green hidden lines, and yet another layer could be for blue centre lines. As well as linetypes and colours, layers can be used for specific drawing purposes, e.g. there may be a layer for dimensions, one for hatching, one for text, etc. Individual layers can be switched on/off by the user to mask out drawing entities which are not required.

The concept of layers can be imagined as a series of transparent overlays, each having its own linetype and colour. The overlay used for dimensioning could be removed without affecting the rest of the drawing.

The following points are important when considering layers:
1. All entities are drawn on layers.
2. Layers must be 'created' by the user before they can be used.
3. New layers are created using the Layer Control dialogue box.
4. Layers are (in my opinion) the most important concept in AutoCAD.

Layers are essential for good and efficient draughting, and the user must become proficient with them. This chapter is therefore rather long, and I make no apology for this.

Getting started

We will discuss several different aspects of layers, and then create several new layers using our standard sheet, so:
1. Start AutoCAD R13 and open your **A:STDA3** drawing.
2. Draw a line and circle anywhere on the screen.

The layer control dialogue box

The 'original' layer control dialogue box is shown in Fig. 16.1 and is activated from the menu bar with **Data–Layers**...
1. The format for layers is:

Layer Name	State	Color	Linetype
0	On . .	white	CONTINUOUS

2. Layer 0 is the layer on which all entities have (so far) been drawn and is 'supplied' with AutoCAD. It is the **CURRENT** layer, and is displayed in the Objects Properties toolbar with a black coloured box. This is an anomaly which the user may find strange – layer 0 is set to colour white, but the entities drawn are black on a grey/white background.

Note: some users may have white lines drawn on a black background, but whatever the entity colours, don't worry.

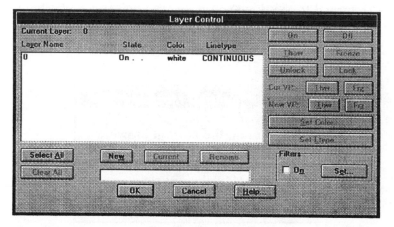

Fig. 16.1. Original Layer Control dialogue box.

3. Certain boxes in the dialogue box are in bold type (e.g. New) and others are in light type (e.g. Set Ltype...). Bold type boxes can be selected (i.e. picked) while light type boxes cannot.
4. Move the pointing device arrow anywhere on the '0,On,white,CONTINUOUS' line and:
   (a) pick it, i.e. left-click
   (b) it will turn blue
   (c) 0 appears in the layer name box towards bottom of dialogue box
   (d) several boxes change to bold type – available for selection.
5. Pick the **Off** box and:
   (a) state now displays ..., i.e. On is not displayed
   (b) **Warning: Current layer is off** is displayed at the lower left-hand corner of the dialogue box
   (c) pick OK.
6. AutoCAD will display the warning message dialogue box Fig. 16.2.
7. Pick OK from the message dialogue box and you will be returned to the drawing screen. The line and circle should have disappeared as they were drawn on layer 0 which is now off.

8. Activate from the menu bar **Data–Layers...** and:
   (a) pick 0 layer line – turns blue
   (b) pick **On** box
   (c) pick OK
   (d) line and circle displayed as layer 0 is now on.

Linetypes

AutoCAD R13 is equipped with several different linetypes, e.g. center, hidden, dashed, etc. and these must be 'loaded' into the system before they can be used.

Note: your system may already have the linetypes loaded, but it will do no harm to work through the following procedure.

1. Activate the Layer Control dialogue box, i.e. Data–Layers...
2. Pick the 0 layer 'line' – turns blue
3. Pick the **Set Ltype...** box which will display the Select Linetype dialogue box as Fig. 16.3.

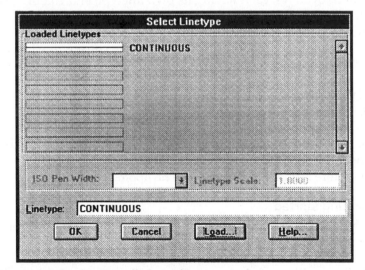

Fig. 16.3. Select Linetype dialogue box.

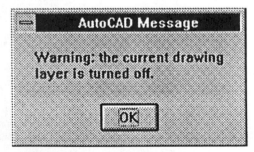

Fig. 16.2. Current layer message box.

4. This dialogue box only displays a CONTINUOUS linetype which means that the other linetypes have not yet been loaded.

   Note that if several linetypes are displayed, then they have already been loaded into the system, and you can cancel the sequence.
5. From the Select Linetype dialogue box pick the **Load...** box which will display the Load or Reload Linetypes dialogue box – Fig. 16.4.
6. Pick the **Select All** box and all the linetypes will turn blue, then pick OK.
7. You will be returned to the Select Linetype File dialogue box with several loaded linetype names displayed.
8. Pick **CENTER** and:
   (a) CENTER picture turns white
   (b) CENTER name displayed at name box
   (c) pick OK.
9. You will be returned to the Layer Control dialogue box which will indicate that layer 0 has a CENTER linetype?

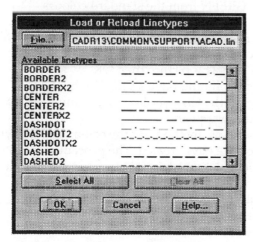

Fig. 16.4. Load or Reload Linetypes dialogue box.

10. Pick OK from the Layer Control dialogue box to return to the drawing screen. The line and circle should be displayed as centre lines. No? Mine did not!

Linetype scale

The appearance of linetypes is controlled by the linetype scale (LTSCALE) variable which must be 'set' by the user. From the menu bar select **Options**
> **Linetypes**
> **Global Linetype Scale**

prompt New scale factor<1.00>
enter **12 <R>**

The line and circle should now be better defined?

Using Options–Linetypes–Global Linetype Scale, enter different scale factors and note the effect on the line and circle. Decide on the value which gives the 'best appearance'. For A3-sized paper, I would recommend that the value be set to between 10 and 15.

Colour

Layers can be used to add colour to a drawing by assigning specific colours to a named layer.
1. Activate the Layer Control dialogue box.
2. Pick the 0 layer line.
3. Select the **Color...** box to display the Select Color dialogue box.
4. Using the Standard Colors pick RED and note that red appears in the Color: box.
5. Pick OK to return to the Layer Control dialogue box, and layer 0 will display color red.
6. Pick OK to return to the drawing screen, and your line and circle will be displayed as red centre lines (I hope).
7. Note the Object Properties toolbar will be displaying red in two icons?

Task

Using the Layer Control dialogue box, set the linetype and colour of layer 0 to CONTINUOUS and white, respectively. The colour white means that you pick the black colour box from the Standard Colours – confusing?

A note on the Select Colours dialogue box

When the Set Color... option is selected from the Layer Control dialogue box, the Set Color dialogue box will be displayed. The appearance of this dialogue box will depend on the type of monitor you have. Many users will have a 'full palette' of 255 colours available for selection, while others will only have about 14. This will not matter to us, as we will only consider the Standard Colours.

All AutoCAD releases designate colours by numbers and the following are the standard colour numbers:

| 1 red | 2 yellow | 3 green | 4 cyan | 5 blue |
| 6 magenta | 7 black (white) | 8 grey? | 9 rust | |

These numbers are used to assign coloured pens in a plotter, thus allowing multicoloured drawings to be obtained.

Creating new layers

Erase the line and circle entities from the screen, and ensure that layer 0 has been returned to colour white and CONTINUOUS linetype. The layers which we will create for future work are:

Usage	Layer name	Layer colour	Layer linetype
General	0	white	CONTINUOUS
Outlines	OUT	red	CONTINUOUS
Centre lines	CL	green	CENTER
Hidden lines	HID	yellow	HIDDEN
Dimensions	DIMEN	blue	CONTINUOUS
Text	TEXT	magenta	CONTINUOUS
Hatching	SECT	cyan	CONTINUOUS

1. Activate the Layer Control dialogue box and note the flashing |. This is where we enter the layer name.
2. Enter **OUT** at the | and then pick the **New** box.
3. The name OUT will be transferred to the layer list and assigned a white colour and a CONTINUOUS linetype. These are the defaults.
4. Enter CL at the | then pick New.
5. Enter HID at the | and pick New.
6. Enter DIMEN,TEXT,SECT at the | then pick New which will transfer the three layer names to the layer list.
7. Select the OUT layer line (turns blue) then:
   (a) pick the Set Color... box
   (b) pick RED from the Standard Colours
   (c) pick OK from the Select Color dialogue box
   (d) layer OUT should display colour red
   (e) deselect the OUT layer by picking it – blue colour disappears.
8. Select the CL layer line and:
   (a) pick the Set Color... box
   (b) pick GREEN from the standard colours
   (c) pick OK
   (d) layer CL colour is green and is still active (in blue)
   (e) pick the Set Ltype... box
   (f) pick CENTER picture then OK
   (g) layer CL should have a CENTER linetype
   (h) deselect the CL layer line by picking the **Clear All** box – blue disappears.
9. Using the above method, set the colour and linetype of the new layers we have created. The procedure is quite simple, and if you make a mistake it is easy to rectify by altering the colour and linetype to the correct setting.
10. When all the colours and linetypes have been set, pick OK from the layer control dialogue box. The layers we have made are now available for use.

The current layer

The current layer is the one on which entities are drawn. Its name and colour appears in the Object Properties toolbar which should always be docked below the Standard toolbar at the top of the screen. The current layer is also named in the Layer Control dialogue box when it is activated. The current layer is set by the user:

1. From the Layer Control dialogue box by:-
   (a) select Data-Layers... from the menu bar
   (b) pick the layer line to be current, e.g. OUT
   (c) pick the **Current** box – Current Layer: OUT at top
   (d) pick OK.
2. Using the pull-down menu from the Objects Properties toolbar
   (a) pick the scroll arrow at right of layer name box
   (b) pick the layer name, e.g. OUT.

The Layer Control dialogue box is used to create new layers with their colours and linetypes. Once created the current layer is best set using the Objects Properties toolbar.

I usually start a drawing with OUT as the current layer, but this a personal preference. Other users may want to start a drawing with layer CL or 0 as the current layer, but it does not matter. At this stage if you activate the Layer Control dialogue box, it will appear as Fig. 16.5, i.e. the created layers are listed alphabetically and not in the order they were made.

Having created layers it is now possible to draw entities with hidden and centre linetypes simply by altering the current layer either from the Layer Control dialogue box or from the Objects Properties toolbar. All future work should be completed with layers used properly, i.e. if text is to be added to a drawing, then the TEXT layer should be current, etc.

Saving the created layers

Now that the required layers have been created, set the current layer to OUT, then pick either

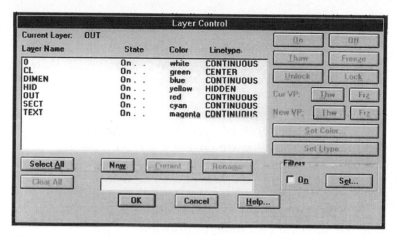

Fig. 16.5. Layer Control with created edges.

(a) the Save icon or
(b) File-Save from the menu bar.

This will automatically update the **A:STDA3** standard sheet drawing opened at the start of the chapter. This standard sheet has now been saved with:

(a) units set to metric decimal to 2DP
(b) limits set to A3 paper with a 'drawing border'
(c) no UCS icon and no pickbox displayed on screen
(d) several variables set, e.g. LTSCALE (12), BLIPS off, etc.
(e) Several layers created.

With the layers now saved in the standard sheet, the layer creation process does not need to be undertaken every time a drawing is started. New layers can be added to the standard A:STDA3 sheet at any time.

The standard sheet should *always be used for a new drawing* and the following options are available to the user:

1. Opening A:STDA3
   (a) select File–Open
   (b) pick A:STDA3 from the drawing list

(c) complete the drawing
(d) pick File–Save As
(e) enter the new drawing name, e.g. A:NEWDRG
(f) drawing will be saved as A:NEWDRG and A:STDA3 will be untouched.

2. Using New
   (a) select File–New
   (b) enter A:STDA3 as the Prototype drawing name
   (c) enter the new drawing name, e.g. A:NEWDRG
   (d) pick OK
   (e) when drawing complete pick the Save icon
   (f) A:NEWDRG will automatically be updated, and A:STDA3 is untouched.

3. Make A:STDA3 the Prototype drawing
   (a) select File–New
   (b) enter A:STDA3 as the Prototype drawing name
   (c) activate the Retain as Default box, i.e. pick to display X
   (d) enter the New drawing name, e.g. A:NEWDRG
   (e) complete drawing then pick the Save icon
   (f) A:NEWDRG will be updated, A:STDA3 will be untouched and retained as the prototype drawing.

Note that at this level I would not recommend the user setting A:STDA3 as the default prototype drawing name. This may be against company policy. Use options 1 or 2 listed above. Option 2 is 'more correct', but Option 1 is quite acceptable. The user should be familiar with using the A:STDA3 standard sheet when opening a drawing.

Task

Using the seven layers (our created 6 and layer 0):
(a) make each layer current in turn
(b) draw a 40 radius circle on each layer
(c) make layer 0 current
(d) proceed to the layer state section.

Layer status

Layers can have six states, these being:
(a) ON or OFF
(b) THAWED or FROZEN
(c) LOCKED or UNLOCKED.

The layer state is displayed in both the Layer Control dialogue box and the Objects Properties toolbar (in icon form) and so far all states have been ON, THAWED and UNLOCKED. We will now investigate the layer state options using the Layer Control dialogue box with the seven coloured circles.

                                         State

1. Activate the Layer Control dialogue box and
   (a) pick the CL layer line
   (b) pick the Off box   . . .
   (c) pick OK – no green circle.
2. Activate the Layer Control dialogue box and
   (a) pick the DIMEN layer line
   (b) pick the Freeze box   **On F .**
   (c) pick Ok – no blue circle.
3. Layer Control dialogue box again and
   (a) pick the HID layer line
   (b) pick the Lock box   **On . L**
   (c) pick OK – yellow circle still displayed.
4. Layer control again and
   (a) pick the SECT layer line
   (b) pick Freeze and Lock boxes **On F L**
   (c) pick OK – no cyan circle.
5. Layer control and
   (a) pick the TEXT layer line
   (b) pick Off, Freeze, Lock boxes **. F L**
   (c) pick OK – no magenta circle.
6. Last time for the Layer Control dialogue box
   (a) make OUT the current layer
   (b) pick Freeze box   **On . .**
   (c) Message – **Cannot freeze the current layer**

(d) pick the Off box   . . .

(e) **Warning: Current layer is off**

(f) pick OK

(g) AutoCAD Message box – pick OK

(h) no red circle.

7. Your drawing should only display a black (layer 0) and yellow (layer HID) circle, i.e. only layers which are ON or LOCKED will be visible. Any layer which is OFF or FROZEN will not display anything.

Task

1. Make layer 0 current.
2. ERASE the yellow circle – you cannot. The prompt displays:
   `1 was on a locked layer.`
3. Draw a line from the centre of the yellow circle to the centre of the black circle using the Snap to center icon. You can reference the yellow circle, even though it is on a locked layer.
4. Make OUT the current layer, and draw a line from 50,50 to 200,200. No line appears on the screen. Why?
5. Using the Layer Control dialogue box
   (a) pick Select All – all layer lines turn blue
   (b) pick On, Thaw, Unlock. State is **On . .**
   (c) pick OK
   (d) circles and red line 'restored'?

Layer icons

While the Layer Control dialogue box is perfectly suitable for making and setting layers, as well as altering the colour and linetype of entities, the same effect can be obtained by icon selection from the Objects Properties toolbar, using the following icons:

(a) Layer – activates the Layer Control dialogue box

(b) Colour – activates the Select Color dialogue box

(c) Linetype – activates the Select Linetype dialogue box

(d) Layer Control – activates the pull down option for setting and altering the layer states – Fig. 16.6. By 'picking' the required icon from the layer line, that layer can be made current, thawed, locked, etc. It is the same as using the dialogue box from the menu bar, but is quicker in operation.

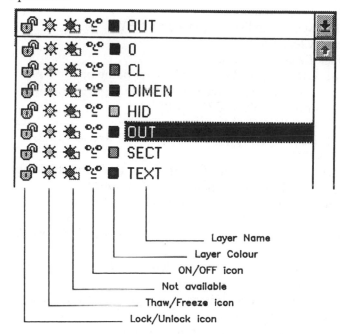

Fig. 16.6. Layer Control from Object Properties toolbar.

Renaming and purging layers

Unwanted, or wrongly named, layers can be renamed or removed by the user at anytime. To demonstrate this:

1. Using Data–Options... make two new layers called L1 and L2. Accept the colour white and CONTINUOUS linetype and pick OK.
2. Activate the Layer Control dialogue box again and:
   (a) pick L1 layer line
   (b) in the layer name box click to left of L1, i.e. **L1|**
   (c) backspace to remove L1, i.e. **|**
   (d) enter NEW1, i.e. **NEW1|**
   (e) pick **Rename** box
   (f) layer L1 in list is replaced by NEW1.
3. Pick Clear All.
4. Pick L2 layer line and:
   (a) layer name L2 appears in layer name box
   (b) delete the L2 name using the backspace key
   (c) enter NEWLAYERNUMBER2
   (d) pick Rename box
   (e) layer L2 is replaced by NEWLAYERNUMBER2.
5. Pick OK.
6. Activate layer control icon from the Objects Properties dialogue box. Two renamed layers there?
7. From the menu bar select **Data–Purge–Layers**
   prompt   `Purge layer NEW1?` and enter **Y<R>**
   prompt   `Purge layer NEWLAYERNUMBER2?` and **Y<R>**
   prompt   `Command line returned?`
8. Activate the Layer Control dialogue box, and two renamed layers have been removed?
9. When using PURGE with layers, you cannot purge:
   (a) the current layer
   (b) layers which have entities on them.

Activity
There are no activities with layers, but all future drawings should be completed using layers used correctly. Exit AutoCAD (but *do not save* anything) and have a break. If you have worked your way through this chapter, you have earned it.

❏ *Summary*
1. Layers are probably the most important concept in AutoCAD.
2. Layers allow entities to be created with different linetypes and colours.
3. Layers are created from the Layer Control dialogue box.
4. There is no limit to the number of layers which can be created, and new layers can be added at any time.
5. The Layer Control dialogue box has two dialogue boxes:
   (a) the Set Color dialogue box
   (b) the Set Ltype dialogue box.
6. Linetypes must be loaded before they can be used.
7. The colour palette allows 255 colours if your monitor system supports them.
8. Layers saved in the standard sheet need only be created once.
9. The LTSCALE variable alters the 'appearance' of linetypes.
10. Layer states can be:
    ON: all entities are displayed and can be edited
    OFF: entities are not displayed
    FREEZE: similar to OFF, but allows faster regeneration
    THAW: undoes a frozen layer
    LOCK: entities are displayed, but **cannot** be edited. They can be referenced.
    UNLOCK: undoes a locked layer.
11. Layers states can be activated from the Layer Control dialogue box, or the Objects Properties toolbar with icon selection.
12. Care must be taken when editing a drawing with layers which are turned off or frozen – more on this later.
13. The layer states in the dialogue box are:
    On . .   layer is ON
     . . .   layer is OFF
    On F .   layer is ON but FROZEN
    On . L   layer is ON and LOCKED
14. Layers can be *purged at any time* providing there are no entities on them. The current layer cannot be purged.

17. User exercise 2

In this chapter we will create a new working drawing using previous commands and then 'take stock' of all drawings so far created, so:

1. Start AutoCAD R13.
2. From the menu bar select **File–New...** and
   (a) enter **A:STDA3** as the prototype name
   (b) enter **A:USEREX** as the new drawing name
   (c) pick OK.
3. Your standard sheet with the created layers will be displayed.
4. Make OUT the current layer – it may be?
5. Refer to Fig. 17.1 and:
   (a) draw the original shape to the sizes given – Fig. 17.1(a). Use the 140,100 start point
   (b) offset three lines using the sizes in Fig. 17.1(b)
   (c) extend four lines as Fig. 17.1(c)
   (d) trim to give the final shape – Fig. 17.1(d).
6. Pick the SAVE icon to save the final shape as **A:USEREX**.

Taking stock

At this stage we have created several drawings:

1. A standard sheet **A:STDA3**.
2. A working drawing **A:WORKDRG** – lines and circles.
3. A user exercise **A:USEREX**.
4. Five tutorials, A:TUT-1; A:TUT-2; A:TUT-3; A:TUT-4 and A:TUT-5.

The **A:STDA3** standard sheet will be used for all new tutorial work, while **A:WORKDRG** and **A:USEREX** will be used throughout the book to demonstrate new AutoCAD R13 commands.

Exercise

Before leaving this chapter, we will use the user exercise drawing to demonstrate an interesting effect.

1. Make CL the current layer.
2. Offset any line of the red shape by 20.
3. Why is the offset line a red continuous line and not a green centre line, when CL is the current layer?
4. The reason is that the line selected to be offset, was created on the OUT layer and is therefore a red continuous line. It will therefore be offset as a red continuous line irrespective of the current layer.
5. This can cause some confusion to new users, and I hope that my explanation will help to overcome any misunderstanding.
6. Now exit AutoCAD **without saving** the changes.

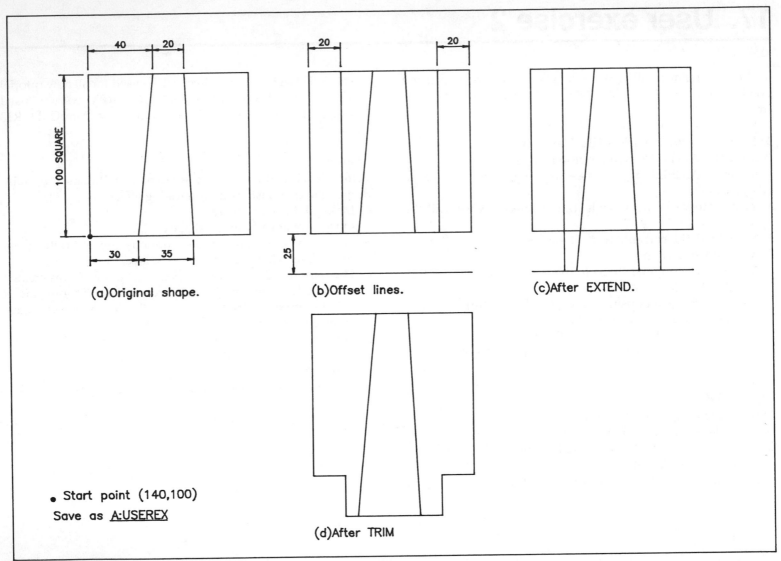

40 20

100 SQUARE

30 35

(a)Original shape.

20 20

25

(b)Offset lines.

(c)After EXTEND.

● Start point (140,100)
Save as A:USEREX

(d)After TRIM

Fig. 17.1. A:USEREX construction.

18. Text

Text should be added to drawings whenever possible. This text may simply be a name and date, but could also be a parts list, a company title block, notes on costing and so on. AutoCAD R13 allows two types of text to be added.
(a) single-line text
(b) dynamic text
We will demonstrate adding text to an existing drawing, so:
1. Start AutoCAD and open drawing **A:USEREX**
2. Make TEXT the current layer and refer to Fig. 18.1.
3. Activate the Draw and Modify toolbars.

Single line text

1. From the menu bar select **Draw**
                     Text
                     Single-Line Text

prompt	Justify/Style/<Start point>
enter	**20,240**
prompt	Height<?> and enter **10**<R>
prompt	Rotation angle<0> and enter **0**<R>
prompt	Text
enter	**TXET EXRECISE**<R> – deliberate misspelling!

2. From the Draw toolbar, activate the TEXT fly-out menu and pick the Single-Line Text icon

prompt	Justify/Style/<Start point>
enter	**25,25**<R>
prompt	Height<10> and enter **8**<R>
prompt	Rotation angle<0> and enter **0**<R>
prompt	Text
enter	**TEXT is single lined**

Dynamic text

1. From the menu bar select **Draw–Text–Dynamic Text** and

prompt	Justify/Style/<Start point> and enter **200,30**<R>
prompt	Height<8> and enter **5**<R>
prompt	Rotation angle<0> and enter **15**<R>
prompt	Text
enter	**AutoCAD is a draughting package**<R>
prompt	Text
enter	**and this is Release 13.**<R>
prompt	Text
enter	**<RETURN>** to end sequence.

2. From the Draw toolbar, activate the TEXT fly-out menu, and pick the Dynamic Text icon and

prompt	Justify/Style/<Start point>
enter	**275,245**<R>
prompt	Height<5>
enter	**6**<R>
prompt	Rotation angle<15>
enter	**0**<R>
prompt	Text
enter	**DYNAMIC TEXT**<R>
prompt	Text
enter	**is**<R>
prompt	Text
enter	**multi-lined**<R>
prompt	Text
enter	**<RETURN>** to end sequence.

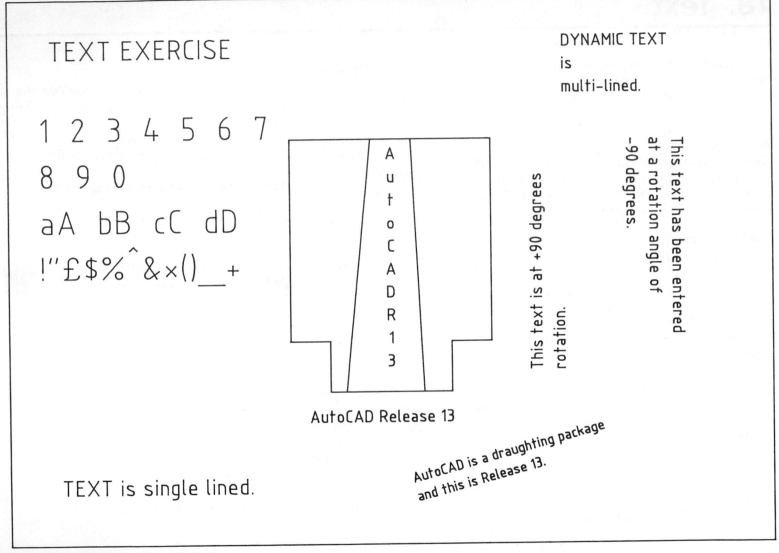

TEXT EXERCISE

DYNAMIC TEXT
is
multi-lined.

1 2 3 4 5 6 7
8 9 0

aA bB cC dD

!"£$%ˆ&×()__+

A
u
t
o
C
A
D
R
1
3

AutoCAD Release 13

This text is at +90 degrees
rotation.

This text has been entered
at a rotation angle of
-90 degrees.

TEXT is single lined.

AutoCAD is a draughting package
and this is Release 13.

Fig. 18.1. Text addition with A:USEREX.

Note

The difference between dynamic and single line text is:
(a) Dynamic – can be 'seen' as the text is entered from the keyboard. It also allows multiple lines of text to be added.
(b) Single – only allows a single text line and is not seen as the text is entered from the keyboard.

Task

Add all other text items shown in Fig. 18.1 using either text command (I prefer the dynamic text). The height of the text is at your discretion, and don't worry if the 'appearance' of your text is slightly different from mine.

Editing existing screen text

Text can be edited as it is entered from the keyboard if the user spots the mistake. Text which needs to be edited when it is on the screen requires a command, and we will demonstrate this using the TXET EXRECISE item wrongly entered.

From the menu bar select **Modify**
                              Edit Text...
prompt   `<Select a TEXT or ATTDEF object>/Undo`
respond **pick the TXET EXRECISE item**
prompt   Edit Text dialogue box – Fig. 18.2
respond (a) move arrow to TX|ET EXRECISE and left click
         (b) backspace to give T|ET EXRECISE
         (c) move arrow to TE|T EXRECISE and left click
         (d) enter X to give TEX|T EXRECISE
         (e) move arrow to TEXT EXR|ECISE and left click
         (f) backspace to give TEXT EX|ECISE
         (g) move arrow to TEXT EXE|CISE and left click
         (h) enter R to give TEXT EXER|CISE
         (i) pick OK
prompt   `<Select a TEXT or ATTDEF object>/Undo`
respond right-click to end sequence.

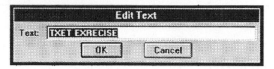

Fig. 18.2. Edit Text dialogue box.

The item of text should be displayed with the correct spelling. This method of editing existing text items is very useful. The user could have erased the text item completely, and then used the TEXT command to re-enter it again – of course it could be re-entered with the wrong spelling!

Now save your text exercise (but *not as* A:USEREX).

Text justification

Text items added to a drawing can be 'justified' (positioned) in different ways, and AutoCAD R13 has 15 justification positions, these being:
(a) six basic: left, aligned, fitted, centred, middled and right
(b) nine extra: TL, TC, TR, ML, MC, MR, BL, BC, BR.
   The justification points can be:
(a) picked with the mouse
(b) entered as co-ordinates
(c) referenced to existing entities.
1. Open your standard sheet A:STDA3 and refer to Fig. 18.3
2. With OUT the current layer, draw the following entities:
   (a) a 100 sided square from the point 50,50
   (b) a circle of radius 50, centre point at 270,150
   (c) five lines: (1) from 220,20 to 320,20; (2) from 220,45 to 320,45; (3) from 120,190 to 200,190; (4) from 225,190 to 275,250; and (5) from 305,250 to 355,100.
3. Make layer TEXT current.
4. Activate the Draw, Modify and Object Snap toolbars.
5. From the menu bar select **Draw–Text–Dynamic Text** and
   prompt   `Justify/Style/<Start point>`
   enter   **25,245**<R>

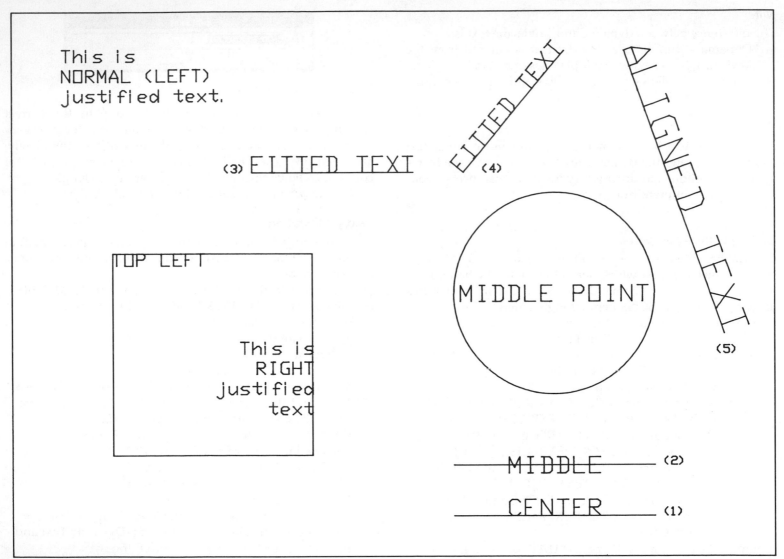

Fig. 18.3. Text justification.

prompt   Height<?> and enter **6** <R>
prompt   Rotation angle<0> and enter **0<R>**
prompt   Text and enter **This is** <R>
prompt   Text and enter **NORMAL (LEFT)** <R>
prompt   Text and enter **justified text.** <R>
prompt   Text and <RETURN>

6. Repeat the Dynamic Text menu bar selection and:

prompt   Justify/Style/<Start point>
enter   **J<R>** – the justify option
prompt   Align/Fit/Center/Middle/Right/TL...
enter   **R<R>** – the right option
prompt   End point
respond   **Snap the Midpoint icon and pick right vertical line of the square**
prompt   Height<6> and <RETURN>
prompt   Rotation angle<0> and <RETURN>
prompt   Text and enter **This is** <R>
prompt   Text and enter **RIGHT** <R>
prompt   Text and enter **justified text** <R>
prompt   Text and <RETURN>

7. Select the Dynamic Text icon from the Draw toolbar and

prompt   Justify/Style/<Start point>
enter   **J<R>**
prompt   Align/Fit/Center...
enter   **C<R>** – the Center option
prompt   Center point
respond   **Snap to Midpoint icon and pick line 1**
prompt   Height<6> and enter **8** <R>
prompt   Rotation angle<0> and <RETURN>
prompt   Text and enter **CENTERED** <R><R> – two returns!

8. Enter **DTEXT<R>** at the command line and:

prompt   Justify/Style/<Start point>
enter   **J**
prompt   Align/Fit/Center...

enter   **M<R>** – the middle option
prompt   Middle point
respond   **Snap to Midpoint icon and pick line 2**
prompt   Height<8> and <RETURN>
prompt   Rotation angle<0> and <RETURN>
prompt   Text and enter **MIDDLE** <R><R>

9. Activate the dynamic text command, and pick the **Fit** justify option and

prompt   First text line point
respond   **Snap to Endpoint and pick left end of line 3**
prompt   Second text line point
respond   **Snap to Endpoint and pick right end of line 3**
prompt   Height and Rotation as default values
prompt   Text and enter **FITTED TEXT** <R><R>

10. Now add the following:
    (a) FITTED TEXT to line 4, with a height of 8.
    (b) ALIGNED TEXT to line 5.

11. Activate the text command and select the **TL** justification option and

prompt   Top/Left point
respond   **Snap to Intersection icon and pick top left of square**
prompt   Height to be 6, Rotation to be 0
prompt   Text to be **TOP LEFT**<R><R>

12. Final item of text is the **MC** justify option and

prompt   Middle point
respond   **Snap to Center icon and pick the circle**
prompt   Height to be 8, angle to be 0
prompt   Text to be **MIDDLE POINT** <R><R>

13. Your drawing should resemble Fig. 18.3. Save it if you want, but we will not refer to this drawing again.

14. The text justification options are easy to use. By entering the justification letter (C, F, TC, BL, etc.) the user can position the text to specific requirements. The letters entered are:
    F: fit   M: middle   C: centre   R: right   A: aligned
    TL: top left   MC: middle centre   BR: bottom right.

The TEXT selection option

When the **Draw–Text** option is activated from the menu bar, the user has three options for selection, these being:

(a) Text
(b) Dynamic Text
(c) Single-Line Text.

Two of these options have already been discussed, and the third option (Text) will be discussed in a later chapter. This is a new R13 option, and pre-R13 users will not yet be aware of it.

Text style

When the text command is activated, one of the options available to the user is **Style**. This option allows to user to set the appearance of the text from different user created styles. At present we will leave this option to another chapter, when we will investigate text fonts and styles.

If the text which is added to your drawings appears slightly different from mine it is due to the text style being used. At this stage, the appearance of the text style is unimportant.

Activity

Attempt Tutorial 6 which is four components with some items of text added. The procedure for drawing should be familiar to you:

1. Open your A:STDA3 standard sheet.
2. Complete the drawings using layers correctly.
3. Save as A:TUT-6.

❏ *Summary*

1. Text is a draw command and can be activated from the menu bar or the Draw toolbar.
2. There are two text options available to the user:
   (a) single-line text
   (b) dynamic text.
3. Dynamic text allows the user to 'see' the text as it is entered from the keyboard. It also allows multiple lines of text to be entered. This is my preferred text option.
4. Text can be entered with varying height and rotation angle. The default rotation angle is 0°, i.e. horizontal text.
5. There are 15 text justification options.
6. The text start point (centred, fitted, aligned, etc.) can be entered as co-ordinates, picked with the mouse, or referenced to existing entities.
7. Screen text can be edited using a dialogue box with Edit Text.
8. Fitted and aligned text are similar as the user selects the line start and end points, but:
   (a) fitted text height is entered by the user
   (b) aligned text height is 'adjusted' to suit the pick points.
9. Centered and middled text are similar, the user selecting the centre/middle point but:
   (a) centred text is about the text BASELINE
   (b) middle text is about the text MIDDLE.
10. Multiple lines of text are justified according to the option selected.

19. Dimensioning

AutoCAD R13 has both automatic and associative dimensioning. For new users, these terms are:

Automatic: the user selects the entity to be dimensioned, and R13 displays the actual dimension with the dimension 'size', arrows, extension lines, etc.

Associative: all the arrows, dimension lines, text, etc. which make up the dimension are treated as a single entity, with the following features:

(a) they change if the entity being dimensioned changes its original size

(b) their appearance can be altered.

Dimensioning has its own nomenclature, and Fig. 19.1 shows the 'types' of dimensioning which are available with R13. These are:

1. Linear (both horizontal and vertical) and aligned.
2. Baseline and continuous.
3. Ordinate – both X and Y datum.
4. Angular.
5. Radial – diameter and radius.
6. Leader – taking the dimension 'outside' the entity.

Dimension exercise

To demonstrate the dimension types we will use our working drawing component, which was last used with offset, extend and trim, so:

1. Open **A:WORKDRG** and erase the four 'centre lines'.
2. Check the layer control dialogue box, i.e. Data–Layers from the menu bar. Only layer 0 is available?
3. Refer to Fig. 19.2 which is rather cluttered due to the number of points which have to be selected – persevere with it.
4. Activate the Modify, Object Snap and Dimensioning toolbars.

Note that the appearance of dimensions depends on the dimension style which will be discussed in the next chapter. Your actual dimensions in this exercise may not be the same as mine, and my dimension 'layout' may not be as you would want it. At this stage we are not interested in the dimension style, only in the dimension process.

Linear dimensioning

1. From the menu bar select **Draw**
                                Dimensioning
                                Linear

prompt	First extension line origin or RETURN to select
respond	**ENDpoint icon and pick point d1**
prompt	Second extension line origin
respond	**ENDpoint icon and pick point d2**
prompt	Dimension line location (...) and drag effect is obtained
respond	**pick a point d3 below the line dimensioned, using the 'pick point' to determine the dimension text position.**

2. Select the Linear icon from the Dimension toolbar and

prompt	First extension line origin...
respond	**ENDpoint icon and pick point d4**
prompt	Second extension line origin
respond	**ENDpoint icon and pick point d5**
prompt	Dimension line location
respond	**pick a point d6 to the left of line dimensioned, using the 'pick point' to position the dimension text.**

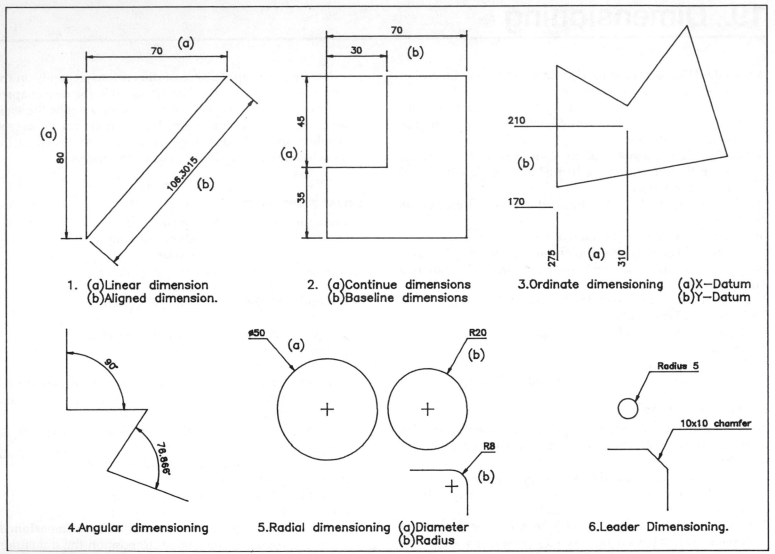

Fig. 19.1. Dimensioning nomenclature.

Baseline dimensioning

This allows dimensions to be taken from a common 'datum' line.

1. From the menu bar select **Draw–Dimensioning–Linear** and

    prompt   First extension line origin...

    respond   **ENDpoint icon and pick point d7**

    prompt   Second extension line origin

    respond   **ENDpoint icon and pick point d8**

    prompt   Dimension line location

    respond   **pick a point d9 above the line**

2. Select from the menu bar **Draw–Dimensioning–Baseline** and

    prompt   Second extension line origin

    respond   **ENDpoint icon and pick point d10**

    prompt   Second extension line origin

    respond   **ENDpoint icon and pick point d11**

    prompt   Second extension line origin

    respond   **press the ESC key**

Continuous dimensioning

1. Select the Linear dimension icon and

    prompt   First extension line origin...

    respond   **ENDpoint icon and pick point d12**

    prompt   Second extension line origin

    respond   **ENDpoint icon and pick point d13**

    prompt   Dimension line location

    respond   **pick point d14 to the right of dimensioned line**

2. Select the Continuous icon from the Dimensioning toolbar

    prompt   Second extension line origin

    respond   **ENDpoint icon and pick point d15**

    prompt   Second extension line origin

    respond   **ENDpoint icon and pick point d16**

    prompt   Second extension line origin

    respond   **press ESCape key**

Diameter dimensioning

From the menu bar select **Draw–Dimensioning–Radial–Diameter**

prompt   Select arc or circle

respond   **pick circle d17**

prompt   Dimension location and <RETURN>

Radius dimensioning

Activate the Radius icon from the Dimensioning toolbar

prompt   Select arc or circle

respond   **pick circle d18**

prompt   Dimension line location and <RETURN>

Aligned dimensioning

Select the Aligned icon from the Dimensioning toolbar

prompt   First extension line origin

respond   **ENDpoint icon and pick point d19**

prompt   Second extension line origin

respond   **ENDpoint icon and pick point d20**

prompt   Dimension line location

respond   **drag and pick point d21 'above' line**

Angular dimensioning

Select the Angular icon from the Dimensioning toolbar

prompt   Select arc, circle or line or RETURN

respond   **pick line d22**

prompt   Second line

respond   **pick line d23**

prompt   Dimension arc line location

respond   **drag and pick a point d24 'above' lines**

Leader dimensioning

From the menu bar select **Draw–Dimensioning–Leader** and

prompt   From point

respond   **NEArest icon and pick line d25**

prompt	To point
respond	**pick a point d26 'above' the selected line**
prompt	To point...
respond	**<RETURN>**
prompt	Annotation...
enter	**10x10**<R>
prompt	MText and <R>

Dimension options

When using the dimension commands, the user will be aware of various options when the prompts are displayed. While it is not my intention to investigate all these options, there are several which are worth discussing.

1. You should still have your dimensioned A:WORKDRG on the screen, so I would recommend that you save it at this stage, but not as A:WORKDRG as we want to use the original drawing again.
2. Draw five horizontal lines towards the right of the screen, about 60 length, as Fig. 19.2.
3. The **RETURN** option. Select the Linear dimension icon and:

prompt	First extension line origin or RETURN to select
respond	**<RETURN>**
prompt	Select object to dimension
respond	**pick the top horizontal line**
prompt	Dimension line location...
respond	**pick point above line** – Fig. 19.1(a).

4. Select the Linear icon, <RETURN>, pick the second line and

prompt	Dimension line location...
enter	**A**<R> – the angle option
prompt	Enter text angle
enter	**15**<R>
prompt	Dimension line location...
respond	**pick point above line** – Fig. 19.1(b).

5. Linear icon, <RETURN>, pick the third line and

prompt	Dimension line location...
enter	**R**<R> – the rotated option
prompt	Dimension line angle<0>
enter	**15**<R>
prompt	Dimension line location...
respond	**pick point above line** – Fig. 19.1(c).

6. Linear icon, <RETURN>; pick fourth line and

prompt	Dimension line location...
enter	**T**<R> – the text option
prompt	Edit MText dialogue box – more on this later
enter	**A LINE** then pick **OK**
prompt	Dimension line location...
respond	**pick above the line**

7. Keyboard dimensioning. Users with pre-R13 knowledge may be surprised at the omission of the 'Dimension Text' prompt when using the dimension commands. The option is available if dimensioning is activated from the command line.
   At the command line enter **DIM**<R>

prompt	Dim
enter	**HOR**<R> – for horizontal dimensioning
prompt	First extension line origin...
respond	**RETURN and pick the fifth line drawn**
prompt	Dimension line location...
respond	**pick a point 'below' the line**
prompt	Dimension text<60>
enter	**123.456**<R> and the dimension is entered
then	Dim
respond	**ESC** to end command.

Hopefully your drawing will resemble Fig. 19.2.

The <RETURN> option is generally easier to use when dimensioning as it only requires the user to select the entity (line, circle, arc) to be dimensioned. I must admit to not using this option very often, preferring to select the entity to be dimensioned using object snap modes.

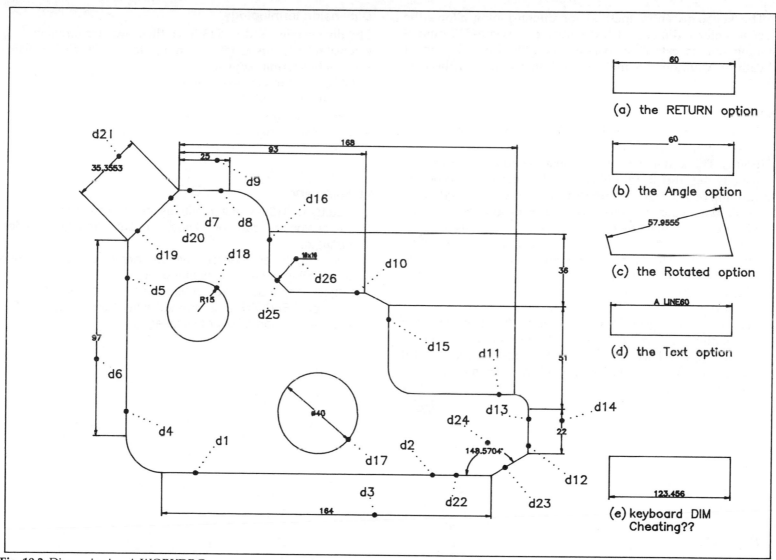

Fig. 19.2. Dimensioning A:WORKDRG.

The keyboard entry method for dimensioning allows the user to enter a dimension text value. This is pre-R13 dimensioning and is extremely useful, but is it dimensioning or cheating? More on this method of dimensioning in the next chapter.

Note

1. In the dimensioning exercises, the user will have been aware of using the object snap icons to select entity reference points. This is when a running object snap is worth using. I usually set the it to ENDpoint. Remember to cancel a running object snap, as problems may occur if it is left on.
2. From the menu bar select **Data–Layers** and observe the Layer Control dialogue box. We have only used layer 0 with our dimensioning exercise, but there is a layer called DEFPOINTS. This layer is automatically created every time any entity is dimensioned. It can be frozen, turned off, changed colour, but this will not affect the screen dimensions.
3. When the dimension line location is 'being picked' the actual dimension text position on this line should be central. If it is not, don't worry. Position the dimension line and if the text item is not central simply select the Home icon from the Dimensioning toolbar.

Dimension terminology

The dimensions used in R13 have their own terminology, e.g. extension line, offset, text location, etc. Figure 19.3 explains some of this terminology for:

1. Dimension and extension lines.
2. Various arrowheads.
3. Centre marking.
4. Text positioning.
5. Interior/basic dimensioning.

❏ *Summary*

1. AutoCAD R13 has automatic. associative dimensions.
2. Dimensioning can be linear, radial, angular, leader, ordinate.
3. The diameter and degrees symbols are automatically added when using radial and angular dimensions.
4. Object snap modes are usually used to select entities.
5. A layer DEFPOINTS is created when dimensioning. The user has no control over this layer.

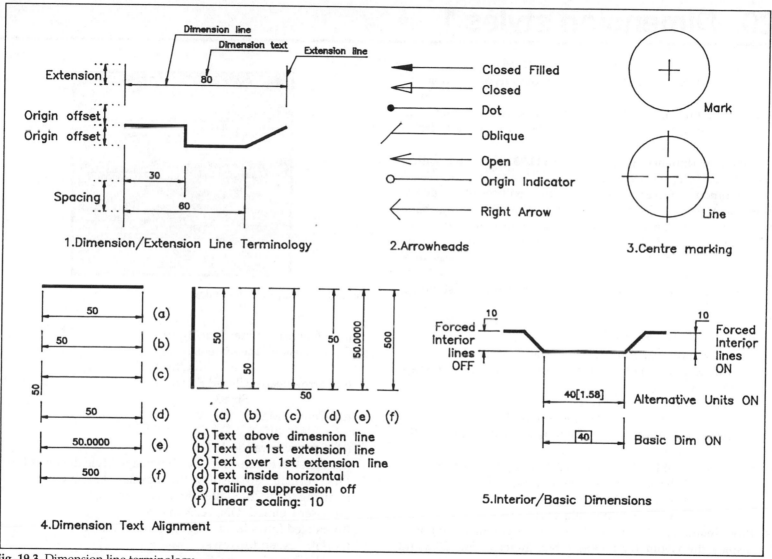

1.Dimension/Extension Line Terminology

2.Arrowheads

Closed Filled
Closed
Dot
Oblique
Open
Origin Indicator
Right Arrow

3.Centre marking

Mark
Line

4.Dimension Text Alignment

(a)
(b)
(c)
(d)
(e)
(f)

(a) (b) (c) (d) (e) (f)

(a) Text above dimesnion line
(b) Text at 1st extension line
(c) Text over 1st extension line
(d) Text inside horizontal
(e) Trailing suppression off
(f) Linear scaling: 10

5.Interior/Basic Dimensions

Forced Interior lines OFF
Forced Interior lines ON
Alternative Units ON
Basic Dim ON

Fig. 19.3. Dimension line terminology.

20. Dimension styles 1

Dimension styles allow the user to set dimension variables to individual standards. This permits styles to be 'saved' for a required standard, e.g. British Standards, ANSI (American), DIN (German) or individual company/customer standards. To demonstrate how a dimension style is 'set and saved', we will create a new dimension style called **STDA3** and save it within our A:STDA3 standard sheet.

The dimension exercise which follows will result in several new dialogue boxes being displayed, and certain settings have to be altered within these dialogue boxes. It is important for the user to be familiar with the Dimension Style dialogue boxes, as a good working knowledge of them is essential if different dimension styles have to be used. The settings used in the exercise are my own, designed for our standard sheet.

Setting dimension style STDA3

1. Start R13 and open your A:STDA3 standard sheet.
2. Activate required toolbars, e.g. Draw, Modify, Object Snap, Dimensioning.
3. From the menu bar select **Data**
   Dimension Style

   prompt   Dimension Style dialogue box with ISO-25 as the Current style

   respond   1. at the Name box, click to right of ISO-25
               2. backspace six times to remove ISO-25
               3. enter STDA3 name
               4. pick Rename – Fig. 20.1

4. Pick **Geometry...** from the Dimension Style dialogue box to display the Geometry dialogue box. Refer to Fig. 20.2 and alter the following values:

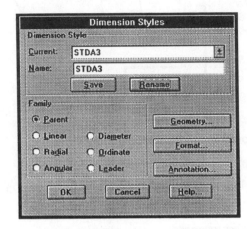

Fig. 20.1. Dimension Styles dialogue box.

(a) Dimension Line: Spacing 10
(b) Extension Line: Extension 2.5
                       Origin Offset 2.5
(c) Arrowheads: Closed Filled
               Size 3
(d) Center: Mark
            Size 2
(e) Scale: Overall scale 1
(f) Pick OK to return to the Dimension Style dialogue box.

5. Pick **Format...** to display the Format dialogue box, and referring to Fig. 20.3, alter the following:
(a) User Defined: ON, i.e. X in box
(b) Forced Lines Inside: OFF, i.e. no X in box
(c) Fit: Text and Arrows
(d) Horizontal justification: Centred

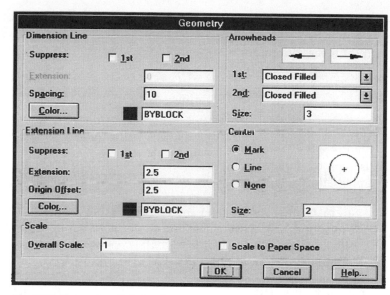

Fig. 20.2. Geometry dialogue box.

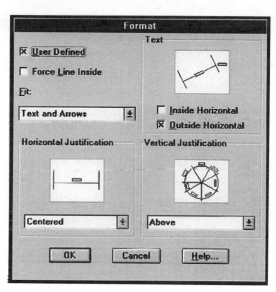

Fig. 20.3. Format dialogue box.

(e) Text: Inside Horizontal OFF, i.e. no X in boxOutside Horizontal ON, i.e. X in box
(f) Vertical justification: Above
(g) Pick OK to return to the Dimension Style dialogue box.
6. Pick **Annotation**... to display the Annotation dialogue box, refer to Fig. 20.4 and alter the following:
(a) Tolerance: None and Middle
(b) Alternate Units: OFF, i.e. no X at Enable Units
(c) Text: Style STANDARD, Height 3, Gap 1.5, Round off 0
(d) Pick Units... to display the Primary Units dialogue box, and set the Dimension Precision to 0.0, then pick OK
(e) Pick OK to return to the Dimension Style dialogue box.
7. As all our 'settings' are now complete:
(a) pick **Save** from the Dimension Style dialogue box
(b) note message **Saved to STDA3** displayed at bottom of box

(c) pick OK from Dimension Style dialogue box to return to the drawing screen.
8. From the menu bar select **File–Save** which will automatically update the A:STDA3 standard sheet.
9. The A:STDA3 standard sheet has the following personal settings:
(a) drawings aids, e.g. snap, grid, no blips
(b) a drawing border within which all drawing work is completed
(c) several layers, e.g. OUT, CL, DIM, etc.
(d) a dimension style STDA3.

Using the STDA3 dimension style

Now that we have created a dimension style, we will 'check' it by dimensioning several entities, so:
1. ensure the A:STDA3 drawing is on the screen

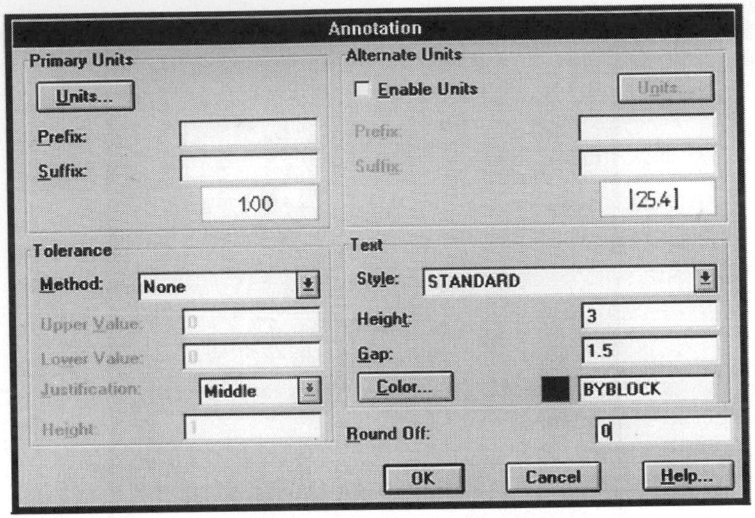

Fig. 20.4. Annotation dialogue box.

2. Check that STDA3 is the dimension style with **Data–Dimension Style** from the menu bar. It should be, so pick OK.
3. Make OUT the current layer – it should be.
4. Use the following commands with absolute co-ordinate input to draw the shape to be dimensioned:

LINE	CIRCLE
From 60,90	1. Centre at 80,160; radius 15
To 95,90	2. Centre at 115,145; radius 10
To   125,120
To   140,80
To   160,200
To   50,185
To   c

5. With DIM the current layer, refer to Fig. 20.5(a) and add the following dimensions:

(a) Linear baseline vertical
(b) Linear continuous horizontal
(c) Linear continuous vertical
(d) Linear baseline horizontal
(e) Three angular
(f) One diameter and one radius.

Ordinate dimensioning

This type of dimensioning was not covered in the previous chapter, and we will investigate it with our STDA3 dimension style.

1. With OUT the current layer refer to Fig. 20.5(a) and create the following shape using absolute co-ordinate input:

LINE	CIRCLE
From point 230,130	Centre point 265,175; radius 12
To point   280,130
To point   330,170
To point   330,230
To point   300,200
To point   250,220
To point   c

2. Make DIM the current layer.
3. From the menu bar select **Draw–Dimensioning–Ordinate–X Datum** and

prompt	Select feature
respond	**pick point A** – snap ON helps
prompt	Leader endpoint
enter	**0,–10**<R>

4. Select **Draw–Dimensioning–Ordinate–Y Datum** from the menu bar and:

prompt	Select feature
respond	**pick point A**
prompt	Leader endpoint
enter	**–10,0**<R>

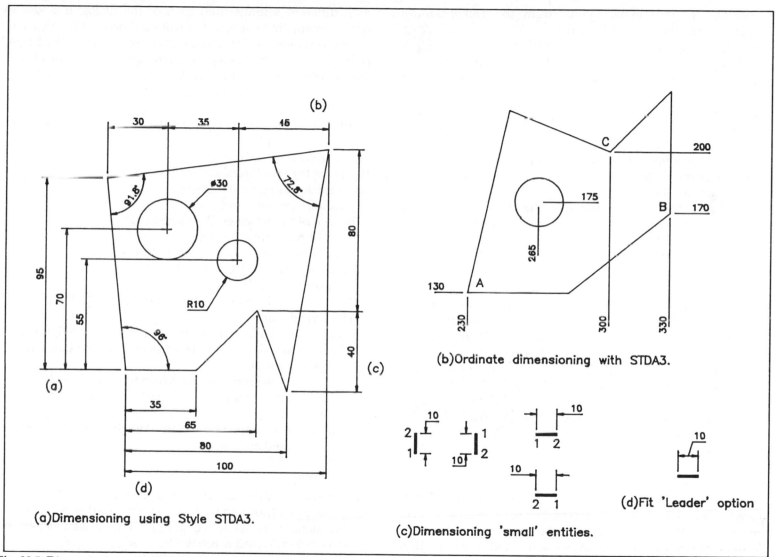

(a)Dimensioning using Style STDA3.

(b)Ordinate dimensioning with STDA3.

(c)Dimensioning 'small' entities.

(d)Fit 'Leader' option

Fig. 20.5. Dimensioning with STDA3 dimension style.

5. Activate the Automatic fly-out from the Dimensioning toolbar and pick the X Datum icon:
   prompt   Select feature and pick point B
   prompt   Leader endpoint and enter 0,–50<R>
6. Select the Y Datum icon from the Dimensioning toolbar
   prompt   Select feature and pick point B
   prompt   Leader endpoint and enter 10,0<R>
7. Now use the X and Y ordinate icons, picking point C and entering the following leader endpoints:
   (a) X Datum 0,–80
   (b) Y Datum 40,0
8. X and Y ordinate again and pick the circle centre as the feature using the CENtre icon, then enter the leader endpoints as:
   (a) X Datum 0,–20
   (b) Y Datum 20,0

Dimensioning small entities

When 'small' entities are being dimensioned the result may not be as expected, as the dimension text may not 'fit between' the dimension extension lines. To demonstrate the effect draw two horizontal and two vertical lines each being 10 units in length. Linear dimension each line, referring to Fig. 20.5(c). The points 1 and 2 refer to the 'pick order'. Note how the dimension text is positioned relative to the pick order. One way of avoiding this type of dimension is to use Leader from the Fit option of the Format dialogue box – Fig. 20.5(d).

Note

There are many options available with the Dimension Style dialogue boxes and it is not possible to investigate every combination. It is in the user's interest to know how the different options affect the dimensions, and I would thus recommend that you create several different dimension styles with different settings from each of the dialogue boxes. By dimensioning line entities, you will soon become familiar with the various options. For all our dimensioning work, the STDA3 style will suffice. Also investigate the dimension styles which are available with R13, i.e. ISO-25, etc.

Activity

As dimensioning is important, I have included three activities. These exercises will give the user practice with:
(a) creating more components
(b) using the standard sheet with layers
(c) opening and saving drawings
(d) adding text and dimensions.
   In each of the activities, the user should:
1. Use the New drawing icon.
2. Enter A:STDA3 as the Prototype drawing name.
3. Enter A:TUT-? as the New drawing name.
4. Complete the drawing.
5. Pick the Save icon to save the drawing as A:TUT-?
   The activities are:
(a) Tutorial 7: two simple shapes to get you started, but the I have included some awkward sizes. Use offset and trim as much as possible.
(b) Tutorial 8: two components which require some thought to complete. The signal arm is particularly interesting to draw.
(c) Tutorial 9: a component which is much easier to complete than it would appear.

❏ Summary

1. Dimension styles can be set to user requirements.
2. Dimension styles can be saved and recalled at any time.
3. Our standard sheet A:STDA3 has a 'customised' dimension style called STDA3 which will be used for all our dimensioning work.

21. Construct and modify

In this chapter we will investigate several of the **Construct** and **Modify** commands and will also investigate other selection set options. The commands which will be discussed are:

Construct Copy, Mirror
Modify   Move, Rotate, Scale

Getting ready for the exercise

1. Start R13 and open your A:WORKDRG which was last used for the dimension exercise. The component was created on the A:STDA3 standard sheet before layers and dimension styles were created.
2. The drawing should consist of:
   (a) the component outline in black – filleted and chamfered
   (b) two circles with four 'centre lines'
   (c) a black border
   (d) layer 0 current – it is the only layer!
3. If you have saved your dimension exercise as A:WORKDRG, then I'm afraid that you will have to delete all your dimensions – we do not want them in this exercise.
4. Activate the Draw, Modify, Object Snap and Select Objects toolbars and position them towards the right of the drawing screen.

Copy

This command allows entities to be copied to other parts of the screen. The command has both single and multiple copy options.

Refer to Fig. 21.1 and select the Copy icon from the Modify toolbar:

prompt Select objects
respond **select Crossing icon** from Select Objects toolbar and
prompt First corner
respond **pick a point d1**
prompt Other corner
respond **pick point d2**
prompt 19 found and selected entities highlighted then Select objects
respond **select Add icon** from the Select Objects toolbar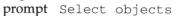
prompt Select objects
respond **pick entities d3,d4,d5** then **right-click**
prompt <Base point or displacement>/Multiple
respond **ENDpoint icon and pick line d6**
prompt Second point of displacement
enter   **@240,60<R>**

The original component will be copied to another part of the screen, and your drawing should resemble Fig. 21.2. You may have to re-arrange some of your toolbars to 'see' the complete copied component.

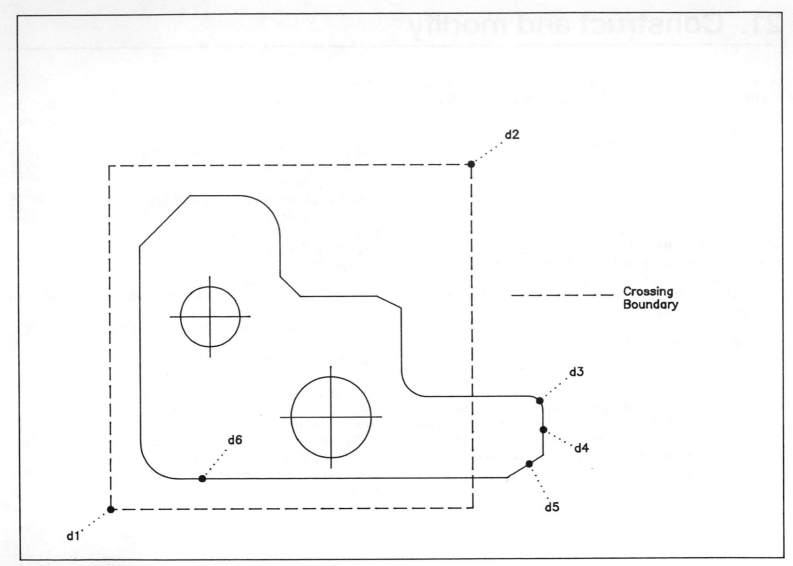

Fig. 21.1. A:WORKDRG with points for the COPY command.

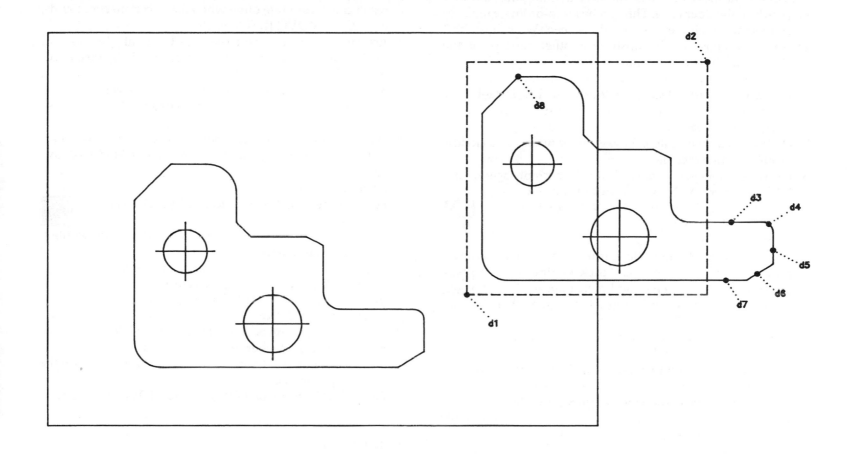

Fig. 21.2. A:WORKDRG after the COPY command, with points for the MOVE command.

Move

This command moves entities, the user defining the start and end points of the operation. This can be by co-ordinate input or by referencing existing entities on the screen. We will use this part of the exercise to demonstrate another concept of the Construct and Modify commands.

1. We have only used layer 0 to draw/dimension our WORKDRG, but select from the menu bar Data–Layers and make a new layer LA1, colour green with continuous linetype and current.
2. Draw a circle, centre at 330,130 with radius 30. This circle is inside the copied circle.
3. Using Data–Layers, make layer 0 current again, and FREEZE layer LA1 No green circle displayed.
4. Refer to Fig. 21.2 and from the Modify toolbar select the Move icon and

    prompt   Select objects
    respond select Windows icon from Select Objects toolbar
    prompt   First corner and **pick a point d1**
    prompt   Other corner and **pick a point d2**
    prompt   17 found and entities highlighted then Select objects
    respond select Add icon from Select Objects toolbar
    prompt   Select objects
    respond **pick entities d3,d4,d5,d6,d7 then right-click**
    prompt   Base point or displacement
    respond **INTersection icon and pick point d8**
    prompt   Second point of displacement and Note 'ghost image' as mouse is moved
    enter   **@–100,200<R>**

5. Your windowed component has disappeared and you are starting to become a bit worried? Don't panic.
6. From the menu bar select **View–Zoom–All**.
7. Your drawing screen will now appear as Fig. 21.3 with the MOVED component displayed at the top of the screen, i.e.

although it 'appeared' to move out of sight, it was on another part of our drawing screen. Note that this type of result can occur quite often when using certain commands, e.g. COPY, MOVE, ROTATE, etc.

8. Activate the Layer Control dialogue box (Data–Layers) and THAW the LA1 layer – the green circle will be displayed, but will be in its original drawn position, i.e. it has not been moved with the MOVE command. This is a very common 'problem' with entities which are on frozen/off layers. Erase the green circle – we will not use it again.
9. We will now move the component to a more realistic part of the screen, so from the menu bar select **Modify–Move** and

    prompt   Select objects
    respond pick the Previous icon (Select Objects toolbar) and
    prompt   22 found and the 'moved' shape is highlighted
    respond **right-click**
    prompt   Base point or displacement
    enter`   **295,330**<R> – a circle centre point
    prompt   Second point of displacement
    enter   **310,130**<R>

10. The component will be moved back into the drawing area – not quite within the border.
11. From the menu bar select **View–Zoom–All** to 'increase the screen' appearance.
12. Figure 21.4 is the result of this second MOVE operation.

Transparency

Using the COPY and MOVE commands involved selecting icons from the Select Objects toolbar while the original command was still active. This type of usage is called *transparency* and is only available with certain commands. It is generally used with the selection set and the zoom commands.

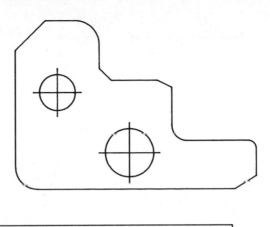

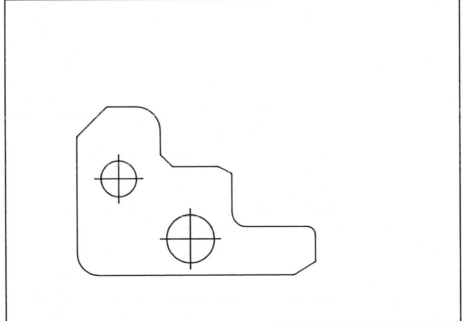

Fig. 21.3. Drawing screen after MOVE and ZOOM, All.

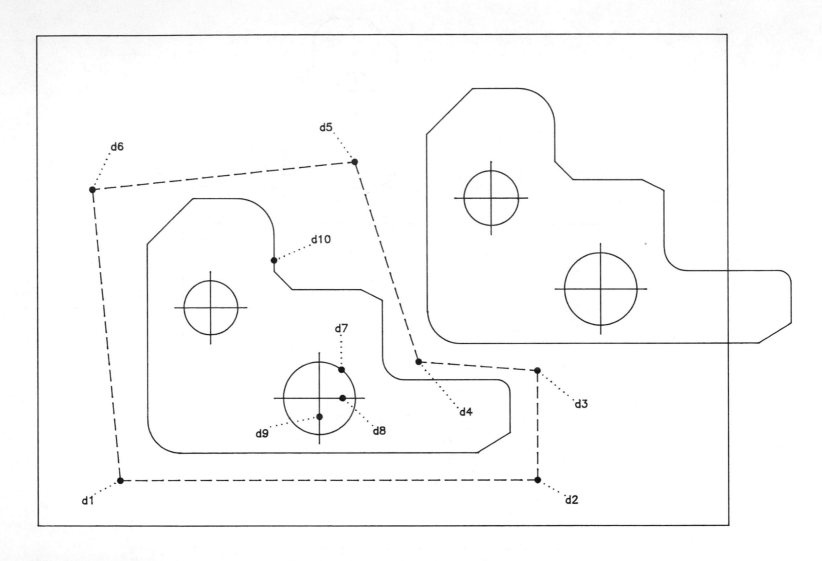

Fig. 21.4. A:WORKDRG after the secon MOVE operation with points for the ROTATE command.

Rotate

Allows the user to 'turn' objects about a designated point. The rotation can be in a clockwise direction (negative) or in an anti-clockwise direction (positive).

Refer to Fig. 21.4 and select the Rotate icon from the Modify toolbar and

prompt   Select objects
respond   pick Window Polygon icon
prompt   First polygon point and **pick a point d1**
prompt   Undo/<Endpoint of line> and **pick point d2**
prompt   Undo/<Endpoint of line> and **pick point d3**
prompt   Undo/<Endpoint of line> and **pick point d4**
prompt   Undo/<Endpoint of line> and **pick point d5**
prompt   Undo/<Endpoint of line> and **pick point d6**
prompt   Undo/<Endpoint of line> and **right-click**
prompt   22 found – highlighted
prompt   Select objects
respond   pick Remove icon from Select Objects toolbar
prompt   Remove objects
respond   **pick entities d7,d8,d9** then **right-click**
prompt   Base point
respond   **ENDpoint icon and pick line d10**
prompt   <Rotation angle>/Reference
enter   **−90<R>**

The original component is rotated, but the selected circle and 'centre lines' are not – Fig. 21.5.

Scale

The scale command allows complete 'shapes' or selected entities to be increased/decreased in size, and when used with dimensions can give some interesting results. To prepare the drawing screen for the command, refer to Fig. 21.5 and

1. Erase the complete component on the right (window selection) and the circle and centre lines 'on their own' to leave the 'rotated' component.
2. Dimension the following using icons:
   (a) Linear icon and pick the left vertical line (164)
   (b) Radius icon and pick circle (R15).
3. At the command line enter **DIM<R>**
   prompt   Dim and enter **HOR<R>**
   prompt   First extension line   and enter **<RETURN>**
   prompt   Select objects and **pick the top horizontal line**
   prompt   Dimension line location and **pick point above line**
   prompt   Dimension text<97> and enter **97<R>**
             NB: *enter* **97**
   prompt   Dim and enter **DIA<R>**
   prompt   Select arc or circle and **pick circle as before**
   prompt   Dimension text<30> and enter **30<R>**
   prompt   Dimension line location and **pick outside circle**
   prompt   Dim and press **ESC**
4. Four dimensions added as Fig. 21.5?
5. MOVE the component and dimensions from a base point of 50,210 by @0,35.
6. Refer to Fig. 21.6 and select the SCALE icon from the Stretch flyout of the Modify toolbar
   prompt   Select objects
   respond   **Window the complete component and dimensions**

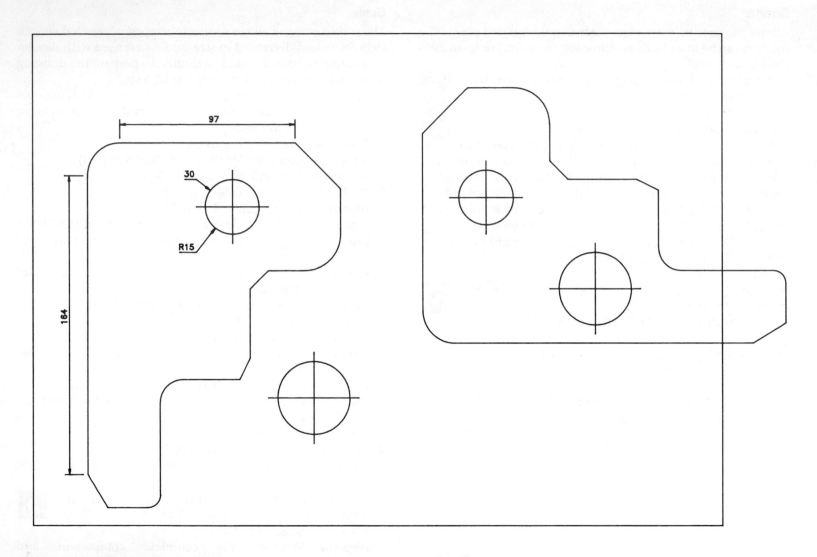

Fig. 21.5. A:WORKDRG after the ROTATE command with dimensions for the SCALE operation.

prompt	`23 found` and then **right-click**
prompt	`Base point`
enter	**0,270<R>** – top LH corner of border
prompt	`<Scale factor>/Reference`
enter	**0.75<R>**

7. The complete component will regenerated at 3/4 size. Note the dimensions:
    (a) vertical dimension of 164 is now 123
    (b) horizontal dimension of 97 is still 97
    (c) radius of 15 is now 11.25
    (d) diameter of 30 is still 30

Why have two dimensions been scaled by 0.75 and two have not? The dimensions which have not been scaled are those which we entered using the keyboard DIM command. Another question: which of the final dimensions are correct – (a) and (c) or (b) and (d)? Think about this!

Multiple copy

This is an option of the COPY command, so from the menu bar select **Construct–Copy** and:

prompt	`Select objects`
respond	from menu bar select **Edit–Select Objects–Previous**
prompt	`23 found` and 'scaled component' highlighted
respond	**right click**
prompt	`<base point or displacement>/Multiple`
enter	**M<R>**
prompt	`Base point`
respond	**CENter icon and pick circle**
prompt	`Second point of displacement` and enter **@90,–90<R>**
prompt	`Second point of displacement` and enter **@230<–15<R>**
prompt	`Second point of displacement` and **right-click**

Now you have two copies of the dimensioned component – Fig. 21.6.

Mirror

Allows components to be mirrored imaged about a line designated by the user by co-ordinate input, referencing existing entities or by picking points on the screen. The command has an option for deleting the original objects if required. Refer to Fig. 21.7 and
(a) erase the two multiple copied components
(b) add the following item of text:
    AutoCAD R13, centred on 55,180; height 5; rotation 0.
(c) draw a line from 135,125 to 135,255.

1. From the menu bar select **Construct–Mirror** and

prompt	`Select objects`
respond	**window the component and dimensions**
prompt	`24 found` and right-click
prompt	`First point of mirror line`
respond	**pick one endpoint of drawn line**
prompt	`Second point`
respond	**pick other endpoint of line**
prompt	`Delete old objects?<N>`
enter	**N<R>**

2. The component is mirrored about the line. Observe:
    (a) dimensions – not mirrored?
    (b) text item – is mirrored?

3. At the command line enter **MIRRTEXT<R>** and

prompt	`New value for MIRRTEXT<1>`
enter	**0<R>**

4. Select the MIRROR icon from the copy flyout of the Modify toolbar and

prompt	`Select objects` and enter **P<R>**
prompt	`24 found` and original highlighted
respond	**right click**
prompt	`First point...` and enter **50,75<R>**
prompt	`Second point` and enter **@50<45<R>**
prompt	`Delete old objects` and enter **N<R>**

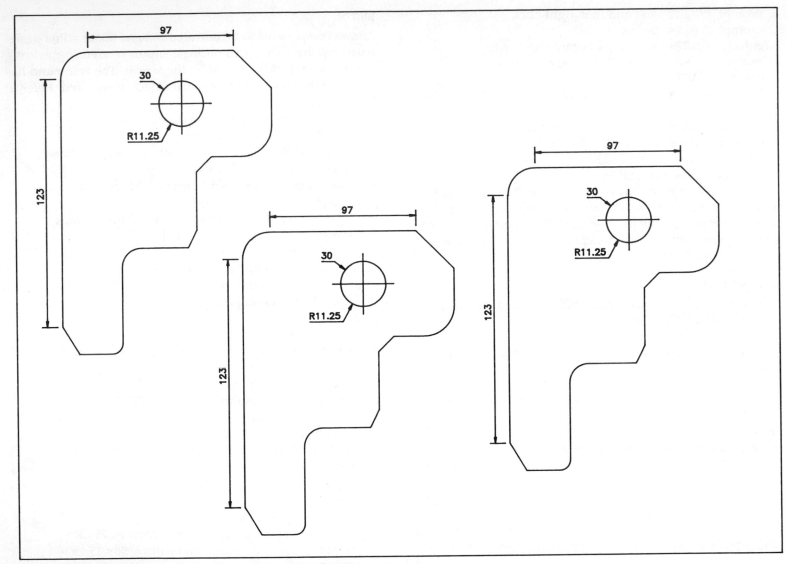

Fig. 21.6. A:WORKDRG after the SCALE and MULTIPLE COPY operations.

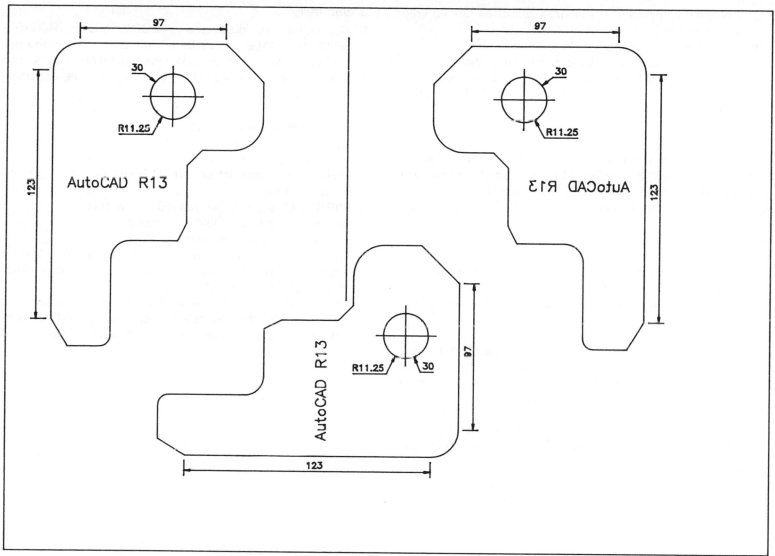

Fig. 21.7. A:WORKDRG after the MIRROR command.

5. The original component is mirrored about the line entered as shown in Fig. 21.7.

Note: (a) dimension positions; (b) text is not mirrored.

This exercise has been quite long, as it has introduced several very common AutoCAD R13 commands. You can now save your work if you want (but not as A:WORKDRG!), but we will not use these modified drawings again.

Activities

Three relatively easy activities are included for this chapter. Each activity should be completed on the A:STDA3 standard sheet, and the method of starting the drawing should be:

(a) A:STDA3 as the Prototype and A:TUT? as the New Drawing
(b) open A:STDA3 and then Save As A:TUT?

The activities are:

1. Tutorial 10: a part decoder circuit which is completed using the multiple copy command.
   Drawing in the lines can be awkward due to the size of the components. Altered SNAP size will help.
2. Tutorial 11: a template drawing.
   This is easier than it looks. Start by drawing the 1/4 of the template given, using the reference sizes. The drawing uses trim quite a bit to obtain the final outline. The mirror command is used twice? I'll let you think about the text item.
3. Tutorial 12: a memory cell.
   Uses mirror, copy and scale. The actual reference drawing is harder than you may think, but should not give any problems.

❏ **Summary**

1. The commands discussed – COPY, MOVE, ROTATE, MIRROR, SCALE can all be activated from the menu bar, the toolbar icons or by direct keyboard entry of the command.
2. The selection set is useful for selecting objects, especially the add/remove options.
3. All of the commands require a base point, and this can be:
   (a) entered as co-ordinates
   (b) referenced to existing entities
   (c) picked on the screen.
4. Entities on layers which are OFF or FROZEN are not copied, moved, etc.
5. MIRRTEXT is a variable with a 0 or 1 value and
   (a) value 1 (default) – text is mirrored
   (b) value 0 – text is not mirrored.
6. Dimensions entered using the icon/menu bar selection are scaled, but dimensions entered using the keyboard (DIM) command are not scaled.
7. The commands used in this chapter demonstrated *transparency* with the Selection Set, i.e. activating other selections while the original command is still active.

22. The selection set

The selection set has been used in previous chapters, allowing the user to 'select objects' when prompted after many commands, e.g. COPY, MOVE, ERASE, etc. The selection set options can be activated by three methods:

1. Menu bar.
   Edit
   Select Objects → Window; Crossing; Group; Previous; Last; All; Window Polygon; Crossing Polygon; Fence; Add; Remove; Selection Filters.
2. Toolbar.
   The Select Objects toolbar has the 12 options available in icon form.
3. Keyboard.
   By entering the letters (W, C, WP, F, etc.) at the prompt line, the selection option will be activated.

The 12 options available with the selection set are:

Window – selects all entities completely within a user specified rectangular window.

Crossing – all entities within or crossing a user specified rectangular window are selected.

Group – predefined entities are selected – dealt with later.

Previous – selects the previous selection set.

Last – the last entity 'drawn' is selected.

All – all entities on the screen are selected.

Window Polygon – selects all entities completely within a user-defined polygon shaped window.

Crossing Polygon – all entities within/crossing a user-defined polygon shaped window are selected.

Fence – selects entities across a fence line boundary.

Add – allows selected entities to be added to the defined selection set.

Remove – selected entities will be removed from the defined selection set.

Selection Filters – allows the user to define 'restrictions' to the selection set.

The selection set usage is shown in:

1. Figure 22.1 using the COPY command with:
   (a) Window then removing three lines
   (b) Crossing Polygon then adding two circles
   (c) Window Polygon then adding two lines and removing one line.
2. Figure 22.2 with the FENCE option using the MIRROR, TRIM and EXTEND commands.

Notes

1. Using the selection set illustrates transparency, i.e. a 'command' being used while 'inside' another.
2. The selection set options should be used at all times, as they improve draughting efficiency.
3. I find that the Select Objects toolbar is the easiest method for selecting the options.

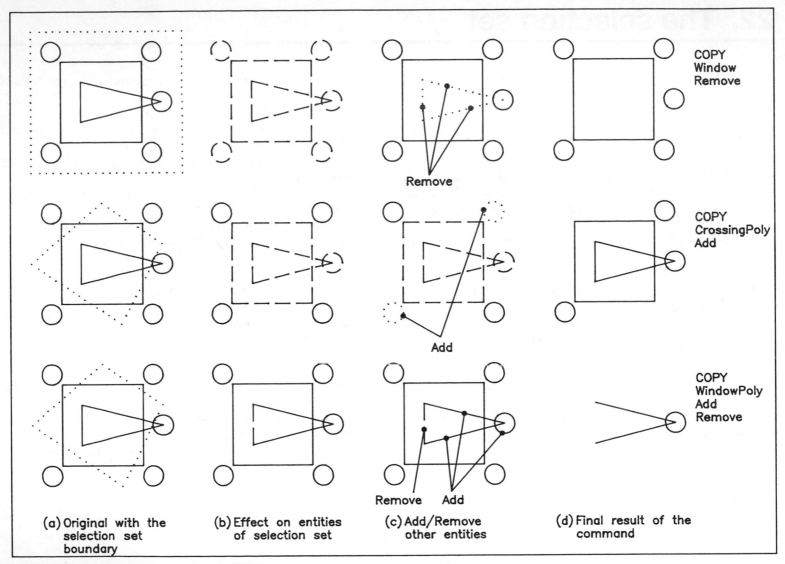

Fig. 22.1. Selection set demonstrated with COPY.

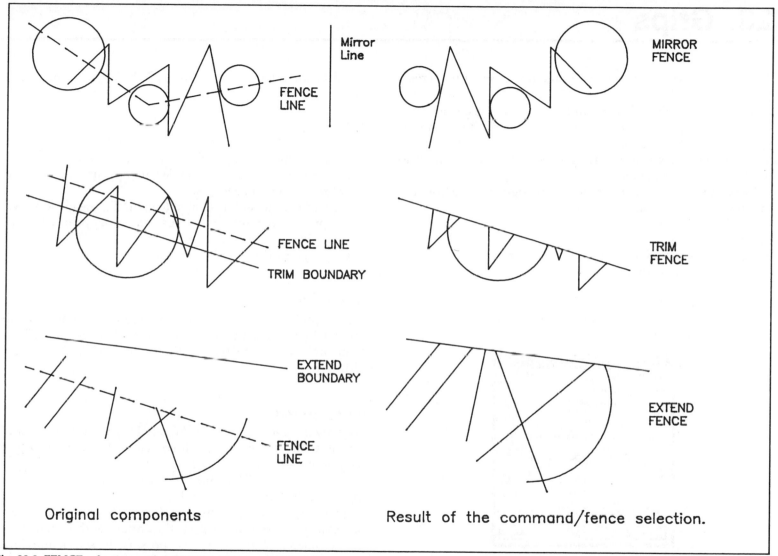

Fig. 22.2. FENCE selection with MIRROR, TRIM and EXTEND.

23. Grips

The small box which is attached to the on-screen cursor cross-hairs is called the grips box, and in an earlier chapter we entered some keyboard commands to 'turn the grips off'. This was because we had no reason to use grips, and they can lead to some difficulties for new AutoCAD users. In this chapter we will investigate what grips are, and how they can be used to modify existing drawings.

Grips can be toggled on/off using a dialogue box, so from the menu bar select **Options**
> **Grips...**

prompt Grips dialogue box
respond 1. pick Enable Grips box, i.e. X in box
2. leave colours as:
   (a) unselected – blue
   (b) selected – red
3. set Grip Size box to suit – Fig. 23.1
4. pick OK.

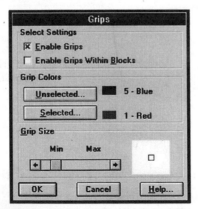

Fig. 23.1. Grips dialogue box.

The drawing screen is returned, with the grip box attached to the cross-hairs.

Notes
1. The grip box should not be confused with the box used for selecting entities, e.g. with the ERASE command for example. Although they are similar in appearance, they are entirely different concepts.
2. When a command is activated (e.g. LINE), the grips box will disappear from the cross-hairs, and re-appear when the command is terminated.
3. Grips are activated with a left-click.

What do grips do?
Grips provide the user with five commands which can be activated without using the icon or menu bar selections. These commands are STRETCH, MOVE, ROTATE, SCALE and MIRROR.

How grips work
To activate a command in AutoCAD, the user first of all activates the command and then selects the entities, e.g. to copy entities, the sequence is:
(a) activate the COPY command – icon or menu bar
(b) select the entities to be copied.
Grips work in the 'opposite sense' from this normal selection process, i.e. the user first selects the entities and then activates the command. With grips, it is possible to select individual entities or entities within a window/crossing boundary.

To demonstrate the grip effect, refer to Fig. 23.2 and
1. Select an area of the screen which has nothing drawn.
2. Move the screen cursor to this area.
3. Pick any point on the screen with a left-click.
4. Move the cursor upwards/downwards to the right of this picked point and note a 'solid window type box' is dragged out.
5. Move the cursor upwards/downwards to the left of the picked point and note a 'dotted crossing type box' occurs.
6. Now press ESC to cancel the grip selection.

When an entity is selected with the grip box, the entity will change appearance and 'blue grip boxes' will appear at the entity snap points as follows:

line: at the endpoints and midpoint
circle: at the circle centre and the four quadrants
arc: at the arc endpoints and midpoint
text: at the text start point.

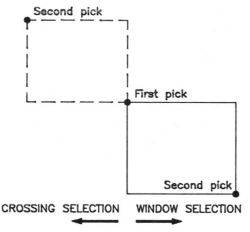

CROSSING SELECTION   WINDOW SELECTION

Fig. 23.2. Selections with grips.

Types of grip

There are three different types of grip as shown in Fig. 23.3. These are:

(a) Cold grip: appear on selected entities in blue, but the entity is not highlighted. The grip options cannot be used with the entity.
(b) Warm grip: appear in blue on highlighted (dashed) entities. The grip options can be used.
(c) Hot grip: appears as a solid red box when a grip box is picked and acts as the base point for the grip options.

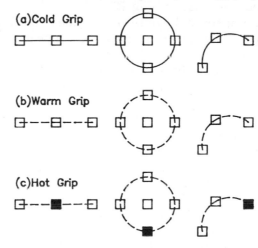

Fig. 23.3. Types of grip.

Draw a line, circle and arc anywhere on the screen to any size and then:

(a) move the cursor to each entity and 'pick them' using the grip box
(b) blue grip boxes appear at the entity 'object snap point' and the entities appear dashed – warm grips
(c) press ESC – blue boxes but no highlight – cold grips
(d) press ESC – no grips on entities.

Grip exercise

The demonstration here is quite simple, but rather long. It is advisable that you work through this exercise without missing any of the steps, so:

1. Open your A:STDA3 standard sheet and refer to Fig. 23.4.
2. De-activate any toolbars which are displayed.
3. Draw the following:
    (a) a 50-unit square, lower left corner at 100,100
    (b) a 15 radius circle, centre point at 125,130
    (c) R13 text item, centred on the point 125,105 with height 4 and zero rotation – Fig. 23.4(a).
4. Move the cursor to the right vertical line of the square and pick it with a left-click. Blue grip boxes appear and the line changes appearance. This is a warm grip – Fig. 23.4(b).
5. Move cursor to the bottom blue grip box and left-click. This box appears as a red solid, i.e. a hot grip – Fig. 23.4(c) and:

    prompt ** STRETCH **
    <Stretch to point>/Base point/Copy/Undo/eXit
    respond **right-click**
    prompt ** MOVE **
          <Move to point>...
    enter   @**20,10**<R>

6. Three 'things' should have happened:
    (a) the command line is returned
    (b) the selected line is moved
    (c) the moved line is still warm – Fig. 23.4(d).
7. Move to the circle and pick it with a left-click. The line and circle are now warm – Fig. 23.4(e).
8. Move to the bottom circle grip box and pick it with a left-click. The box becomes hot – Fig. 23.4(f) – and

    prompt ** STRETCH **
          <Stretch to point>...

    respond **right-click**
    prompt ** MOVE **
          <Move to point>...
    respond **right-click**
    prompt ** ROTATE **
          <Rotation angle>...
    enter   **90**<R>

9. The line and circle are rotated about the 'circle base quadrant' and are both still warm – Fig. 23.4(g).
10. Move to circle centre grip box, and pick it – Fig. 23.4(h) – and

    prompt ** STRETCH **
          <Stretch to point>
    enter   **SC**<R> – the scale option
    prompt ** SCALE **
          <Scale factor>...
    enter   **0.5**<R>

11. The circle and line are scaled by 0.5 about the circle centre, and are both still warm – Fig. 23.4(i).
12. Add the text item to the circle and line selection, by picking it with a left click, i.e. line, circle and text item are warm.
13. Make the right box of the highlighted line hot and

    prompt ** STRETCH **
    enter   **MI**<R>
    prompt ** MIRROR **
          <Second point>...
    enter   @**50<–45**<R>

14. Press ESC – cold grips on the three entities?
15. Press ESC – removes the grips and leaves Fig. 23.4(j).

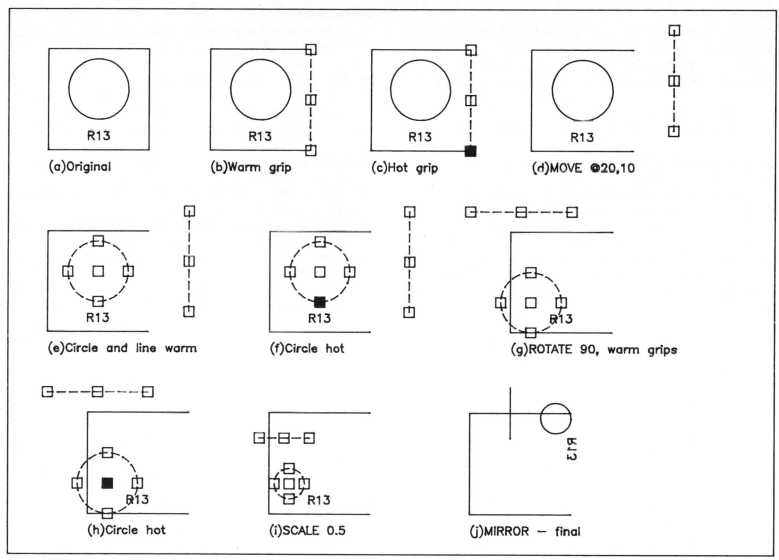

Fig. 23.4. Grip exercise.

Activity

The grip activity is a robot arm – Tutorial 13 which displays the reference sizes for drawing the robot arm and

(a) the arm after it has been drawn – original position
(b) upper arm rotation of 45° – need to 'pick' the two circles and two lines. The base point for rotation is the centre grip of the larger circle
(c) both arms mirrored about the vertical axis of the robot. Three circles and four lines required?
(d) both arms rotated to a horizontal position
(e) three grip operations:
    1. upper arm rotation to the vertical position
    2. upper arm movement to the right
    3. lower arm stretch to the upper arm position.

This activity should be attempted with grips, although it can be completed with other commands. The sizes given are only a guide, as you should be able to create a robot arm to your own sizes. The last part of the tutorial (e) may required some thought!

❏ *Summary*

1. Grips allow the user access to the commands STRETCH, MOVE, ROTATE, SCALE and MIRROR without icon or menu bar selection.
2. The order is always as listed above.
3. Grips work in the 'opposite sense' from normal AutoCAD commands, i.e. object first then command.
4. Grips allow the user access to entities which may not be easily selected using the selection set.
5. Grips *do not have to be used* – they are an alternative to the normal selection.
6. Grips are enabled/disabled using the Grips dialogue box.
7. Grips can be cold, warm or hot.
8. The grip box colours can be changed, but are defaulted with blue for cold/warm and red for hot.
9. If grips are not to be used, I recommend that they be disabled.
10. The grip option can be activated by entering the first two letters of the option and the prompt, e.g. SC, MI, etc.

24. Drawing assistance

All entities created so far have been drawn by:
(a) picking points on the screen
(b) using co-ordinate input from the keyboard
(c) referencing existing entities, e.g. ENDpoint.
There are other methods which enable entities to be created, and in this section we will investigate three new ideas, these being:
(a) point filters
(b) construction lines
(c) ray lines.

Point filters

1. Open the A:STDA3 standard sheet with layer OUT current, and refer to Fig. 24.1.
2. Display the Draw, Modify, Object Snap and Point Filters toolbars towards the right of the drawing screen.

Example 1

1. Draw a 50-unit square, the lower left corner being at the point 30,200.
2. Multiple copy this square by @70,0 and @140,0.
3. We want to draw a circle of diameter 30 and the 'centre' of each square, and will use three different methods:
   (a) Coordinates: activate the CIRCLE icon, enter 55,225 as the centre point and 15 as the radius – Fig. 24.1(a)
   (b) Object Snap: draw a diagonal line in the second square, then select the CIRCLE icon and
   prompt   Center point
   respond **MIDpoint icon and pick diagonal**
   prompt   Radius and enter **15<R>** – Fig. 24.1(b)

(c) Point Filters: select the CIRCLE icon and
prompt   Center point
respond **pick .X icon from Point Filters toolbar**
prompt   of
respond **MIDpoint icon and pick line AB**
prompt   (need YZ)
respond **MIDpoint icon and pick line AC**
prompt   Diameter/<Radius> and note snap is at 'square centre'
enter   **15<R>** – Fig. 24.1(c).

Example 2

Figure 24.1 gives a top, end and isometric view of a shaped block. We want to construct the front view of the block using point filters. The exercise is given as a sequence of point filter instructions and is quite long and repetitive, but persevere with it.
1. Draw the top and end views to the sizes given, in any suitable area of the screen – SNAP ON will assist.
2. Select the LINE icon and
   prompt   From point
   respond **pick .X point filter icon**
   prompt   .X of
   respond **pick point (a)**
   prompt   (need YZ)
   respond **pick .YZ point filter icon**
   prompt   .YZ of
   respond **pick point (k)** and cursor 'jumps' to selected point on screen
   prompt   To point
   respond **pick .X point filter icon**
   prompt   .X of

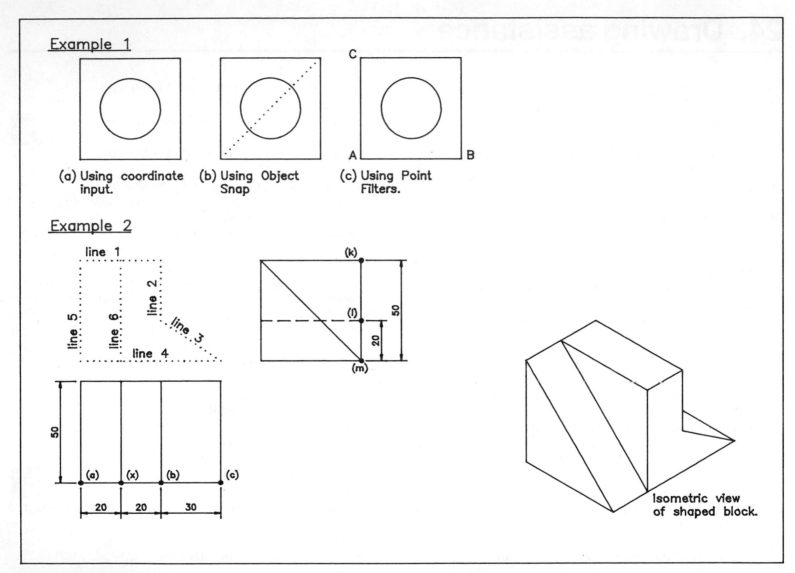

Example 1

(a) Using coordinate input.

(b) Using Object Snap

(c) Using Point Filters.

Example 2

line 1
line 2
line 3
line 4
line 5
line 6

(k)
(l)
(m)
50
20

50
(a) (x) (b) (c)
20 20 30

Isometric view of shaped block.

Fig. 24.1. Point filter examples.

respond	**pick point (b)**
prompt	(need YZ)
respond	**pick .YZ point filter icon**
prompt	.YZ of
respond	**pick point (k)** and line 1 is drawn
prompt	To point
respond	.X icon and pick point (b)
prompt	(need YZ)
respond	.YZ icon and pick point (l) and line 2 is drawn
prompt	To point
respond	.X icon and pick point (c)
prompt	(need YZ)
respond	.YZ icon and pick point (m) and line 3 is drawn
prompt	To point
respond	.X icon and pick point (d)
prompt	(need YZ)
respond	.YZ icon and pick point (m) and line 4 drawn
prompt	To point
respond	.X icon and pick point (a)
prompt	(need YZ)
respond	.YZ icon and pick point (k) and line 5 is drawn
prompt	To point and right click.

3. The outline of the shaped block is complete.
4. The vertical line can be easily drawn, but we will use the point filter technique so select the LINE icon and

prompt	From point
respond	.Y icon and pick point (k) then .XZ icon and pick point (x) then .Y icon and pick point (m) then .XZ icon and pick point (x) and line 6 is drawn then right click.

5. The front view of the block is now complete.
6. The drawing can be saved if required.

Construction lines

Construction lines are lines that extend to infinity in both directions from a selected point. They can be referenced to assist in the creation of other entities.

1. Open your A:SDTA3 standard sheet, activate the Draw, Modify and Object Snap toolbars and refer to Fig. 24.2(a).
2. With OUT the current layer, draw:
   (a) a 100-sided square, lower left corner at 50,50
   (b) a 50 radius circle, centre at 250,150.
3. Create a new layer (Data–Layers) called **CONLINE**, colour yellow and linetype DASHED. Make this new layer current.
4. Check the global linetype scale is 12–14.
5. Select the construction line icon from the LINE flyout of the Draw toolbar and

prompt	Hor/Ver/Angle/Bisect/Offset/<From point>
enter	**50,50<R>** and note line 'attached' to cursor
prompt	Through point
enter	**80,200<R>**
prompt	Through point
respond	**MIDpoint icon and pick top line of square**
prompt	Through point
respond	**CENter icon and pick circle**
prompt	Through point and right-click.

6. The screen will display three yellow dashed lines, all passing through the 50,50 selected point. These lines 'extend in both directions' from this point.
7. From the menu bar select **Draw–Construction Line** and

prompt	Hor/Ver/Angle...
enter	**H<R>** – the horizontal option
prompt	Through point and enter 50,180<R>
prompt	Through point and MIDpoint icon, pick square side
prompt	Through point and QUADrant icon, pick top circle
prompt	Through point and right-click.

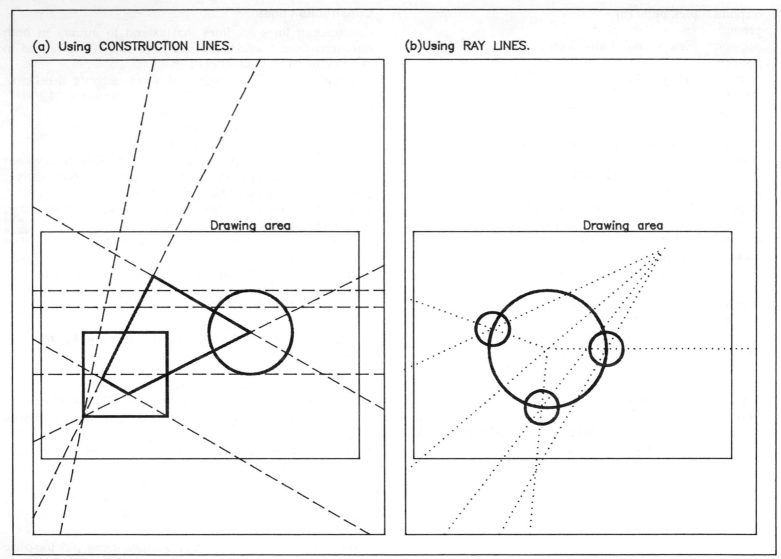

Fig. 24.2. Construction and ray lines.

8. At the command line enter **XLINE**<R>

prompt	Hor/Ver...
enter	**A**<R> – the angle option
prompt	Reference/<Enter angle <0>>
enter	**–30**<R>
prompt	Through point and CENter icon and pick circle
prompt	Through point and INTersection icon and pick the lower right corner of square
prompt	Through point and right-click.

9. The construction lines can be copied, moved, reference by the user to created other shapes. I have added a simple shape to the square and circle drawing as shown in Fig. 24.2(a).

Note

Construction lines are usually created on their own layer, and this layer is then frozen to avoid 'screen clutter'. I have left the construction layer on, so that we can 'see' the lines. I've also made them yellow and dashed, so that they can easily be identified.

Task

Try the following:
1. At the command line enter **LIMITS**<R> and

prompt	<Lower left corner> and enter **0,0**<R>
prompt	Upper right corner and enter **10000,10000**<R>

2. From the menu bar select **View–Zoom–All** and
   (a) our drawing appears very small in the lower left corner
   (b) the construction lines are 'radiating outwards'.
3. Enter LIMITS and
   (a) –10000,–10000 as the lower left corner
   (b) 0,0 as the upper right corner.
4. View–Zoom–All to 'see' the construction lines.
5. Return limits to 0,0 and 420,297 then Zoom All – original?
6. Save if required, but we will not use this drawing again.

Rays

Rays are similar to construction lines, but they only extend to infinity in one direction from the selected point.

1. Open A:STDA3 and draw a circle at the point 160,130 with a radius of 70.
2. Make a new layer called RAY, colour magenta and linetype dot. Make this new layer current and refer to Fig. 24.2(b).
3. Select the RAY icon from the LINE flyout of the Draw toolbar and

prompt	From point
respond	**CENter icon and pick circle** and as you move the mouse, the screen is covered with black ray lines radiating from the circle centre – don't panic
prompt	Through point and enter **@100<0**<R>
prompt	Through point and enter **@100<160**<R>
prompt	Through point and enter **150,30**<R>
prompt	Through point and right-click

4. Select the REDRAW icon and
   (a) black radiating lines disappear
   (b) you feel better
   (c) three new dotted magenta lines have been created.
5. With OUT the current layer, draw three circles of radii 20 at the ray line and circle intersection.
6. At the command line enter **RAY**<R> and

prompt	From point and enter **300,250**<R>
prompt	Through point
respond	**CENter icon and pick the four circles** then right-click

7. REDRAW to remove any black ray lines – Fig. 24.2(b).

Note

Rays are normally created on their own layer and frozen when not required. As they are only drawn in 'one direction' they do not cause as much 'screen clutter' as the construction lines. The black 'radiating effect' of rays when the mouse is moved always causes concern, but the effect is removed with REDRAW.

❏ *Summary*

1. Point Filters allow the user a method of accessing existing entity co-ordinates.
2. Point filters should be activated from the toolbar, although they can be activated from the menu bar.
3. Point filters do not have to be used. They allow the user another method of creating entities.
4. Construction lines and rays can be useful. They allow lines to be drawn to infinity from a selected point and
   (a) construction lines are extended in both directions
   (b) rays only extend in one direction.
5. Construction lines and rays can be referenced to create other entities. They should have their own named layer.
6. Both construction lines and rays can be activated from the toolbar, the menu bar or from the keyboard.
7. As with point filters, construction lines and rays do not have to be used. They are aids for the AutoCAD user.

25. Viewing a drawing

In the chapter dealing with COPY, MOVE, etc. we had to 'zoom all' to see the complete drawing due to certain co-ordinate input, but up until now we have not really investigated how to view a drawing

AutoCAD R13 has three methods of viewing a drawing, these being:

(a) pan
(b) zoom
(c) aerial view.

The commands are usually activated by using the mouse, selecting points on the screen as required. They can also be used with co-ordinate input.

As usual we will demonstrate the commands by example, so open your **A:WORKDRG** which should display:

(a) a four line border
(b) the component which is filleted and chamfered
(c) two circles with four 'centre lines'
(d) no dimensions.

Pan

1. From the Standard toolbar select the Pan Point icon and
   prompt   Displacement
   respond **pick any two points on the screen**
2. Drawing appears to have moved?
3. Note that the Pan Point icon has a flyout facility which allows access to another eight icons.
4. Investigate some of these icon options, and you may find that your drawing quickly disappears from the screen.
5. The PAN options are also available from the menu bar with **View–Pan** which accesses the nine options.

6. Finally PAN the screen so that your drawing is visible – the lower left corner at least.
7. At the command line enter **PAN<R>**
   prompt   Displacement
   respond **INTersection and pick lower left corner of border**
   prompt   Second point
   enter   0,0<R>
8. Drawing back to its original position, but not at corner of the screen?
9. From the menu bar select **View–Pan–Point** and
   prompt   Displacement and enter 0,0<R>
   prompt   Second point and enter **@500,500<R>**
10. No drawing on screen?

Zoom

Allows the user zoom in/out on selected areas of a drawing obtaining different 'magnification' effects. The ZOOM command can be activated:

(a) from the menu bar with View–Zoom
(b) from the Zoom flyout menu of the Standard toolbar
(c) by entering ZOOM<R> at the command line.

Refer to Fig. 25.1 which displays six zoom options for our A:WORKDRG.

Zoom all

A very useful option, as it 'restores' a complete drawing:
1. Screen still blank?
2. From the menu bar select **View–Zoom–All**.
3. Original A:WORKDRG restored at the origin? – Fig. 25.1(a).

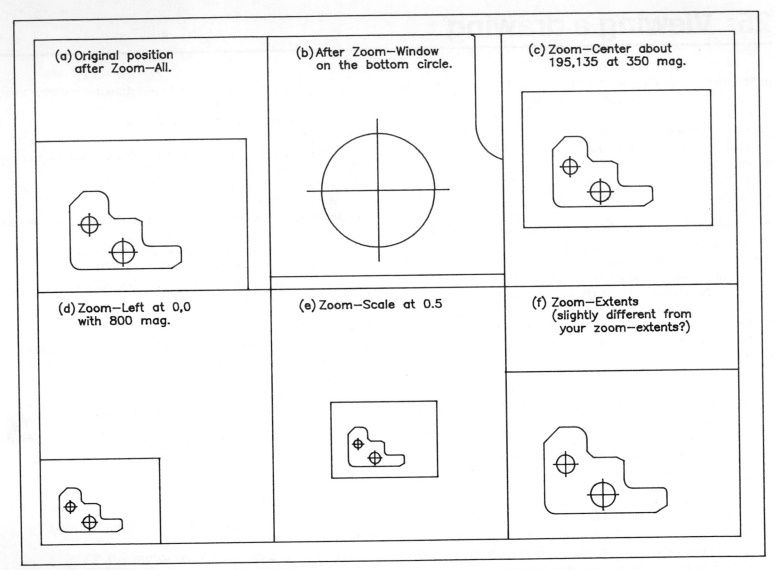

Fig. 25.1. Some ZOOM options.

Zoom window

Perhaps the most useful of the zoom options, as it allows the user to 'magnify' parts of a drawing for clarity/closer work, etc. This option is generally activated by the user selecting a window on the screen.

1. Select from the menu bar **View–Zoom–Window** and
   prompt　　First corner
   respond　**window the bottom circle and 'centre lines'**
2. The circle and lines 'fill the screen'.
3. Circle appears as lines? – 16 perhaps?
4. At the command line enter **REGEN**<R> – Fig. 25.1(b).
5. At the command line enter **ZOOM**<R>
   prompt　　All/Center...
   enter　　　**W**<R>
   prompt　　First corner and enter **150,60**<R>
   prompt　　Other corner and enter **170,80**<R>
6. You have now 'zoomed in' on the centre line intersection.
7. If the snap is ON, the cursor movement is very jerky, due to the snap setting and the small drawing area displayed.

Zoom previous

Returns the screen to the display before the last zoom command. It can be used until all the zoom options are 'removed'.

1. From the menu bar select **View–Zoom–Previous** to return to the circle screen.
2. View–Zoom–Previous again, to display the original drawing.
3. Don't do it, but you could Zoom–Previous again. What would be displayed?

Zoom center

Allows drawings to be zoomed about a user-defined centre point. Our border is 380 × 270, so the drawing 'centre' is at the point 195,135.

1. At the command line enter **ZOOM**<R>
   prompt　　All/Center/Dynamic...
   enter　　　**C**<R> – the centre option
   prompt　　Center point
   enter　　　**195,135**<R>
   prompt　　Magnification or height<297.00>
   enter　　　**350**<R>
2. The drawing is displayed at the centre of the screen and is smaller than the original – Fig. 25.1(c). The 'size' of the drawing is dependent on the magnification value entered relative to the <...> default which was 297 for our drawing:
   (a) a value less than 297 will magnify the drawing
   (b) a value greater than 297 will reduce the size of the drawing.
3. Note the grid effect for the centre option.
4. Now select from the menu bar **View–Zoom–Center** and try these:
   (a) centre point at 195,135 with 500 magnification
   (b) 0,0 as the centre point with a magnification of 1000
   (c) centre point: 380,270; magnification: 400.
5. Zoom–Previous four times – original drawing?

Zoom left

1. Select from the menu bar **View–Zoom–Left** and:
   prompt　　Lower left corner point and enter **0,0**<R>
   prompt　　Magnification or height and enter **800**<R>
   　　　　　　Fig. 25.1(d).
2. Select View–Zoom–Left and enter
   (a) 380,270 as the lower left corner point
   (b) 800 as the magnification
3. Drawing displayed? – think about it!
4. Now Zoom–Previous twice.

Zoom scale

This option is similar to Zoom–Center, but is probably 'easier to understand'.

1. From the menu bar select **View–Zoom–Scale** and
   prompt   `All/Center/.../<scale (X/XP)>`
   enter **0.5<R>**
2. Drawing is displayed at the screen centre and scaled half-size as Fig. 25.1(e).
3. At the command line enter **ZOOM<R>**; then **S<R>**; then **0.25<R>**.
4. Zoom–Previous twice to return to original.

Zoom limits

Zooms the drawing to the existing limits, but is only really useful if the drawing limits have been altered.

1. From the menu bar select **View–Zoom–Limits** and there should be no apparent change to the drawing. The drawing is zoomed to the existing limits.
2. From the menu bar select **Data–Drawing Limits**
   prompt   `Lower left corner` and enter **0,0<R>**
   prompt   `Upper right corner` and enter **600,500<R>**
3. Now View–Zoom–Limits and smaller drawing due to increased limits?
4. Set limits back to 0,0 (lower left) and 420,297 (upper right) then View–Zoom–Limits again. Original drawing?
5. Question: why did we not just Zoom–Previous, rather than alter the drawing limits?

Zoom extents

This option zooms the drawing to the extents of the drawing screen, and the drawing 'fills the screen'.

1. Select **View–Zoom–Extents** and the drawing may appear slightly larger.
2. De-activate the Standard and Object Properties toolbars then View–Zoom–Extents again. Drawing fills the screen? – Fig. 25.1(f).

3. Set drawing limits of 0,0 to 600,500 then
   (a) View–Zoom–All
   (b) View–Zoom–Extents.
4. Activate the Standard and Object Properties toolbars and dock them at the top of the screen. Remember this?
5. Set the drawing limits back to 0,0 and 420,297 then View–Zoom–All to restore the original A:WORKDRG drawing – I hope!

Zoom Vmax and Zoom Dynamic

I will not discuss these two options as I have never found them of great relevance, and indeed the Dynamic Zoom can be a 'bit fiddly' to new AutoCAD users. The other options are more than sufficient for the user's zoom requirements.

Aerial view

The aerial view command allows the user to pan and zoom a drawing interactively, i.e. by using the aerial view dialogue box, the actual screen drawing can be panned and zoom. The command is really only suited for very large drawings, allowing the user to 'see' different areas before selecting the one to work on.

1. Your original A:WORKDRG position should be on the screen?
2. From the Standard toolbar select the Aerial View icon and
   prompt   `Aerial View interactive dialogue box or Aerial View Unavailable` message.
3. The first time that I used the Aerial View command, I was rather surprised when the unavailable message was displayed as Fig. 25.2. If you are faced with this message, select from the menu bar **Options–Configure**, pick the Video display number, then pick a new Video display option, e.g. Accelerated Display Driver.

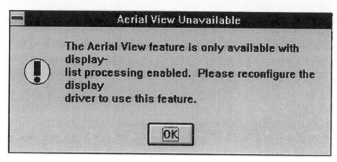

Fig. 25.2. Aerial View message.

4. When the Aerial View is used with the A:WORKDRG drawing, the screen will be as Fig. 25.3, i.e. the Aerial View 'dialogue box' is placed to the right of the screen and also displays the A:WORKDRG.
5. To use Aerial View:
   (a) move the cursor into the Aerial View screen
   (b) the cursor becomes dashed
   (c) window any area of the drawing – the **view box**
   (d) the main drawing will also change
   (e) note the appearance of the 'black line' in the dialogue box. This black rectangle controls the drawing display.

Aerial view options

The 'commands' available with the Aerial View dialogue box are:
(a) menu bar: View – Zoom in, Zoom Out, Global
   mode – Pan or Zoom
   * – indicates current mode
   options – of no interest to us at this stage.
(b) Icons: from left to right the icons are:
   Pan, Zoom, Locator, Zoom in. Zoom out, Global, Statistics.

Note

I would suggest that although the Aerial View is very useful, it is not required at our level with our A3-size drawings. The Zoom Window and Zoom All commands should cover all users requirements.

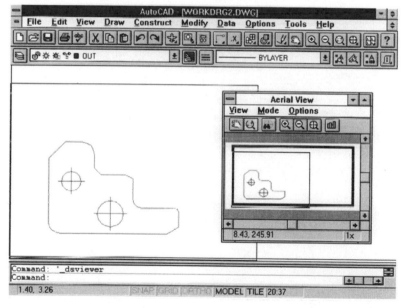

Fig. 25.3. Aerial View of A:WORKDRG.

❏ *Summary*

1. Pan, Zoom and Aerial View are DISPLAY commands, usually activated from the menu bar or the Standard toolbar.
2. Pan appears to move a drawing but this is not the case. The pan command is usually activated by picking points on the screen. It can also be used with co-ordinate input.
3. With the pan command, the drawing can 'disappear' from the screen.
4. The zoom command allows areas of a drawing to be looked at in greater detail, i.e. zooming in on a drawing.
5. The main zoom options are:
   ALL – displays the complete drawing
   CENTER – zooms a drawing about a centre point defined by the user. The option also requires a magnification factor.
   WINDOW – zooms in on selected areas and is probably the most useful option to the user.
   EXTENTS – zooms the drawing to the screen extents.
   PREVIOUS – displays the screen as it was before the zoom command was used. It can be used repetitively.
   SCALE – zooms the drawing to a user defined scale factor.
6. The Aerial View allows areas of a large drawing to be viewed interactively.

26. Hatching

AutoCAD R13 has associated boundary hatching. The hatching (or sectioning) must be added by the user, and R13 has three types:
(a) predefined
(b) user defined
(c) custom – not considered in this book.
When hatching, the user has two methods of defining the hatch pattern boundary:
(a) by selecting objects which make the boundary
(b) by picking points within the boundary.
The hatch command is activated by selecting:
(a) from the menu bar **DrawHatch**
          Hatch...
(b) the HATCH icon from the Draw toolbar

Both selection methods will display the Boundary Hatch dialogue box.

User-defined hatch patterns – Select Objects option

User-defined patterns are line hatch patterns, the user defining:
(a) the hatch line angle, relative to the horizontal
(b) the distance between the hatch lines.
To demonstrate how the Select Objects option is used when hatching, refer to Fig. 26.1 and:
1. Open the A:STDA3 standard sheet with layer OUT current. Display the Draw and Modify toolbars.
2. Draw a 50-unit square and multiple copy it to nine other places on the screen. Add the other lines within the required squares.
3. Make layer SECT (cyan) current.

4. From the Draw toolbar select the HATCH icon and
   prompt   Boundary Hatch dialogue box
   respond 1. pick arrow at Pattern Type Predefined
            2. pick User-defined
            3. alter Angle to 45
            4. alter Spacing to 3 – Fig. 26.2
            5. pick Boundary Select Objects<
   prompt   drawing screen and Select objects
   respond **pick the four lines of first square then right-click**
   prompt   Boundary Hatch dialogue box
   respond **pick Preview Hatch<**
   prompt   hatching added to square and Boundary Hatch
   then   Continue message
   respond **pick Continue**
   prompt   Boundary Hatch dialogue box
   respond **pick Apply**
5. Hatching is added to the square – Fig. 26.1. **Note** that in Fig. 26.1 I have displayed two sets of squares to show both the Select Object option and the hatch result.
6. Repeat the HATCH icon selection, and using the Boundary Hatch dialogue box:
   (a) User-defined, 45 angle, 3 spacing
   (b) pick Select Objects<
   (c) pick four lines of small square then right-click
   (d) pick Preview–Continue–Apply
   (e) hatching as Fig. 26.1(b).
7. Using the same procedure, hatch the middle square as Fig. 26.1(c). Eight lines need to be selected?
8. Using the fourth square – Fig. 26.1(d) – select the HATCH icon and
   prompt   Boundary Hatch dialogue box

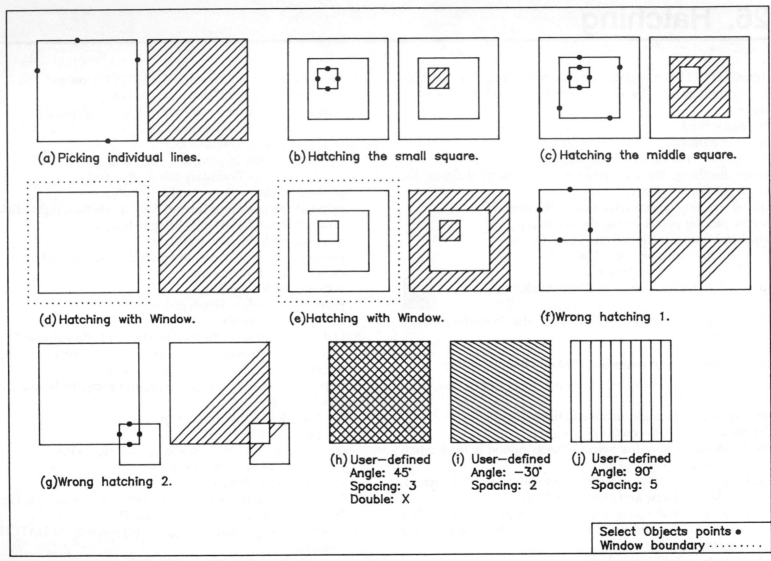

(a) Picking individual lines.

(b) Hatching the small square.

(c) Hatching the middle square.

(d) Hatching with Window.

(e) Hatching with Window.

(f) Wrong hatching 1.

(g) Wrong hatching 2.

(h) User—defined
Angle: 45°
Spacing: 3
Double: X

(i) User—defined
Angle: −30°
Spacing: 2

(j) User—defined
Angle: 90°
Spacing: 5

Select Objects points •
Window boundary · · · · · · · ·

Fig. 26.1. User-defined hatching with Select Objects option.

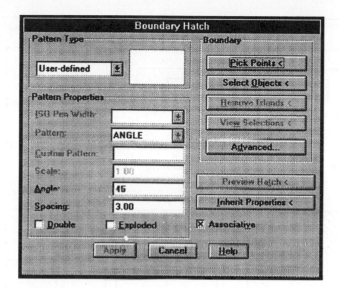

Fig. 26.2. Boundary Hatch dialogue box.

respond **pick Select Objects<**
    prompt   Select objects
    respond **from the menu bar select Edit–Select Objects–Window**
    prompt   First corner
    respond **window the square**
    prompt   4 found then Select objects
    respond **right click**
    prompt   Boundary Hatch dialogue box
    respond **Preview–Continue–Apply**

9. Using the Window selection method, hatch the next square – Fig. 26.1(e) – and note the result.
10. Figure 26.1 also displays other hatching effects, which you should attempt using the other squares drawn.
Figure (f): wrong hatching – we want to hatch the small top left square and have picked the four lines indicated.
Figure (g): wrong hatching – small square should have been hatched.
Figure (h): picking the Double option (X in box) from the Boundary Hatch dialogue box.
Figure (i): altering the Angle and·Spacing.
Figure (j): altering the Angle and Spacing.
11. Save this drawing if you want to.

User-defined hatch patterns – Pick Points option

1. Open A:STDA3, layer OUT current.
2. Refer to Fig. 26.3 and draw a 50-unit square. Multiple copy this square to six other places and add the other lines. This drawing is similar to Fig. 26.1, so you could simply erase the hatching which was added in the previous exercise.
3. Make layer SECT current.
4. Select the HATCH icon and
    prompt   Boundary Hatch dialogue box
    respond   1. User-defined
              2. Angle 45
              3. Spacing 3
    then   **pick Pick Points<**
    prompt   Select internal points
    respond   **pick any point within the first square**
    prompt   Selecting everything visible...
              Analyzing the selected data...
              Analyzing internal islands...
    then   Select internal points and square outline is highlighted
    respond   **right-click**
    prompt   Boundary Hatch dialogue box
    respond   **pick Preview<**
    prompt   correct hatching added?
    respond   **Continue–Apply** – Fig. 26.3(a).

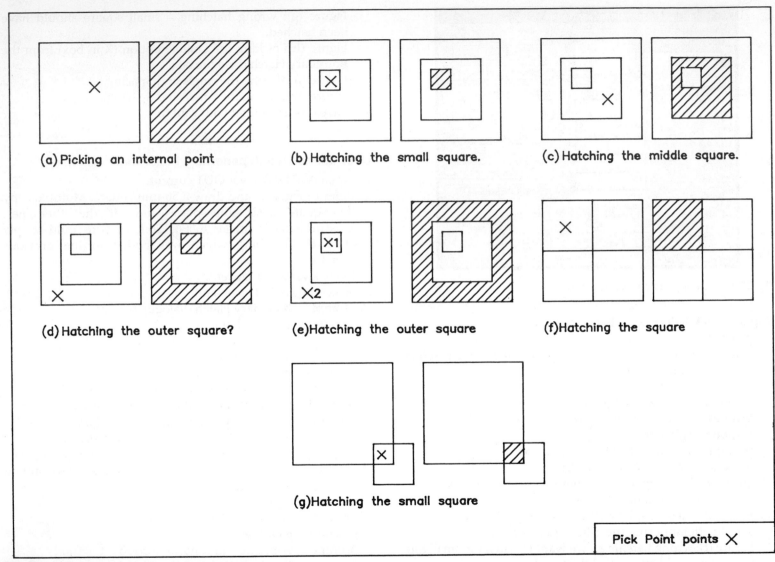

Fig. 26.3. User-defined hatching with Pick Points option.

5. Using the HATCH icon with the Pick Points option, select points within the inner, middle and outer squares to produce the hatching as Fig. 26.3(b)–(d).
6. The hatching in Fig. 26.3(d) may not be as the user would expect, and to obtain hatching in the 'outer square' only, it is necessary to select two internal points – Fig. 26.3(e). Another method of hatching the outer square will be discussed shortly.
7. Now use the pick points option to hatch the squares in Fig. 26.3(f) and (g).

Select Objects vs Pick Points

With the two options available for hatching, new users to this type of boundary command sometimes become confused as to whether they should Select Objects or Pick Points. In general the Pick Points option is the simpler to use, and will allow complex shapes to be hatched with a single pick within the area to be hatched. To demonstrate the effect:
1. Open A:STDA3 and refer to Fig. 26.4.
2. Draw two sets of three intersecting circles, any size and anywhere on the screen. We want to hatch the intersection area of the three circles.
3. Select the HATCH icon and from the Boundary Hatch dialogue box, set User-defined, Angle of 45 and Spacing of 3 then:
   (a) pick the Select Objects option
   (b) pick the three circles
   (c) preview–continue–apply to give Fig. 26.4(a).
4. Using the HATCH icon again:
   (a) pick the Pick Points option
   (b) pick an internal point within the 'area' to be hatched
   (c) preview–continue–apply to give Fig. 26.3(b).

Hatch style

R13 has a hatch style option which allows the user to control three 'variants' to the hatch command. To demonstrate the hatch style, refer to Fig. 26.4 and draw a 70-unit square, adding other squares inside it (Snap on will help.) Copy the squares to two other places.
1. Select the HATCH icon and
   prompt   Boundary Hatch dialogue box
   respond User-defined, Angle 45, Spacing 3 then **pick Advanced...**
   prompt   Advanced options dialogue box
   respond **check Style is Normal** and note the 'picture' then **pick OK**
   prompt   Boundary Hatch dialogue box
   respond **pick Select Objects**
   prompt   Select objects
   respond **window the first 70 sided square** then Preview and Apply – Fig. 26.4(c).
2. Using the HATCH icon:
   (a) pick Advanced
   (b) alter Style to Outer then pick OK
   (c) pick Select Objects and window the second 70 sided square
   (d) apply to give Fig. 26.4(d).
3. Repeat the HATCH icon selection, pick Advanced and set the Style to Ignore. Window the third 70 sided square – Fig. 26.4(e).
4. Usually the Style is left at Normal, and the user 'controls' the hatch area by picking points within the are to be hatched.
5. Save if required, but we will not use this drawing again.

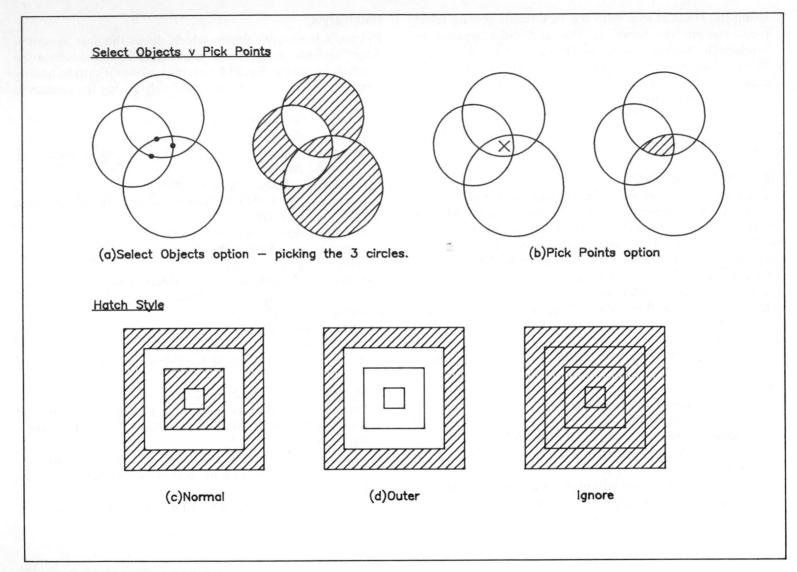

Fig. 26.4. Using the hatch command.

R13's predefined hatch patterns

AutoCAD R13 has several stored hatch patterns which are accessed from the Boundary Hatch dialogue box, by selecting the appropriate hatch pattern name from the list provided. With predefined hatch patterns, the user defines:

(a) the scale of the pattern

(b) the angle of the pattern.

We will demonstrate these predefined patterns by example, so:

1. Open A:STAD3, layer OUT current and refer to Fig. 26.5.
2. Draw a 50-unit square and multiple copy it to several other places. Add some lines and circles within the squares to make the exercise more interesting.
3. Layer SECT current.
4. Select the HATCH icon and

prompt	Boundary Hatch dialogue box
respond	1. pick Pattern Type: Predefined
	2. Pattern: ANSI33
	3. Scale: 1
	4. Angle: 0
	5. pick Pick Points
prompt	Select internal point
respond	**pick a point in area to be hatched then right-click**
prompt	Boundary Hatch dialogue box
respond	**pick Preview**
prompt	*Dense black hatching?*
respond	pick Continue
prompt	Boundary Hatch dialogue box
respond	**alter Scale to 5 then Preview**
prompt	Hatching still quite dense?
respond	1. Continue
	2. alter Scale to 25
	3. Preview
	4. hatching satisfactory?
	5. continue
	6. apply – Fig. 26.5(a).

5. HATCH icon again and

prompt	Boundary Hatch dialogue box
respond	**pick arrow at Pattern**
prompt	other hatch pattern names
respond	scroll down until HONEY appears
then	**pick HONEY**
and	1. HONEY appears in Pattern box
	2. Preview box displays the honey pattern
respond	1. Scale: 25, Angle: 0 – should be?
	2. **pick Pick Points**
prompt	Select internal point
respond	pick point in area to be hatched then right-click
prompt	Boundary Hatch dialogue box
respond	**pick Preview**
prompt	suitable hatching added?
respond	**Continue–Apply** – Fig. 26.5(b).

6. By referring to Fig. 26.5, select the hatch pattern name, scale and angle, and add hatching to the other areas.
7. Save if required?

Hatch exercise

Now that we have discussed both user-defined and predefined hatching, it is time for you to try a simple hatching exercise, so:

1. Open the **A:USEREX** drawing which was last used when text was being discussed. Move the component to one side of the screen, then copy it to another part of the screen.
2. Refer to Fig. 26.6.
3. Using the SECT layer add the following hatching to the three areas of the component using the Pick Points option:

(a) User-defined	(b) Predefined
1. angle: 60, spacing: 2	1. AR-HBONE, scale:1, angle: 0
2. angle: 90, spacing: 4	2. SACNCR, scale: 40, angle: 0
3. angle: –15, spacing: 6	3. HOUND, scale: 50, angle: 0

4. Save your exercise if you want to.

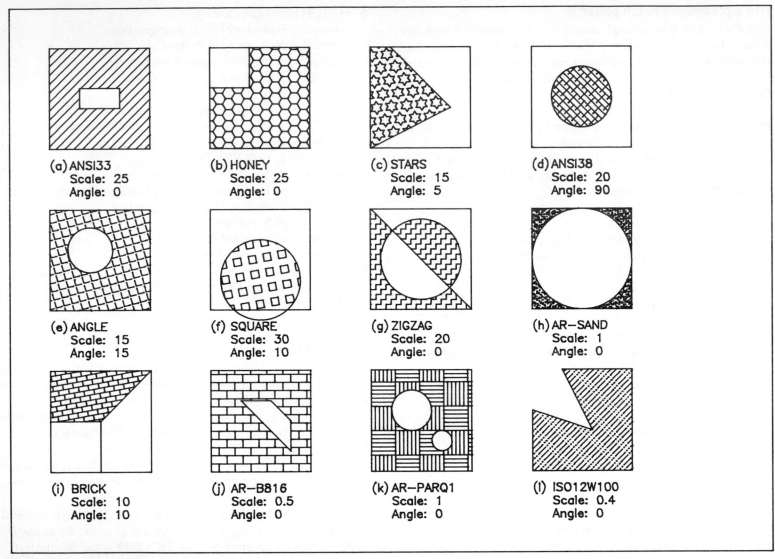

(a) ANSI33
Scale: 25
Angle: 0

(b) HONEY
Scale: 25
Angle: 0

(c) STARS
Scale: 15
Angle: 5

(d) ANSI38
Scale: 20
Angle: 90

(e) ANGLE
Scale: 15
Angle: 15

(f) SQUARE
Scale: 30
Angle: 10

(g) ZIGZAG
Scale: 20
Angle: 0

(h) AR—SAND
Scale: 1
Angle: 0

(i) BRICK
Scale: 10
Angle: 10

(j) AR—B816
Scale: 0.5
Angle: 0

(k) AR—PARQ1
Scale: 1
Angle: 0

(l) ISO12W100
Scale: 0.4
Angle: 0

Fig. 26.5. Using predefined hatch patterns.

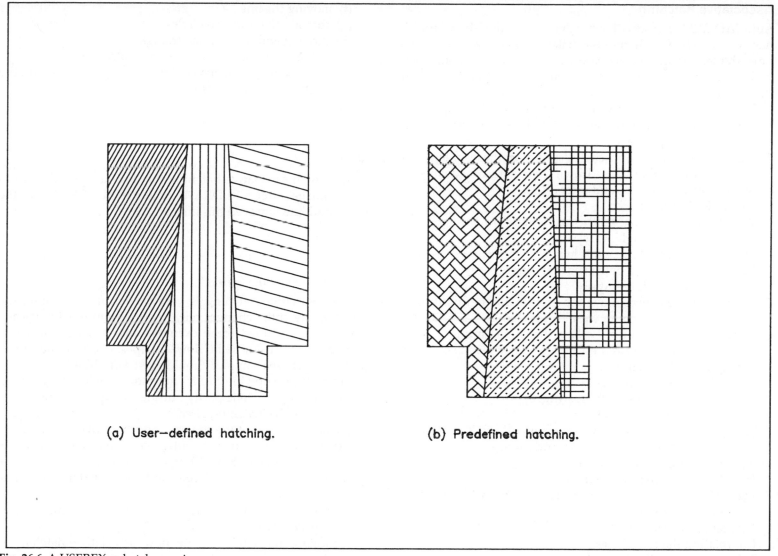

(a) User—defined hatching.   (b) Predefined hatching.

Fig. 26.6. A:USEREX as hatch exercise.

Associative hatching

AutoCAD R13 has associative hatching, i.e. if the 'shape' which has been hatched is altered, the hatching will also alter to the new shape. Associative hatching is applicable to both user-defined and predefined hatch patterns, irrespective of whether the Select Objects or Pick Points option is used.

To demonstrate associative hatching try the following:

1. Open A:STDA3 standard sheet, OUT layer current with the toolbars you require active.
2. Draw some squares and circles similar to those in Fig. 26.7 but remember that I've drawn two sets of squares to demonstrate the before and after effect.
3. Layer SECT current.
4. With the HATCH icon, set the following:
   (a) User-defined, angle: 45, spacing: 8
   (b) Associative OFF, i.e. no X in box
   (c) use Pick Points to hatch the first square
   (d) Preview–Continue–Apply.
5. Use the MOVE icon to move the circle to another position in the square. The hatching should not change – Fig. 26.7(a). Note that the reason for the large hatch spacing is to allow you to 'pick' the required entities. You can also zoom-in of the appropriate squares.
6. Select the HATCH icon again and
   (a) User-defined, angle: 45, spacing: 0
   (b) Associative ON, i.e. X in box
   (c) Advanced – check Island Detection ON (ie X in box)
   (d) Pick Points and hatch the second square
   (e) Preview–Continue–Apply
   (f) MOVE the circle and hatching changes – Fig. 26.7(b).
7. Figure 26.7 displays some other associative hatching, which you should attempt:
   (c): scaling the circle
   (d): rotating the two circles
   (e): two moves with the circles

(f): moving the line
(g): rotating the trimmed circles
(h): moving and rotating the triangle
(i): two different hatch patterns and scaled circle.
8. In all the examples displayed, the hatching changes with the entity changes. This is associative hatching.

Note

I found with associative hatching that I sometimes obtained a 'ghost image' after a REDRAW. Entering **REGEN**<R> at the command line removed this image.

Associative hatching 'quirks'

While associative hatching is very powerful and useful, the result of any entity changes may not be as you would logically expect. I've included some examples in Fig. 26.8 which you should attempt using some simple shapes. I've kept the square and circle. These examples should make you think!
   (a): multiple copy the circle – no associative hatching
   (b): moving the circle partly outside the square – interesting associative hatching effect
   (c): filleting sides of the square – no associative hatching
   (d): moving two circles to intersect – note hatching at the circle intersection. Compare to Fig. 26.7(e) where the spacing was large and not evident at circle intersection
   (e): moving the line – no associative hatching. Compare with Fig. 26.7(f)
   (f): scaling the circle – note how associative hatching is drawn.

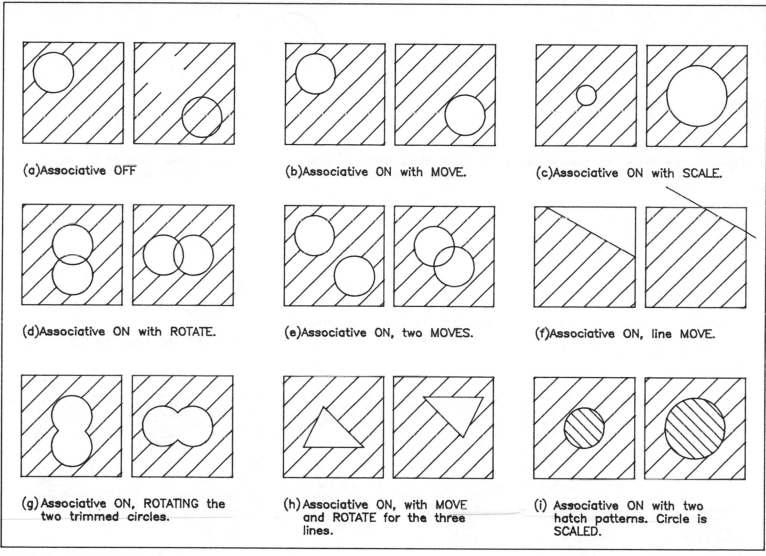

(a) Associative OFF

(b) Associative ON with MOVE.

(c) Associative ON with SCALE.

(d) Associative ON with ROTATE.

(e) Associative ON, two MOVES.

(f) Associative ON, line MOVE.

(g) Associative ON, ROTATING the two trimmed circles.

(h) Associative ON, with MOVE and ROTATE for the three lines.

(i) Associative ON with two hatch patterns. Circle is SCALED.

Fig. 26.7. Associative hatching.

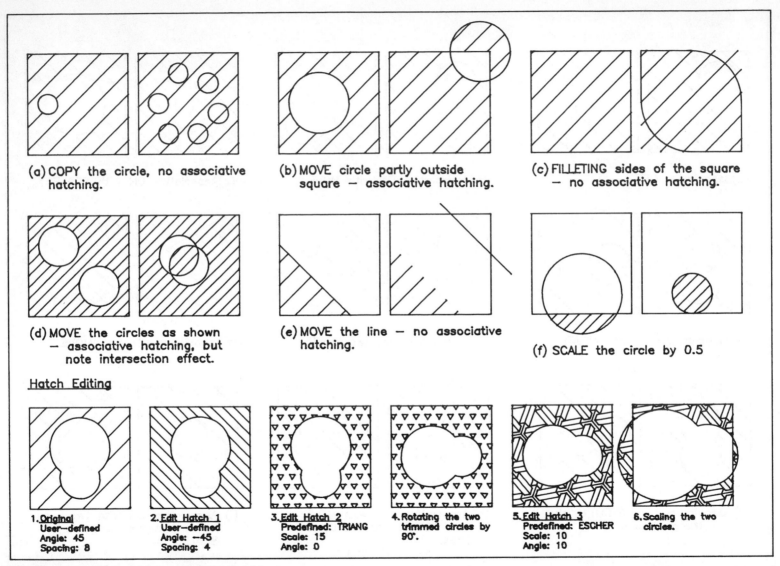

(a) COPY the circle, no associative hatching.

(b) MOVE circle partly outside square — associative hatching.

(c) FILLETING sides of the square — no associative hatching.

(d) MOVE the circles as shown — associative hatching, but note intersection effect.

(e) MOVE the line — no associative hatching.

(f) SCALE the circle by 0.5

Hatch Editing

1. Original
   User—defined
   Angle: 45
   Spacing: 8

2. Edit Hatch 1
   User—defined
   Angle: —45
   Spacing: 4

3. Edit Hatch 2
   Predefined: TRIANG
   Scale: 15
   Angle: 0

4. Rotating the two trimmed circles by 90°.

5. Edit Hatch 3
   Predefined: ESCHER
   Scale: 10
   Angle: 10

6. Scaling the two circles.

Fig. 26.8. Associative hatching and editing hatching.

Editing hatching

Hatching which has been added to a drawing can be edited, i.e. the angle and spacing can be altered, or a user-defined pattern can be replaced by a predefined pattern.

To demonstrate how hatching can be edited, refer to Fig. 26.8 and

1. Draw a square (any size) with two trimmed circles. Add user-defined hatching as shown, angle 45 and spacing 8.
2. Select from the menu bar **Modify–Edit Hatch...**
   prompt   `Select hatch object`
   respond   **pick the hatch just drawn**
   prompt   Hatchedit dialogue box – as Boundary Hatch with User-defined, Angle 45, Spacing 8
   respond   1. alter angle to –45
                2. alter spacing to 4
                3. pick Apply
   The added hatching is altered to the new values.
3. Modify–Edit Hatch again and select the edited hatch pattern, then change:
   (a) User-defined to Predefined
   (b) Pattern to TRIANG
   (c) Scale to 15
   (d) Angle to 0
   (e) Apply
4. Zoom in on the square, and rotate the trimmed circles by 90° and the hatching will alter accordingly.
5. Edit the TRIANG hatching to:
   (a) Predefined: ESCHER
   (b) Scale: 10
   (c) Angle: 10
6. Finally scale the trimmed circles by a factor of 1.5 or 2 and note the associative hatching effect.
7. As this completes our hatching demonstration, save your work if required.

Hatching with text

Text which is placed in an area to be hatched will be displayed with a 'clear boundary' around it when the hatching is added.

1. Refer to Fig. 26.9 and draw four 70-unit squares. Add any suitable text to the squares, e.g. centred, fitted, etc. The text size is at your discretion, but make it quite large, e.g. 12–15 or more.
2. Select the HATCH icon and
   (a) Predefined: STARS pattern, scale 25, angle 0
   (b) Pick Points option and pick a point in first square
   (c) Apply – Fig. 26.9(a).
3. Repeat the HATCH icon selection and
   (a) Predefined: BRSTONE, scale 20, angle 20
   (b) Pick Points option and pick point in next square
   (c) Apply – Fig. 26.9(b).
4. HATCH again and
   (a) User-defined, angle 45, spacing 4
   (b) Select Objects option and pick the four sides of next square
   (c) Apply – Fig. 26.9(c).
5. With the same user-defined pattern, use the Select Objects option and
   (a) pick four lines of next square
   (b) pick all the text item lines
   (c) right-click, apply – Fig. 26.9(d).
6. Associative hatching works with text items, e.g.
   (e): moving the text items
   (f): rotating the text item
   (g): mirroring the text items, but deleting old objects.

Note

There are other commands which affect associative hatching, e.g. polylines, stretch. These commands will be discussed in later chapters.

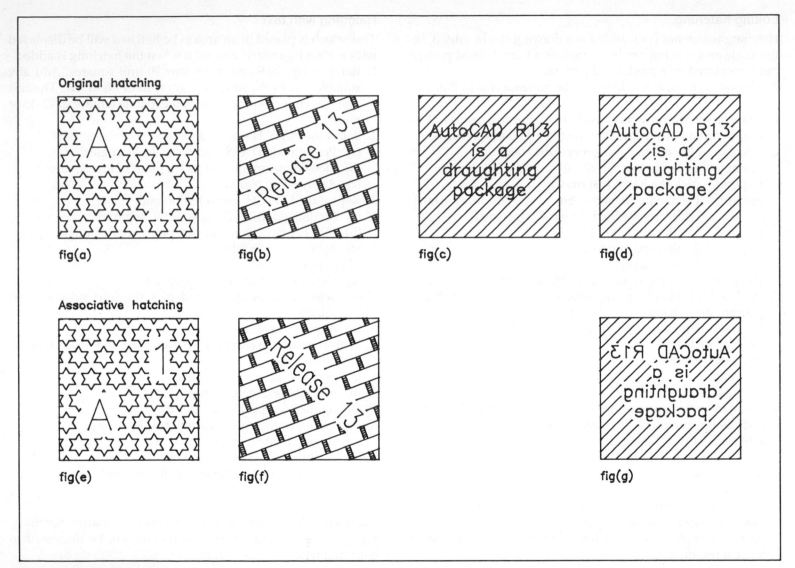

Original hatching

fig(a)　　fig(b)　　fig(c)　　fig(d)

Associative hatching

fig(e)　　fig(f)　　fig(g)

Fig. 26.9. Hatching with text.

❏ *Summary*

1. Hatching is a draw command, activated from the menu bar or the hatch icon from the Draw toolbar. Both methods result in the Boundary Hatch dialogue box being displayed.
2. AutoCAD R13 allows three types of hatching:
   (a) User-defined: line hatching, the user specifying the angle for the hatch lines and the spacing between these lines.
   (b) Predefined: are stored hatch patterns, the user specifying the pattern scale and angle.
   (c) Custom: which has not been covered in this book.
3. The hatch boundary can be specified by:
   (a) Selecting the objects which make the boundary
   (b) Picking points within the boundary.
4. Hatching added is a single entity and is erased by a single pick.
5. R13 has associative hatching, which allows the hatching to change when the hatch boundary changes.
6. Added hatching can be edited.
7. The recommended procedure for hatching is to use the pick points option.
8. When using predefined hatch patterns *always use a large scale factor initially* and work to a lower value until the desired hatching is obtained. Using a low value for the scale factor can result in serious disk problems, e.g. *disk full!*

Activities

Some users may not use hatching in their draughting work, but they should still be familiar with the process. R13's pick points option makes hatching fairly straightforward, and for this reason I have included three interesting (I hope) exercises for you to attempt. These should test your CAD draughting and dimensioning skills.

1. Tutorial 14: a simple cover plate drawing. The MIRROR command is useful and the hatching is fairly easy. The hatching added is user-defined at 45 degrees with a spacing of 3. Watch the centre line when adding the hatching.
2. Tutorial 15: a protected bearing housing. The component is easy to draw and the hatching should give you no problems. The dimensioning is interesting.
3. Tutorial 16: the steam expansion box which has been successful in my other books. This component is much easier than it would appear. The construction of the outline uses many commands, e.g. fillet, trim, offset, mirror, etc. I have added ANSI34 hatching at a scale of 20. Why should the hatching not be mirrored?

27. Point, polygon and solid

These three drawing commands allow a certain amount of scope to the user and are quite interesting. As usual we will demonstrate them by example, so:

1. Open your A:STDA3 standard sheet with layer OUT current.
2. Activate the Draw, Modify and Object Snap toolbars.
3. Refer to Fig. 27.1.

Point

A point is an entity whose size and appearance can be controlled by the user.

1. From the Draw toolbar pick the POINT icon and
   prompt   Point and enter **50,50**<R>
   prompt   Point and enter **60,200**<R>
   prompt   Point and **ESC** to end command.
2. Two point entities will be displayed in red? You may have to toggle the grid off (F7) to 'see' these points.
3. From the menu bar select **Options**
   Display
   Point Style...
   prompt   Point Style dialogue box as Fig. 27.2
   respond   1. pick the point style indicated
            2. set Point Size to 5
            3. check – Relative to screen
            4. pick OK
4. From the menu bar select **Draw**
   Point
   Point
   prompt   Point and enter **30,85**<R>
   prompt   Point and enter **270,210**<R>
   prompt   Point and ESC.

5. From the Standard toolbar pick REDRAW icon – no change in points?
6. At the command line enter **REGEN**<R> and all four points have the new style?
7. Using the LINE command:
   prompt   From point
   respond   **Snap to Node icon and pick lower left point**
   prompt   To point
   respond   **Snap to Node icon and pick upper right point**
   prompt   To point and right-click.
8. Finally set the point appearance to another style and size then REGEN.

Polygon

A polygon is a multi-sided figure, each side having the same length. Polygons can be drawn by the user specifying:
(a) a centre point and an inscribed/circumscribed radius
(b) the endpoints of an edge of the polygon.

1. Select the POLYGON icon from the rectangular flyout of the Draw toolbar and
   prompt   Number of sides<4>
   enter   **6**<R>
   prompt   Edge/<Center of polygon>
   respond   **Snap to MIDpoint icon and pick the drawn line**
   prompt   Inscribed in circle/Circumscribed about circle(I/C)<I>
   enter   **I**<R> – the inscribed (default) option
   prompt   Radius of circle
   enter   **40**<R>
2. Repeat the polygon icon selection and

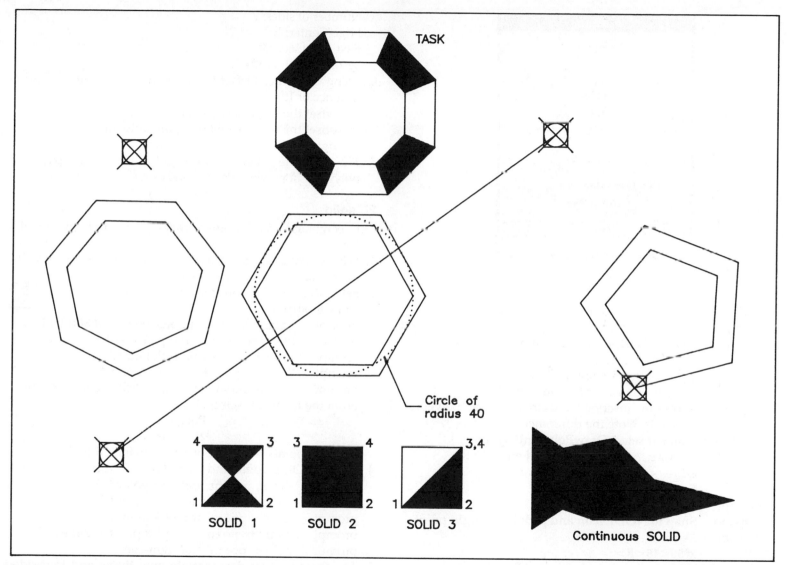

Fig. 27.1. Point, polygon and solid.

Fig. 27.2. Point Style dialogue box.

prompt Number of sides<6> and enter **6<R>**
   prompt   Edge/<Center of polygon>
   respond **Snap to MIDpoint icon and pick the line**
   prompt   Inscribed in...
   enter   **C<R>** – the circumscribed option
   prompt   Radius of circle and enter **40<R>**
3. Figure 27.1 shows the inscribed and circumscribed polygons for a 40 radius circle. Note the difference.
4. From the menu bar select **DrawPolygonPolygon**
   prompt   Number of sides<6> and enter **5<R>**
   prompt   Edge/<Center of polygon>
   enter   **E<R>** – the edge option
   prompt   First point of edge
   respond **Snap to NODE icon and pick lower right point**
   prompt   Second point of edge
   enter   **@50<15<R>**
5. Enter **POLYGON<R>** at the command line then:

Number of sides: 7
Edge/Center: E
First point: 60,100
Second point: @30<25
6. Using **Construct–Offset** from the menu bar, enter an offset distance of 10 then:
   (a) offset the five-sided polygon 'inwards'
   (b) offset the seven-sided polygon 'outwards'
   (c) right-click to end offset command.
7. The complete polygons are offset with a single pick as a polygon is a polyline entity (later).

2D solid

This command 'fills-in' lined shapes according to the pick order.
1. With SNAP ON, draw three squares of side 30 towards the lower part of the screen – see Fig. 27.1
2. Select the 2D solid icon from the Polygon flyout of Draw toolbar and
   prompt   First point and pick point 1 of SOLID 1
   prompt   Second point and pick point 2
   prompt   Third point and pick point 3
   prompt   Fourth point and pick point 4
   prompt   Third point and right-click to end command.
3. From the menu bar select **Draw**
                  Polygon
                  2D Solid
and pick points 1–4 in the order given in SOLID 2.
4. Use the SOLID command with SOLID 3 and:
   prompt   First point and pick point 1
   prompt   Second point and pick point 2
   prompt   Third point and pick point 3
   prompt   Fourth point and pick point 4 (same as 3)
   prompt   Third point and right-click.
5. The three squares demonstrate how three- and four-sided

shapes are filled with the 2D solid command.

6. The prompts Fourth point/Third point allow continuous solid creation, so activate the command and

prompt	First point and enter 260,15
prompt	Second point and enter 260,65
prompt	Third point and enter 275,25
prompt	Fourth point and enter 275,55
prompt	Third point and enter 290,20
prompt	Fourth point and enter 300,60
prompt	Third point and enter 320,20
prompt	Fourth point and enter 320,40
prompt	Third point and enter 360,30
prompt	Fourth point and enter 360,30
prompt	Third point and right-click.

Task

1. (a) Draw an eight-sided polygon, centre at 170,220 circumscribed in a 40 radius circle.
   (b) Offset the polygon inwards by 15.
   (c) Use the 2D SOLID command to produce the effect in Fig. 27.1 – a running ENDpoint snap will help.
2. What are the minimum and maximum number of sides allowed with the POLYGON command?
3. From the menu bar select **Options–Drawing Aids** and
   (a) Solid Fill OFF, i.e. no X in box
   (b) REDRAW – any change?
   (c) REGEN – any change?
4. Toggle solid fill ON, then restore the drawing to its original appearance.

❑ *Summary*

1. A point is an entity whose appearance and size can be altered using the Point Style dialogue box.
2. The NODE snap mode is used to reference points.
3. All points appear as the last point style selected.
4. Two variables control the style and size of points. These are PDMODE and PDSIZE.
5. A polygon is an equal multi-sided figure.
6. A polygon is a polyline.
7. Line shapes can be 'filled' with the 2D solid command.
8. The pick order is important with 2D solid.
9. Only three- and four-sided shapes can be filled.
10. Point, Polygon and 2D Solid can be drawn by picking with the mouse, entering co-ordinates or referencing existing entities.

28. Polylines and splines

A polyline is an entity which can consist of line and arc segments and can also be drawn with varying width. It has its own editing facility and is activated by icon or from the menu bar.

Polyline is one of the most powerful AutoCAD draw commands and yet is probably one of the most under-used. As usual we will investigate by example.

1. Open A:STDA3 with the Draw, Modify and Object Snap toolbars. Refer to Fig. 28.1.

2. Select the POLYLINE icon from the Draw toolbar and

   prompt   From point
   enter   **15,205<R>**
   prompt   Arc/Close/Halfwidth/Length/Undo/
            Width/<Endpoint of line>
   enter   **@50,0<R>**
   prompt   Arc/Close... and enter **@0,50<R>**
   prompt   Arc/Close... and enter **@–50,0<R>**
   prompt   Arc/Close... and enter **@0,–50<R>**
   prompt   Arc/Close... and right-click.

3. From the menu bar select **Draw–Polyline**
   prompt   From point and enter **80,205**
   prompt   Arc/Close... and enter **@50<0<R>** – polar
   prompt   Arc/Close... and enter **130,255<R>** – absolute
   prompt   Arc/Close... and enter **@–50,0<R>** – relative
   prompt   Arc/Close... and enter **C<R>** – close option.

4. Select the COPY icon and
   prompt   Select objects
   respond **pick any line on second square** and all four lines are highlighted
   prompt   Select objects and **right-click**
   prompt   Base point...Multiple and enter **M<R>**

5. prompt   Base point and enter **80,205<R>**
   prompt   Second   point and enter 145,205; 210,205; 290,205; 15,105; 80,105; 145,105; 220,105; 290,105 then right-click.

5. Select from the menu bar Construct–Fillet and set a fillet radius of 8, then Construct–Chamfer and set the chamfer distances to 8.

6. Select the FILLET icon and
   prompt   Polyline/Radius/Trim/<Select first object>
   enter   **P<R>** – the polyline option
   prompt   Select 2D polyline
   respond **pick the first square**
   prompt   3 lines were filleted – Fig. 28.1(a).

7. Repeat the fillet icon selection, enter **P<R>** and pick the second square drawn and
   prompt   4 lines were filleted – Fig. 28.1(b).

8. Note the difference between: Fig. 28.1(a) – not a 'closed' shape, so three corners filleted and Fig. 28.1(b) – a 'closed' shape, so four corners filleted.

9. Select the CHAMFER icon and
   prompt   Polyline/Distance...
   enter   **P<R>**
   prompt   Select 2D polyline
   respond **pick the third square**
   prompt   4 lines were chamfered – Fig. 28.1(c).

10. Repeat the CHAMFER icon selection, enter **D<R>** then
    (a) first chamfer distance and enter **12<R>**
    (b) second chamfer distance and enter **5<R>**

11. Now chamfer the fourth square, remembering to enter **P<R>** to activate the polyline option – Fig. 28.1(d). Note the orientation of the 12 and 5 chamfer distances.

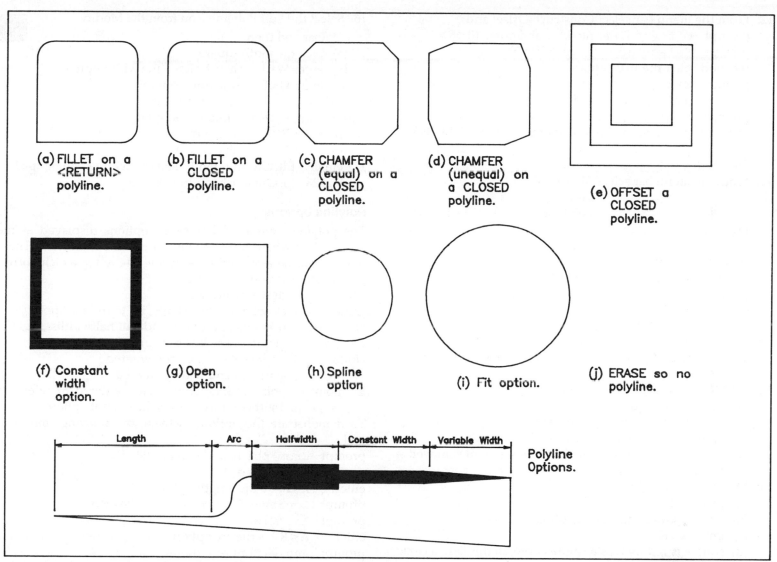

Fig. 28.1. Polyline examples.

12. From the menu bar select Construct–Offset and
    prompt   Offset distance... and enter **10**<R>
    prompt   Select object to offset
    respond **pick the fifth square**
    prompt   Side to offset?
    respond **pick a point 'outside' the square**
    prompt   Side to offset?
    respond **pick a point 'inside' the square** then right-click
    The complete square is offset with a single pick –
    Fig. 28.1(e).
13. From the menu bar select **Modify**
    Edit
    Polyline
    prompt   Select polyline
    respond **pick the sixth square**
    prompt   Open/Join...eXit<X>
    enter   **W**<R> – the width option
    prompt   Enter new width for all segments
    enter   **5**<R>
    prompt   Open/Join...eXit<X>
    enter   **X**<R> – the exit command option.
    The complete square is drawn with a line width of 5 –
    Fig. 28.1(f).
14. Select Modify–Edit Polyline and
    (a) pick the next square
    (b) enter **O**<R> – the Open option
    (c) enter **X**<R> – end command
    (d) square is drawn with the last line segment removed –
        Fig. 28.1(g).
15. Modify–Edit Polyline and
    (a) pick next square (eighth)
    (b) enter **S**<R> – the spline option
    (c) enter **X**<R>
    (d) square is redrawn as a spline curve, in this case a circle
        as Fig. 28.1(h).

16. Select the Edit Polyline icon from the Modify
    toolbar and then
    (a) pick the ninth square
    (b) enter **W**<R> then **2**<R> – the width option
    (c) enter **U**<R> – the undo option
    (d) enter **S**<R> – the spline option
    (e) enter **U**<R> – undoes the spline
    (f) enter **F**<R> – the fit option
    (g) enter **X**<R> – Fig. 28.1(i).
17. Finally ERASE the tenth square with a single pick –
    Fig. 28.1(j). Obviously nothing there!

Polyline options

The polyline command has seven options displayed at the prompt line when the start point of the line is selected. These options can be activated by entering the letter which corresponds to the option. The options are:

Arc	draws an arc segment
Close	closes a polyline shape, i.e. to the start point
Halfwidth	user enters the start and end halfwidths
Length	length of the line segment is entered
Undo	undoes the last option entered
Width	start and end widths entered
Endpoint	point picked, co-ordinates entered or reference another entity. This is the default option.

To demonstrate the options, activate the polyline command and
prompt   From point and enter **25,20**<R>
prompt   Arc/Close...
enter   **L**<R> – the length option
prompt   Length of line and enter **78**<R>
prompt   Arc/Close...
enter   **A**<R> – the arc option
prompt   Angle/CEnter/CLose...
enter   **@10,10**<R> – the arc endpoint

then   @10,10<R> – second arc endpoint
then   L<R> – the line option
prompt   `Arc/Close...`
enter   H<R> – the halfwidth option
prompt   `Starting half width` and enter 6<R>
prompt   `End half width` and enter 6<R>
prompt   `Arc/Close...`
enter   @43,0<R> – endpoint of halfwidth segment
prompt   `Arc/Close...`
enter   W<R> – the width option
prompt   `Starting width <12.00>` and enter 6<R>
prompt   `Ending width` and enter 6<R>
prompt   `Arc/Close...`
enter   @43,0<R> – endpoint of width segment
prompt   `Arc/Close...` and enter W<R>
prompt   `Starting width` and enter 6<R>
prompt   `Ending width` and enter 0<R>
prompt   `Arc/Close...` and enter @43,0<R>
prompt   `Arc/Close...` and enter @0,34<R> – line drawn upwards?
prompt   `Arc/Close...` and enter U<R> – drawn line removed
prompt   `Arc/Close...` and enter @0,–34<R>
prompt   `Arc/Close...` and enter C<R> – closes shape and ends the command.

Before leaving this exercise:
1. MOVE the complete polyline shape with a single pick on any part of it, from 25,20 by @50,0.
2. Options–Drawing Aids–Solid Fill OFF, i.e. no X.
3. REDRAW – any difference?
4. REGEN – any difference?
5. Solid Fill ON, then REDRAW, REGEN.
6. Save if required but it will not be used again.

Line and arc segments

A continuous polyline entity can be created from a series of line and arc segments of varying width. In the example that follows we will employ several of the options and the resultant shape will be used in the next chapter. The exercise is given as a *long* series of stepped sequences, so open A:STDA3, layer OUT current with toolbars Draw, Modify and Object Snap.

Refer to Fig. 28.2, select the POLYLINE icon and

Prompt	*Enter*	
1. `From point`	25,45	– pt 1
2. `Arc/Close...`	L	
3. `Length of line`	45	– pt 2
4. `Arc/Close...`	W	
5. `Starting width<0>`	0	
6. `Ending width<0>`	10	
7. `Arc/Close...`	@120,0	– pt 3
8. `Arc/Close...`	A	
9. `Angle/CEnter...`	@40,60	– pt 4
10. `Angle/CEnter...`	L	
11. `Arc/Close...`	W	
12. `Starting width<10>`	10	
13. `Ending width<10>`	0	
14. `Arc/Close...`	@–10,110	– pt 5
15. `Arc/Close...`	175,215	– pt 6
16. `Arc/Close...`	W	
17. `Starting width<0>`	0	
18. `Ending width<0>`	5	
19. `Arc/Close...`	@30<-90	– pt 7
20. `Arc/Close...`	A	
21. `Angle/CEnter...`	@–40,0	– pt 8
22. `Angle/CEnter...`	CE	
23. `Center point`	100,185	– pt 9
24. `Angle/CEnter...`	A	
25. `Included angle`	120	– pt 10
26. `Angle/CEnter...`	L	

27. `Arc/Close...`	W	
28. `Starting width<5>`	5	
29. `Ending width<0>`	0	
30. `Arc/Close...`	25,185	– pt 11
31. `Arc/Close...`	C	– pt 1 again

32. A closed polyshape.
33. And that's all there is to it!

With a bit of luck your polyshape will be the same as that in Fig. 28.2. The steps are involved, but this is normal when constructing a polyshape with line and arc segments. The line segments have their own options as do the arc segments. Mistakes can be easily rectified with the **UNDO** option, but it is not uncommon to erase the shape and start again. The sequence of commands introduced the user to the arc options, allowing angles, arc centre, length of arc, etc. to be specified.

To demonstrate an arc only polyshape, select the icon and

Prompt	*Entry*
1. `From point`	60,120
2. `Arc/Close...`	A
3. `Angle/CEnter...`	W
4. `Staring width<0>`	0
5. `Ending width<0>`	5
6. `Angle/CEnter...`	D
7. `Direction...`	@0,–10, i.e. downwards
8. `End point`	120,80
9. `Angle/CEnter...`	CE
10. `Center point`	110,105
11. `Angle/Length...`	A
12. `Included angle`	90
13. `Angle/CEnter...`	W
14. `Starting width<5>`	5
15. `Ending width<5>`	15
16. `Angle/CEnter...`	95,105
17. `Angle/CEnter...`	<RETURN>

18. A nice curly polyshape?

At this stage save your drawing as **A:POLY** as it will be used in the next chapter to demonstrate polyline editing.

Task

Select a suitable area on the screen and draw a 100-unit square as a closed polyline. With the sizes given in Fig. 28.2, use the OFFSET, FILLET and CHAMFER commands to complete the component. It is much easier than you may think.

Return vs close

A polyline shape can be 'closed' with <RETURN> or with the Close option and the fillet exercises demonstrated the difference between the two methods. The difference can also be seen in the following example:

1. Select a clear area on the screen and draw two 40-unit polyline squares with the width set to 3 using:

(a) From select point		(b) From select point	
To	@40,0	To	@40,0
To	@0,40	To	@0,40
To	@–40,0	To	@0,–40
To	@0,–40	To	C<R>
To	<RETURN>	closes square and ends	
ends command		command	

2. The difference between a 'return polysquare' and a 'closed polysquare' is apparent at the lower left corner of the squares.

Spline curve

A spline is a smooth curve which passes through a given set of points. These points can be picked, entered as co-ordinates or referenced to existing entities. The spline is drawn as a non-uniform rational B-spline or **NURBS**. Splines have uses in many CAD application areas, e.g. car body design, contour mapping, etc.

A spline is *not* a polyline but is a continuous entity.

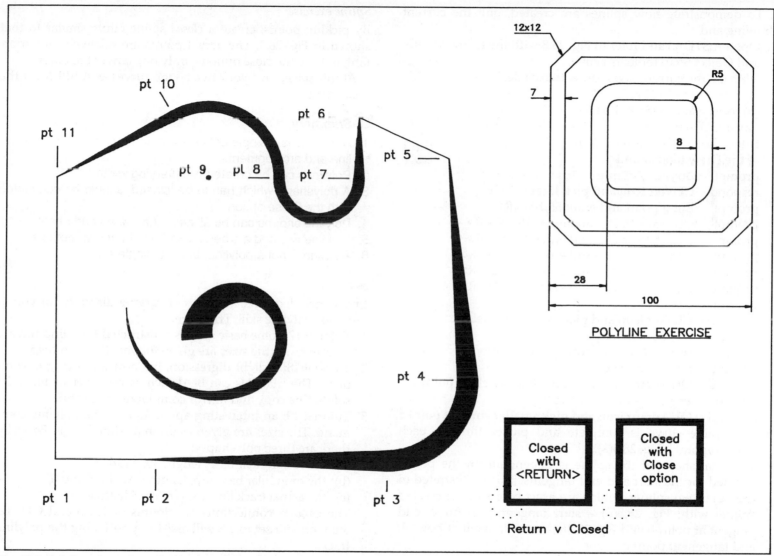

Fig. 28.2. Polyline shape from line and arc segments.

POLYLINE EXERCISE

Return v Closed

To demonstrate how splines are created, quit the current drawing and

1. Open A:STDA3 and refer to Fig. 28.3 with the Draw, Modify and Object Snap toolbars active.
2. With CL the current layer, draw two circles:
   (a) centre at 45,135 radius 30
   (b) centre at 215,155 radius 15
3. Layer OUT current.
4. Select the SPLINE icon from the polyline flyout of the Draw toolbar and

prompt	Object/<Enter first point>
respond	**CENter icon and pick larger circle**
prompt	Enter point and enter **55,100**<R>
prompt	Close/Fit... and enter **75,170**<R>
prompt	Close/Fit... and enter **95,115**<R>
prompt	Close/Fit... and enter **125,155**<R>
prompt	Close/Fit... and enter **165,125**<R>
prompt	Close/Fit... and enter **195,175**<R>
prompt	Close/Fit...
respond	**CENter icon and pick smaller circle**
prompt	Close/Fit...
respond	**right-click** – no more points to enter
prompt	Enter start tangent
respond	**QUAdrant icon and pick large circle at point 1**
prompt	Enter end tangent
respond	**QUAdrant icon and pick smaller circle at point a**

5. The spline curve is complete and passes through each entered point – Fig. 28.3(a).
6. The final shape of the spline is dependent on the points selected for the start and end tangents. This is illustrated in the other two splines (which are exact copies of the created spline) with: Fig. 28.3(b) – start tangent at point 2, end tangent at point b and Fig. 28.3(c) – start tangent at point 3, end tangent at point c.

Spline exercise

By picking points, create a *closed* spline curve similar to that shown in Fig. 28.3. The actual points are relatively unimportant, but use the close option – only one tangent to enter?

At this stage, save your two spline curves as **A:SPLN** for the next chapter.

❑ *Summary*

1. A polyline is a single entity which can be made from several line and arc segments.
2. Polylines can be created with varying width.
3. A polyshape which has to be 'closed' should be completed with the Close option.
4. Polyline shapes can be filleted, chamfered and offset.
5. Polyline line and arc segments have their own options.
6. A spline is not a polyline, but is a single entity.

Activity

I have included three activities of varying difficulty for you to test your polyline skill. These are:

1. Tutorial 17: some basic shapes constructed from line and arc segments. All the sizes are given for you. Snap on helps.
2. Tutorial 18: a slight digression, but a nice drawing to complete. The triangles can be drawn as polylines or filled 2D solids. The copy and mirror commands are useful.
3. Tutorial 19: an interesting application of the polyline command. The sizes are given as ordinate dimensions. Basically there are three polyshapes:
   (a) the rectangular base, length 30, width 5
   (b) the triangular base top, length 5, width 5 and 0
   (c) the actual track line, drawn at 0.5 halfwidth.

The circular connections are donuts of ID: 3 and OD: 12. Snap on and set to 2.5 will assist in positioning the polyline track.

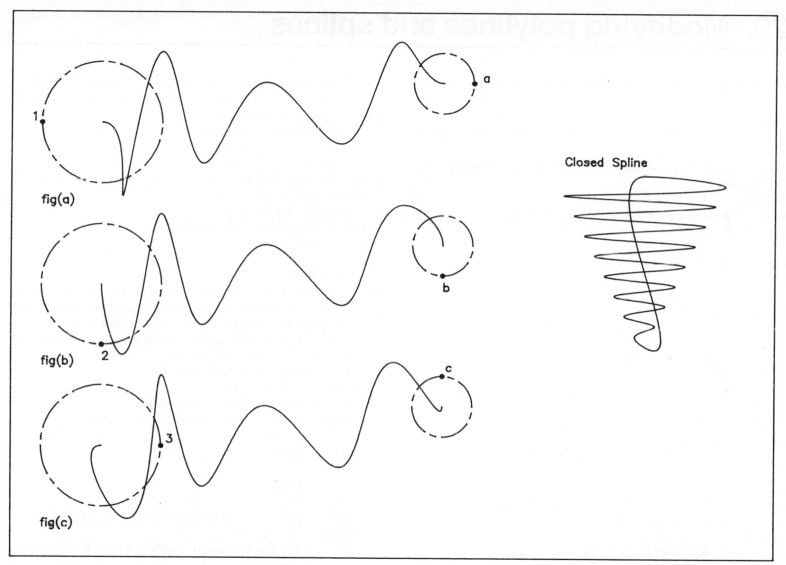

Fig. 28.3. Spline curves.

29. Modifying polylines and splines

Polylines have their own editing command (Edit Polyline) which was discussed briefly in the previous chapter. There are several options available to the user and these are best demonstrated by example, so open the **A:POLY** drawing saved from the previous chapter.

Refer to Fig. 29.1 and from the menu bar select **Modify–Edit Polyline** and

prompt   Select polyline
respond **pick any point on the large polyshape**
prompt   Open/Join/Width/Edit vertex/Fit/Spline/
              Decurve/Ltype gen/Undo/eXit<X>
enter   **W<R>** – the width option
prompt   Enter new width for all segments
enter   **3<R>** – Fig. 29.1(b)
prompt   Open/Join...
enter   **D<R>** – the decurve option – Fig. 29.1(c)
prompt   Open/Join...
enter   **S<R>** – the spline option – Fig. 29.1(d)
prompt   Open/Join...
enter   **F<R>** – the fit option – Fig. 29.1(e)
prompt   Open/Join...
enter   **D<R>** – decurve again – Fig. 29.1(f)
prompt   Open/Join...
enter   **O<R>** – the open option – Fig. 29.1(g)
prompt   Open/Join...
enter   **W<R>**
prompt   Enter new width for all segments
enter   **0<R>** – Fig. 29.1(h)
prompt   Open/Join...
enter   **X<R>** to end command.

The Edit Polyline command is very interactive and if the result is not as expected, the undo option (U) is very useful.

We will now edit the polyarc shape, so activate the Edit Polyline icon, pick any point on the polyarc then enter:

1. W for width, then 2 – Fig. 29.1(b)
2. D for decurve – Fig. 29.1(c)
3. S for spline – Fig. 29.1(d)
4. F for fit – Fig. 29.1(e)
5. D for decurve – Fig. 29.1(f)
6. C for close – Fig. 29.1(g)
7. W for width then 0 – Fig. 29.1(h)
8. X to end command.

The join option

This is a very useful option as it allows several polylines to be joined into one entity. It can also be used to 'convert' an ordinary entity into a polyline. Refer to Fig. 29.1 and

1. Select a suitable area of the screen and draw about six *lines* in a 'saw tooth' pattern – Fig. 29.1(x).
2. Select the Edit Polyline icon and

prompt   Select polyline
respond **pick the first line segment**
prompt   Object selected is not a polyline
          Do you want to turn it into one?<Y>
enter   **Y<R>**
prompt   Close/Join...
enter   **J<R>**
prompt   Select objects
respond **pick the six line segments then right-click**
prompt   Close/Join...
enter   **W<R>** and a new width of **3** then **X<R>** to end command.

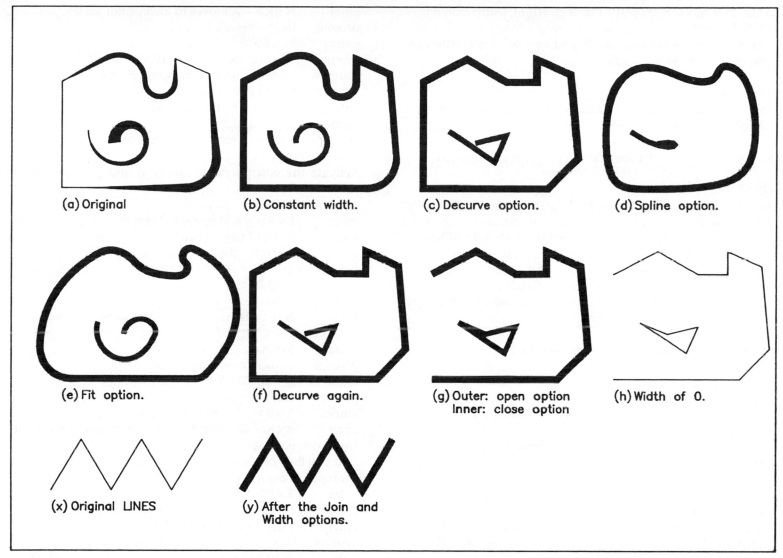

(a) Original

(b) Constant width.

(c) Decurve option.

(d) Spline option.

(e) Fit option.

(f) Decurve again.

(g) Outer: open option
Inner: close option

(h) Width of 0.

(x) Original LINES

(y) After the Join and
Width options.

Fig. 29.1. Edit polyline example using A:POLY.

3. The saw tooth is displayed as a constant width polyline – Fig. 29.1(y).
4. This exercise is now complete and can be saved, although we will not refer to it again.

Notes

When the Edit Polyline command is activated and a polyline selected, the prompt is either:
(a) `Open/Join...` if the selected polyshape is 'closed'
(b) `Close/Join...` if the selected polyshape is 'opened'.

Edit vertex option

The options available with the Edit Polyline command usually 'redraw' the selected polyshape after a single entry, e.g. (F)it, (S)pline, etc., but the (E)dit vertex option is slightly different. When **E** is entered from the options, the user has another set of options. We will demonstrate the edit vertex options by example, so open A:STDA3 and refer to Fig. 29.2.
1. Draw an 80-unit *closed* square polyshape, and multiple copy it to three other places on the screen.
2. Variable width.
   Activate the Edit Polyline command and

prompt	`Select polyline`
respond	**pick the first square**
prompt	`Open/Join...`
enter	**W<R>** then **5<R>** as constant width
prompt	`Open/Join...`
enter	**E<R>** – the edit vertex option
prompt	`Next/Previous/Break/Insert/Move/` `Regen/Straighten/Tangent/Width/eXit` and an X is placed at the start vertex (lower left?)
enter	**W<R>**
prompt	`Enter starting width<5>` and enter **5<R>**
prompt	`Enter ending width<5>` and enter **0<R>**
prompt	`Next/Previous...`

enter	**N<R>** – X moves to lower right vertex
prompt	`Next/Previous...`
enter	**W<R>**
prompt	`Starting width` and enter **0<R>**
prompt	`Ending width` and enter **5<R>**
prompt	`Next/Previous...`
enter	**X<R>** – to end edit vertex option
prompt	`Open/Join...`
enter	**X<R>** – to end edit polyline command – Fig. 29.2(a).

3. Move a vertex.
   Activate the edit polyline command and pick the second square:

prompt	`Open/Join...`
enter	**E<R>** – X at lower left vertex?
prompt	`Next/Previous...`
enter	**M<R>** – the move option
prompt	`Enter new location`
enter	**@20,20<R>**
prompt	`Next/Previous...`
enter	**N<R>** then **N<R>** – X at top right vertex?
prompt	`Next/Previous...`
enter	**M<R>**
prompt	`Enter new location`
enter	**@–20,–20<R>**
prompt	`Next/Previous...`
enter	**X<R>** – to exit edit vertex
enter	**X<R>** – to exit edit polyline command – Fig. 29.2(b).

4. Insert a new vertex
   Edit polyline, pick the third square, constant width to 2 then:

prompt	`Open/Join...`
enter	**E<R>**
prompt	`Next/Previous...` (X at lower left corner)
enter	**I<R>** – the insert option
prompt	`Enter location of new vertex`
enter	**@20,20<R>**

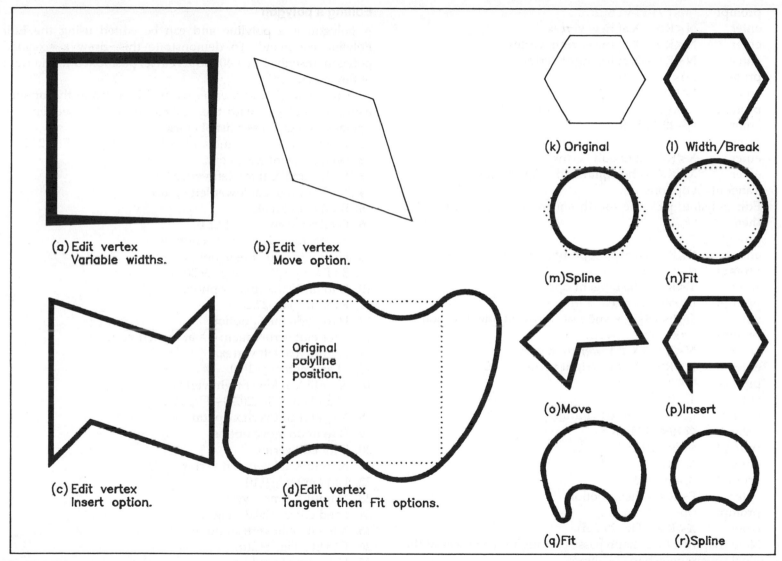

(a) Edit vertex
Variable widths.

(b) Edit vertex
Move option.

(c) Edit vertex
Insert option.

(d) Edit vertex
Tangent then Fit options.

Original
polyline
position.

(k) Original

(l) Width/Break

(m) Spline

(n) Fit

(o) Move

(p) Insert

(q) Fit

(r) Spline

Fig. 29.2. Edit vertex options.

prompt	Next/Previous...
enter	**N**<R> – X at new vertex
enter	**N**<R> – X at lower right vertex
enter	**N**<R> – X at top right vertex
prompt	Next/Previous...
enter	**I**<R>
prompt	Enter location of new vertex
enter	**@–20,–20**<R>
prompt	Next/Previous...
enter	**X**<R> – end edit vertex
enter	**X**<R> – end command – Fig. 29.2(c).

5. Tangent–fit options

Edit polyline, pick the fourth square, constant width of 2 then:

prompt	Open/Join...
enter	**E**<R> – X at start point (lower left?)
prompt	Next/Previous...
enter	**T**<R> – the tangent option
prompt	Direction of tangent
enter	**@10<45**<R> and note arrowed line direction
prompt	Next/Previous...
enter	**N**<R> – X at lower right vertex
enter	**N**<R> – X at top right vertex
prompt	Next/Previous...
enter	**T**<R>
prompt	Direction of tangent
enter	**@10<–135**<R>
prompt	Next/Previous...
enter	**X**<R>
prompt	Open/Join...
enter	**F**<R> – the fit option
prompt	Open/Join...
enter	**X**<R> – Fig. 29.2(d).

Note that the fitted shape passes through the vertices of the original square polyshape position.

Editing a polygon

A polygon is a polyline and can be edited using the Edit Polyline command. To demonstrate this, draw a six-sided polygon, inscribed in a 40 radius circle, positioned to the right of the screen.

In the following sequence, we will investigate the options using this polygon with the UNDO option. The sequence of operations is given as a list of entries.

1. Edit polyline command and pick the polygon – Fig. 29.2(k).
2. Set a constant width of 2.
3. E<R> and X at top left vertex?
4. N<R> until X at lower left vertex.
5. B<R> for break.
6. G<R> for go – Fig. 29.2(l).
7. X<R> to end edit vertex option.
8. U<R> to undo break option.
9. S<R> for spline – Fig. 29.2(m).
10. U to undo the spline option.
11. F for fit – Fig. 29.2(n).
12. U to undo the fit option.
13. E for edit vertex again – X at top left vertex.
14. N until X at left vertex.
15. M and enter @–10,0.
16. N until X at lower right vertex.
17. M and enter @–20,20 – Fig. 29.2(o).
18. X to end edit vertex option.
19. U to undo move option.
20. E for edit vertex.
21. N until X at lower left vertex.
22. I and enter @0,10.
23. N until X at new vertex.
24. I and enter @20,0 – Fig. 29.2(p).
25. X to end edit vertex option.
26. F to fit – Fig. 29.2(q).
27. U to undo fit option.

28. S for spline – Fig. 29.2(r).
29. X to end the edit polyline command.

The edit vertex and polygon exercises are now complete.

Editing spline curves

Spline curves can be edited in a manner which is similar to editing a polyline. Open drawing **A:SPLN** to display the two spline curves from the previous chapter and refer to Fig. 29.3

1. From the menu bar select **Modify–Edit Spline**

prompt	`Select spline`
respond	**pick the first spline curve** – Fig. 29.3(a)
prompt	`Fit Data/Close/Move Vertex...` and blue (grip) boxes displayed
enter	**F<R>** – the fit option and blue grip boxes now at entered spline points
prompt	`Add/Close/Delete/Purge...`
enter	**A<R>** – the add option
prompt	`Select point`
respond	**pick fifth box from left** and fifth and sixth grip boxes hot – red
prompt	`Enter new point`
enter	**135,95<R>**
prompt	`Enter new point`
enter	**150,195<R>**
prompt	`Enter new point` and right-click – Fig. 29.3(b)
prompt	`Select point` and right-click
prompt	`Add/Close...`
enter	**X<R>** – end add option
prompt	`Fit Data/Close...`
enter	**F<R>** – to fit grips on curve
prompt	`Add/Close...`
enter	**D<R>** – the delete option
prompt	`Select point`
respond	**pick the third blue box from left**
prompt	`Select point`

respond	**pick second blue box from right**
prompt	`Select point` and right-click – Fig. 29.3(c)
prompt	`Add/Close...`
enter	**X<R>**
prompt	`Fit Data/Close...`
enter	**F<R>** – fit grips to curve
prompt	`Add/Close...`
enter	**M<R>** – the move option
prompt	`Next/Previous...` and left grip box hot?
enter	**@0,40<R>**
prompt	`Next/Previous...`
respond	**N<R>** until second right box is hot then **@40<45<R>**
prompt	`Next/Previous...`
enter	**X<R>** – to end move option
prompt	`Add/Close...` and enter **X<R>**
prompt	`Fit Data/Close...` and enter **X<R>** – Fig. 29.3(d).

2. Select the EDIT SPLINE icon from the Edit Polyline icon of the Modify toolbar and
   (a) select the spline exercise curve – Fig. 29.3(e)
   (b) F – to fit the data
   (c) M – and move the top grip box by @0,50
   (d) M – and move the bottom box by @0, 15
   (e) M – and move the 'side vertices' into the same vertical position as Fig. 29.3(f).
3. Save your edited splines in required.

❏ *Summary*

1. Polyshapes and splines can be copied, scaled, moved, etc.
2. Both have their own edit command – Edit Polyline or Edit Spline.
3. The commands can be activated from the Modify menu bar or by icon.
4. Each command has several options.

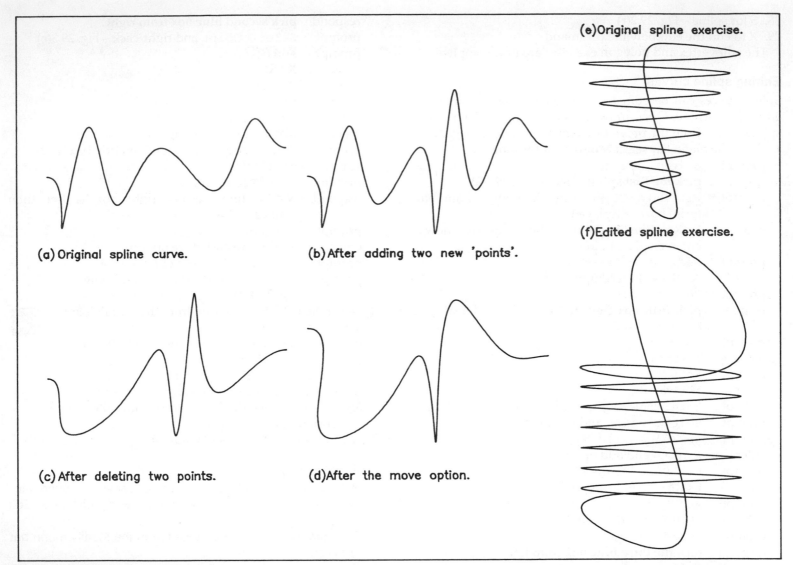

(a) Original spline curve.

(b) After adding two new 'points'.

(c) After deleting two points.

(d) After the move option.

(e) Original spline exercise.

(f) Edited spline exercise.

Fig. 29.3. Spline editing with A:SPLN.

30. Divide, measure and break

These are three commands which allow existing entities to be 'modified' by the user.

1. Open A:STDA3, layer OUT current with toolbars Draw, Modify and Object Snap active.
2. Set a point style and size as indicated in Fig. 30.1.
3. Draw the following entities:
   (a) LINE: from 25,225 to @60<15
   (b) CIRCLE: centre at 125,230 with radius 25
   (c) POLYLINE: from 165,245 to 215,245
      arc to 215,215
      line to 185,215
   (d) SPLINE: any shape.
4. Copy the four entities by @0,–90.

Divide

A selected entity is 'divided' into an equal number of segments, the user specifying this number. The current point style is 'placed' at the division points.

1. From the menu bar select **Draw**
   Point
   Divide
   prompt   Select object to divide
   respond **pick the line**
   prompt   <Number of segments>/Block
   enter   3<R>
   The line is divided into three equal parts and a point is placed at each segment division – Fig. 30.1(a).

2. Select the DIVIDE icon from the Point flyout of the Draw toolbar and
   prompt   Select object to divide
   respond **pick the circle**

prompt   <Number of segments>/Block
enter   7<R>
The circle is divided into seven equal arc lengths and seven points placed on the circumference – Fig. 30.1(b).

3. Using the command, divide:
   (a) the polyline into 5 segments – Fig. 30.1(c)
   (b) the spline into 9 segments – Fig. 30.1(d).

Measure

A selected entity is 'divided' into a number of user-specified lengths and the current point style is placed at each measure length.

1. From the menu bar select **Draw–Point–Measure** and
   prompt   Select object to measure
   respond **pick the line**
   prompt   <Segment length>/Block
   enter   18<R>
   The selected line is divided into measured lengths of 18 units from the start point of the line – Fig. 30.1(e).

2. Select the MEASURE icon from the Modify toolbar and
   prompt   Select object to measure
   respond **pick the circle**
   prompt   <Segment length>/Block
   enter   19<R>
   The circle circumference displays points every 19 units – Fig. 30.1(f).
   Question: where is the circle start point for measure?

3. Using the command, measure:
   (a) the polyline: 17 – Fig. 30.1(g)
   (b) the spline: 31 – Fig. 30.1(h)

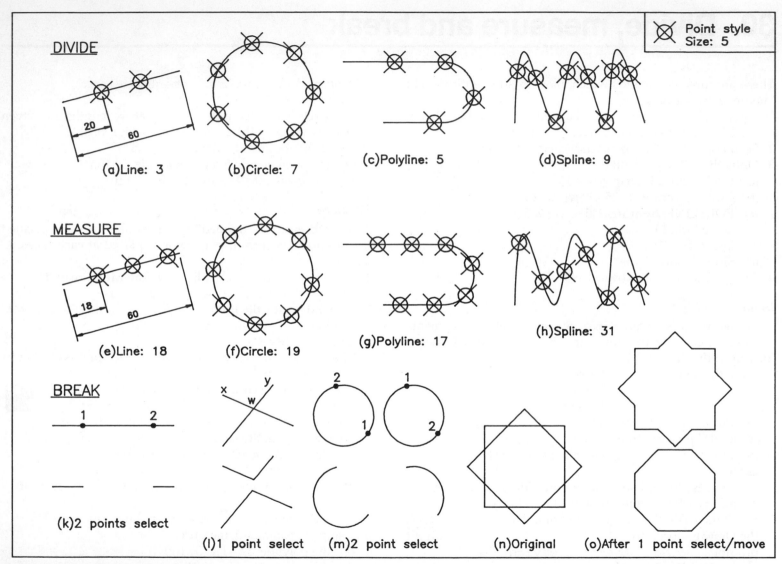

Fig. 30.1. Divide, measure and break.

Task

Using the aligned dimension with the baseline option, add the four dimensions to the lines to check the divide/measure command. Remember NODE is used to reference points.

Break

This command allows an entity to be broken in one or two selected points, the user specifying these points. To demonstrate the command, draw the following entities:

(a) Line: from 20,50 to 80,50

(b) Two lines: from 105,60 to 140,45
          from 105,35 to 130,65

(c) Two circle: centres at (165,50) and (200,50) with radii 15.

1. From the menu bar select **Modify–Break–2 Points Select**
   prompt   Select object
   respond   **pick the horizontal line**
   prompt   Enter first point
   respond   **pick any point 1 on the line**
   prompt   Enter second point
   respond   **pick any point 2 on the line**
   The selected line is 'broken' between the two points – Fig. 30.1(k).

2. (a) Select the 1 Point Select icon from the Break flyout of the Modify toolbar and
      prompt Select object
      respond **pick line x**
      prompt Enter first point
      respond **INTersection icon and pick point w**
   (b) Repeat the 1 Point Select icon and
      (i) pick line y
      (ii) INTersection icon and pick point w
   (c) Use the MOVE icon to move the two upper line segments from the two bottom line segments – Fig. 30.1(l).

3. Using the 2 Point Select break command, pick the circle circumference in the order 1 and 2 and note the result.

Break exercise

1. Draw a 40-unit line square at any suitable point with snap on.
2. Copy the four lines 'onto themselves'.
3. Rotate (previous) by 45° about the square 'centre point'.
4. Redraw – interesting ? – Fig. 30.1(n).
   Question: could you draw the two squares by another method?
5. Using the break command – 1 point select option – break the lines at the intersection points. Command has to be used 16 times?
6. Finally move the 'outside' away from the 'inside' – Fig. 30.1(o).

Note

The divide and measure prompts refer to the term 'Block' which will be discussed during the chapter on blocks.

❏ Summary

1. Divide is a command which 'divides' an entity into an equal number of parts.
2. Measure is a command which 'divides' an entity into equal length segments.
3. The current point style is displayed on divided and measured entities.
4. Break is a command which allows entities to be broken using either one or two point selection.
5. All three commands can be activated by keyboard entry, menu bar selection or icon selection.
6. The three commands can be used on line, arc, circle, polyline and spline entities.

31. Lengthen, align and stretch

Lengthen, align and stretch are three useful commands which greatly increase draughting efficiency.

Lengthen

This command changes the length of lines, arcs and polylines, allowing several options for the user.
1. Open A:STDA3 with Draw, Modify and Object Snap toolbars.
2. Draw a horizontal line of length 80 and multiple copy it to three other places. Refer to Fig. 31.1.
3. From the menu bar select **Modify**

                           Lengthen

    prompt   DElta/Percent/Total/DYnamic...
    enter   **T<R>** – the total option
    prompt   Angle/<Enter total length(?)>
    enter   **120<R>**
    prompt   <Select object to change>/Undo
    respond   **pick second line**
    prompt   <Select object to change>/Undo
    respond   **right-click** – Fig. 31.1(b).
4. Select the LENGTHEN icon from the Stretch flyout of the Modify toolbar and
    prompt   DElta/Percent...
    enter   **P<R>** – the percent option
    prompt   Enter percent length<?>
    enter   **75<R>**
    prompt   <Select object to change>/Undo
    respond   **pick the third line then right-click** – Fig. 31.1(c).
5. Now lengthen the fourth line with:
    (a) enter DE – delta option
    (b) enter 15 as delta length
    (c) pick line and right-click – Fig. 31.1(d).

6. In the example I've dimensioned the lines purely to show that the lengthen entries are 'correct'.

Dynamic lengthen

This is an interactive lengthen option which is very easy to use.
1. Refer to Fig. 31.1 and draw a Z-shape (snap on) then copy it to another part of the screen.
2. Activate the lengthen command and
    prompt   DElta/Percent...
    enter   **DY<R>** – the dynamic option
    prompt   <Select object to change>/Undo
    respond   **pick point 1 on first shape** – SNAP ON
    prompt   Specify new end point
    respond   **pick point 2 then right-click** – Fig. 31.1(e).
3. For the second Z-shape, repeat lengthen and:
    (a) enter DY
    (b) pick line at point 3 then pick point 4
    (c) pick line at point 5 then pick point 3
    (d) pick line at point 6 then pick point 7
    (e) pick line at point 8 then pick point 6
    (f) right-click – Fig. 31.1(f).

Align

A very powerful command which combines move and rotate into one operation.
1. Refer to fig. (g) and draw two triangles (any length) in the orientation shown – SNAP ON. Copy the triangles to two other places on the screen. The numbers added are for reference only.
2. We are going to align:
    (a) side 13 of triangle A onto side xy of triangle B

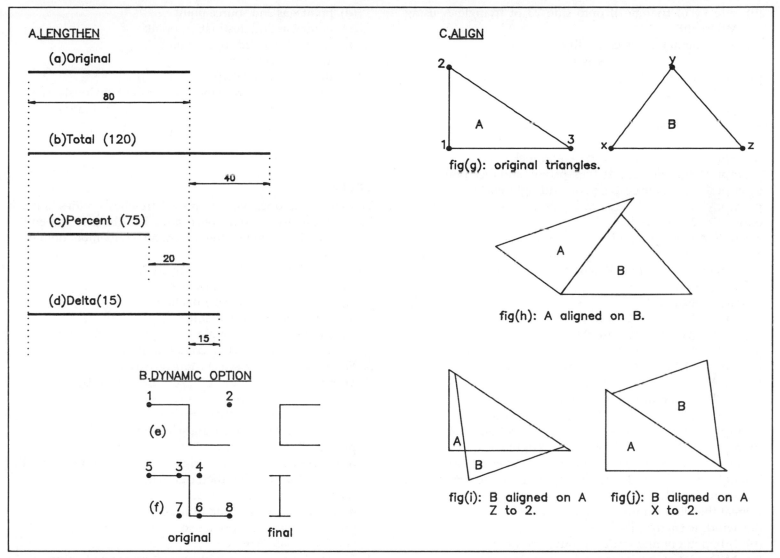

A. LENGTHEN

(a) Original

80

(b) Total (120)

40

(c) Percent (75)

20

(d) Delta (15)

15

B. DYNAMIC OPTION

1   2

(e)

5   3 4

(f) 7 6   8

original   final

C. ALIGN

2   y

A   B

1   3   x   z

fig(g): original triangles.

A

B

fig(h): A aligned on B.

A   B

B   A

fig(i): B aligned on A   fig(j): B aligned on A
Z to 2.   X to 2.

Fig. 31.1. Lengthen and Align commands.

(b) side xy of triangle B onto side 23 of triangle A using MIDpoint.

3. From the menu bar select **Modify**
    Align

prompt   `Select object`
respond   **window triangle A** then right-click
prompt   `1st source point and pick point 1 –`
           snap on helps
prompt   `1st destination point` and pick point *x*
prompt   `2nd source point` and pick point 3
prompt   `2nd destination point` and pick point *y*
prompt   `3rd source point` and right-click
prompt   `<2d> or 3d transformation`
enter   **2d** or 2D<R>

4. Triangle A is moved and rotated onto triangle B with sides 13 and xy in alignment – Fig. 31.1(h). Note the two 'ghost alignment lines'. REDRAW icon to remove them.

5. Select the ALIGN icon from the Rotate flyout of the Modify toolbar and

prompt   `Select objects`
respond   **window triangle B** then right-click
prompt   `1st source point`
respond   **MIDpoint icon and pick line xy**
prompt   `1st destination point`
respond   **MIDpoint icon and pick line 23**
prompt   `2nd source point` and pick point z
prompt   `2nd destination point` and pick point 2
prompt   `3rd source point` and right-click
prompt   `<2d> or 3d transformation` and enter 2d<R>.

6. Triangle B is aligned onto triangle A in the orientation shown in Fig. 31.1(i).

7. Repeat the align command and
    (a) window triangle B
    (b) MIDpoint of line xy as 1st source point
    (c) MIDpoint of line 23 as 1st destination point

(d) point x as 2nd source point
(e) point 2 as 2nd destination point
(f) right-click at 3rd source point
(g) 2d transformation
(h) Redraw – Fig. 31.1(j).

8. The orientation of an aligned component obviously depends on the selection order of the source and destination points.

9. Save if required.

Stretch

This command does what it says, it 'stretches' entities. If hatching and dimensions have been added to the selected entities they are both affected by the command – remember both hatch and dimension are associative.

1. Open A:STDA3 and refer to Fig. 31.2.
2. Draw the components shown ie
    (a) a dimensioned horizontal line
    (b) a variable width polyline
    (c) a dimensioned triangle
    (d) an L-shaped hatched component.
3. From the menu bar select **Modify–Stretch**

prompt   `Select object to stretch by crossing`
           `-window or -polygon`
           `Select object`
enter   **C<R>** – crossing selection
prompt   `First corner`
respond   **window the right end of line including dimension** then right-click
prompt   `Base point or displacement`
respond   **pick right end of line**
prompt   `Second point of displacement`
enter   **@5.75,0<R>**

4. Line and dimension are 'stretched' by entered value.

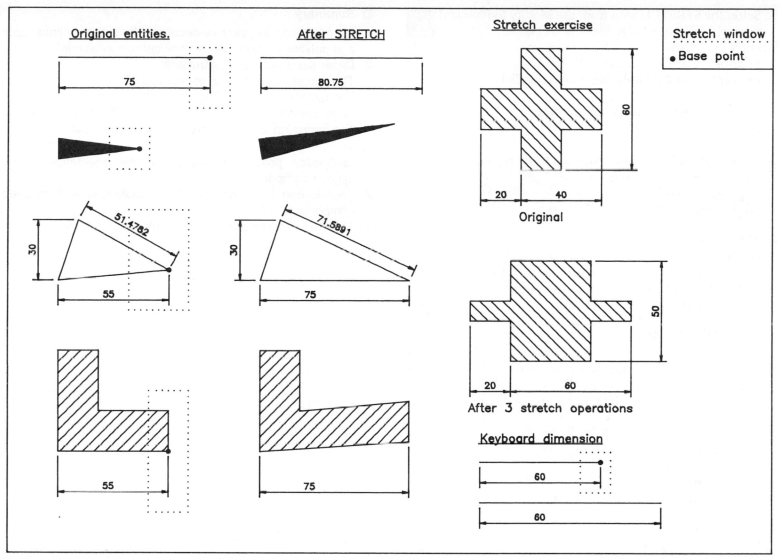

Fig. 31.2. The STRETCH command.

5. Select the STRETCH icon from the Modify toolbar and

prompt	Select object to stretch...
enter	**C\<R\>**
prompt	First corner
respond	**window polyline** then right-click
prompt	Base point...
respond	**pick any point on polyline**
prompt	Second point...
enter	**@30\<25\<R\>**

6. Use the STRETCH command, enter C, then pick the crossing window indicated then enter:
   (a) triangle: @20,–5
   (b) L-shape: @20,5

Stretch exercise

Draw the + shape in Fig. 31.2 and add the three dimensions and hatching. Using the stretch-crossing selection, alter the component to that shown. I used three stretch operations! Use the home dimension icon to 'tidy up'.

Keyboard dimensions

Dimensions are stretched because they are associative, but if dimensions are added from the keyboard they are not stretched – remember the scale examples?

Draw a horizontal line, then at the command line enter:

(a) DIM\<R\>
(b) HOR\<R\>
(c) pick the two end points
(d) enter dimension text, e.g. 60
(e) stretch-crossing by @30,0
(f) dimension text will not be altered.

❏ *Summary*

1. Lengthen can increase or decrease the length of lines, arcs and polylines. There are several options available.
2. Dimensions are not 'lengthened'.
3. The dynamic lengthen is very useful.
4. The lengthen angle option is for arcs.
5. Align combines the MOVE and ROTATE commands into one operation to give a very powerful command.
6. With align, the order of selection of the source and destination points will affect the final orientation of the aligned component.
7. Stretch can be used with lines, polylines and hatched components.
8. The stretch command will alter dimension values.

32. Enquiring into a drawing

AutoCAD R13 allows the user the ability to interrogate a drawing to obtain information about co-ordinates, distances and areas. To demonstrate these facilities:
1. Open A:STDA3 with Draw, Modify and Object Snap toolbars.
2. Draw the following:
    (a) A rectangle with the LINE command, the lower left corner placed at 35,185. The sides have to be 80 horizontal and 50 vertical. Draw in the diagonal.
    (b) Two circles: (1) centre at 175,215 with radius 30; (2) centre at 225,235 with radius 15. Draw in a tangent line between the two circles.
    (c) A square of 80-unit sides and 'inside it' a 20-unit square and a 10 radius circle – position is not important, but draw with SNAP ON. Draw a 30 unit square 'outside'.
    (d) A right-angle triangle, vertical side 80, horizontal side 60.
    (e) A closed polyshape, straight side 70 long and arc radius 30. Offset the polyshape 15 'inwards'.
3. Increase the command prompt area to a three-line display – easy?
4. The letters in Fig. 32.1 are for reference only.

Point identification
Displays the co-ordinates of a selected entity.
1. From the menu bar select **Edit**

    Inquiry

    Locate point

prompt   id Point
respond   **INTersection icon and pick point A**
The command area displays: X = 35.00, Y = 185.00, Z = 0.00.
2. Repeat the **Edit–Inquiry–Locate point** selection and
prompt   id Point
respond   **CENter icon and pick large circle.**
          Display X = 175.00, Y = 215.00, Z = 0.00.
3. Now find the co-ordinates of the midpoint of line AC.
X = 75.00, Y = 210.00, Z = 0.00?

Distance
This command display the distance and angle to the horizontal for a line between two selected points.
1. From the menu bar select **Edit–Inquiry–Distance** and
prompt   First point and pick point A
prompt   Second point and pick point C
The command line displays: Distance = 94.34, Angle in XY Plane = 32, Angle from XY Plane = 0, Delta X = 80.00, Delta Y = 50.00, Delta Z = 0.00.
2. Repeat the Distance command and
prompt   First point
respond   **CENter icon and pick large circle**
prompt   Second point
respond   **CENter icon and pick circle nearest large circle**
The command line will display: Distance = 53.88, Angle in XY Plane = 22, Angle from XY plane = 0, Delta X = 50.00, Delta Y = 20.00, Delta Z = 0.00.

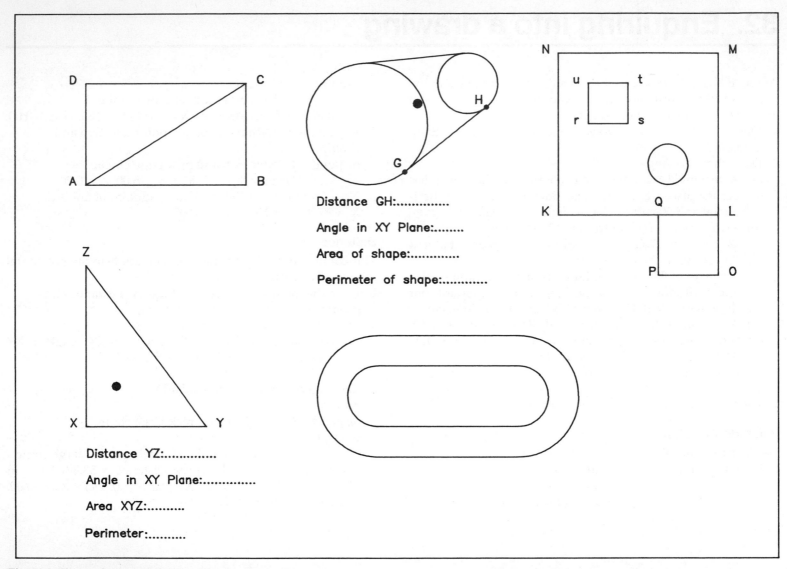

Distance GH:..............

Angle in XY Plane:........

Area of shape:.............

Perimeter of shape:............

Distance YZ:..............

Angle in XY Plane:..............

Area XYZ:..........

Perimeter:..........

Fig. 32.1. Shapes for use with Point, Distance and Area.

Area

Returns the area and perimeter of a selected shape or poly-shape and has the facility to allow composites shapes to be selected.

1. From the menu bar select **Edit–Inquiry–Area** and

prompt	`<First point>/Object/Add/Subtract`
respond	pick point A – snap on helps
prompt	`Next point` and pick point B
prompt	`Next point` and pick point C
prompt	`Next point` and pick point D
prompt	`Next point` and right-click

   Command area displays: Area = 4000.00, Perimeter = 260.00. Correct for an 80×50 rectangle?

2. Repeat the Edit–Inquiry–Area selection and

prompt	`<First point>/...`
enter	**O<R>** – the object option
prompt	`Select objects`
respond	**pick large circle**

   Display Area = 2827.43, Circumference = 188.50. Correct for a circle of 30 radius?

3. Repeat the area command, enter the Object option (O) and

prompt	`Select objects`
respond	**pick the 'inside' polyshape**

   Display Area = 2806.86, Perimeter = 234.25. Could you calculate the area and perimeter for this shape?

4. This example is long as it involves calculating the area of a composite shape. Activate the area command and

prompt	`<First point>/...`
enter	**A<R>** – the add option
prompt	`<First point>/Object/Subtract`
respond	**pick point K of the square** – snap on helps?
prompt	`(ADD mode) Next point` and pick point L
prompt	`(ADD mode) Next point` and pick point M
prompt	`(ADD mode) Next point` and pick point N
prompt	`(ADD mode) Next point` and right-click

Display Area = 6400.00, Perimeter = 320.00, Total area = 6400.00

prompt	`<First point>/Object/Subtract`
enter	**S<R>** – the subtract option
prompt	`<First point>/Object/Add`
respond	pick point r of small square
prompt	`(SUBTRACT mode) Next point` and pick point s
prompt	`(SUBTRACT mode) Next point` and pick point t
prompt	`(SUBTRACT mode) Next point` and pick point u
prompt	`(SUBTRACT mode) Next point` and right-click

Display Area = 400.00, Perimeter = 80.00, Total area = 6000.00

prompt	`<First point>/Object/Add`
enter	**A<R>** – the add option again
prompt	`<First point>/Object/Subtract`
respond	pick point L
prompt	`(ADD mode) Next point` and pick point O
prompt	`(ADD mode) Next point` and pick point P
prompt	`(ADD mode) Next point` and pick point Q
prompt	`(ADD mode) Next point` and right-click

Display Area = 900.00, Perimeter = 120.00, Total area = 6900.00

prompt	`<First point>/Object/Subtract`
enter	**S<R>** – subtract again
prompt	`<First point>/Object/Add`
enter	**O<R>** – the object option
prompt	`(SUBTRACT mode) Select objects`
respond	pick circle inside square. Display Area = 314.16, Circumference = 62.83, Total area = 6585.84
prompt	`(SUBTRACT mode) Select objects` and right-click
prompt	`<First point>/...` and right-click.

5. Finally enter **AREA**<R> and the command line then:
   (a) enter A<R>
   (b) enter O<R>
   (c) pick outer polyshape. Area = 7027.43, Perimeter = 328.50, Total area = 7027.43
   (d) enter S<R>
   (e) enter O<R>
   (f) pick inner polyshape. Area = 2806.86, Perimeter = 234.28, Total area = 4220.58
   (g) right-click
   (h) right-click.

Exercise

1. For the triangle shape, find:
   (a) length of side yz – distance?
   (b) angle of yz in the XY plane
   (c) area and perimeter of triangle xyz.
2. Find the length of the tangent line GH and its angle in the XY plane.
3. Can you find the total area and perimeter of the shape consisting of the two circles and the two tangent lines? Possible ideas:
   (a) draw a polyshape around the outline?
   (b) trim the circles and then convert the four entities into a single polyline?

Mass properties

From the menu bar select **Edit–Inquiry–Mass Properties** and
prompt   Select objects
respond **pick any entity** then right-click
prompt   No solids or regions selected
   These topics will not be covered in this book.

List

A command which gives information about a selected entity.
1. From the menu bar select **Edit–Inquiry–List** and
   prompt   Select objects
   respond **pick line AB** then right-click
   prompt   AutoCAD 'flips' to the Text Window and displays certain information about the line AB
   respond **F2 to flip back to drawing screen**
2. Select the LIST icon from the Object Properties toolbar and
   prompt   Select objects
   respond **pick the large circle** the right-click
   prompt   Text Window with information about the circle
   respond F2
3. Figure 32.2 is a screen dump of the Text Window display for the line AB and the large circle.
4. Note that the LIST icon from the Object Properties toolbar has a flyout selection, which allows access to all the commands in icon form, i.e. Locate Point, Distance, Area and Mass Properties.

Time

A command which gives 'time' information about the current drawing
(a) when it was originally created
(b) when it was last updated
(c) the length of time worked on it.
From the menu bar select **Data–Time** and the Text Window displays the information for the drawing, similar to Fig. 32.3. There are options available with the command
1. ON – turns the timer on
2. OFF – turns the timer off
3. Reset – resets the timer.
Toggle back to the drawing screen with F2.

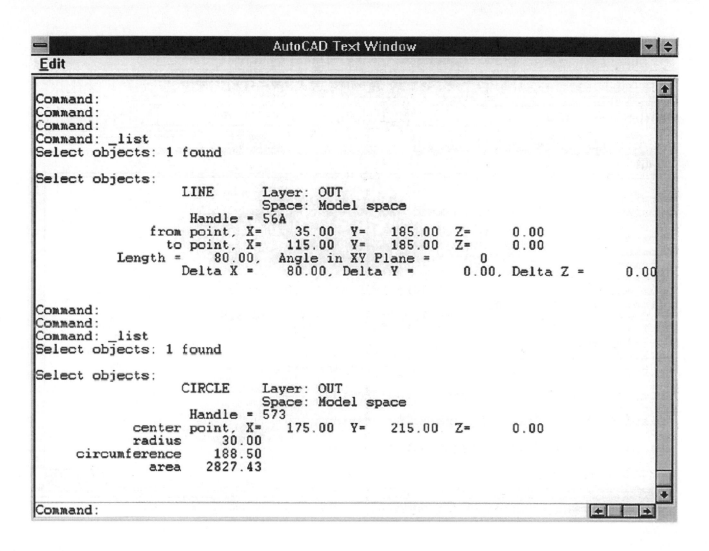

```
─                          AutoCAD Text Window                      ▼ ⬍

Edit

Command:                                                              ⬆
Command:
Command:
Command: _list
Select objects: 1 found

Select objects:
                    LINE        Layer: OUT
                                Space: Model space
                        Handle = 56A
                from point, X=     35.00  Y=     185.00  Z=       0.00
                  to point, X=    115.00  Y=     185.00  Z=       0.00
          Length =      80.00,   Angle in XY Plane =        0
                    Delta X =       80.00, Delta Y =        0.00, Delta Z =       0.00


Command:
Command:
Command: _list
Select objects: 1 found

Select objects:
                    CIRCLE      Layer: OUT
                                Space: Model space
                        Handle = 573
                center point, X=    175.00  Y=     215.00  Z=       0.00
             radius        30.00
      circumference       188.50
             area       2827.43
                                                                     ▼
Command:                                                        ← ▮ ▮ →
```

Fig. 32.2. LIST text screen.

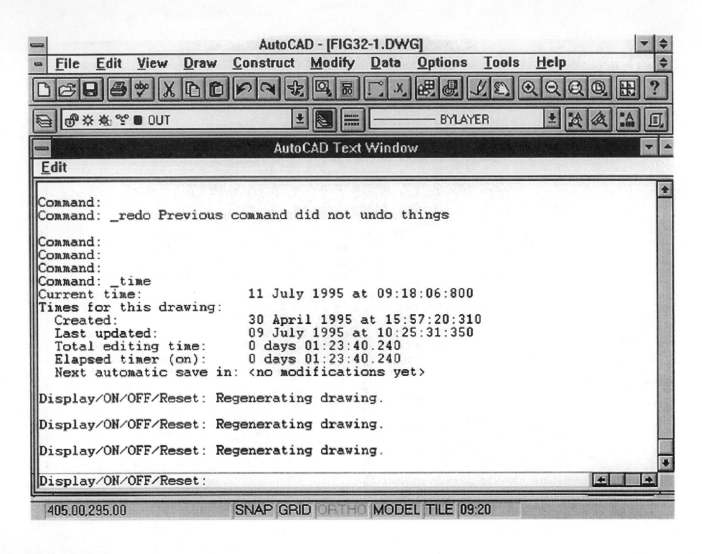

Fig. 32.3. TIME text screen.

Status

Useful as it gives information about the current drawing, e.g. limits, grid, snap, etc., as well as disk information. Figure 32.4 is a typical status screen. The command is activated from the menu bar with **Data–Status**.

Calculator

AutoCAD R13 has a built-in calculator which can be used:
(a) to evaluate mathematical expressions
(b) to assist in the calculation of point data.
The mathematical operations obey the usual order of preference.
1. From the menu bar select **Tools**

   Calculator

   prompt   >> Expression
   enter   **5 ∗ (2 + 3) ^ 2<R>**
   prompt   125.0
2. Repeat the calculator selection and
   prompt   >> Expression
   enter   **(5 ∗ (2 + 3)) ^ 2<R>**
   prompt   625.0
3. Select the CALCULATOR icon from the Object Snap toolbar and
   prompt   >> Expression
   enter   **((7 − 4)+(2 ∗ (8 + 1)))/3**
   prompt   ? – what is the answer?

Transparent calculator

A transparent command is one which can be used while 'in another command' and is activated from the command line by entering ('). For example, '**ZOOM** allows the zoom command to be used while drawing entities.

The transparent calculator command is very powerful as it allows the user to enter an expression to define points. To demonstrate how it works:

1. Select the donut command and set the ID to 0 and the OD to 4 then:
   prompt   Center of doughnut
   enter   '**cal**<R> – transparent calculator
   prompt   >> Expression
   enter   **(cen + cen)/2<R>**
   prompt   >> Select entity for CEN snap
   respond   **pick large circle through G**
   prompt   >> Select entity for CEN snap
   respond   **pick circle through H** and a donut is displayed at the calculated point.
2. The prompt is still 'Center of doughnut' so:
   enter   '**cal**<R>
   prompt   >> Expression
   enter   **(MID + MID)/2<R>**
   prompt   >> Select entity for MID snap
   respond   **pick line XY**
   prompt   >> Select entity for MID snap
   respond   **pick line XZ** and doughnut displayed.
3. Prompt still active, so ESC.

❏ *Summary*
1. Drawings can be 'interrogated' to obtain information about:
   (a) co-ordinate details
   (b) distance between points
   (c) areas and perimeters of composite shapes
   (d) entity status
   (e) time spent.
2. Areas are returned for selected shapes/polyshapes. Areas can be added/subtracted to/from the original shape.
3. The distance is returned between two selected points and
   (a) the angle to the horizontal is given
   (b) the X and Y distances between the selected points is given.
4. The calculator command can be used transparently (') and gives the user a powerful draughting aid.

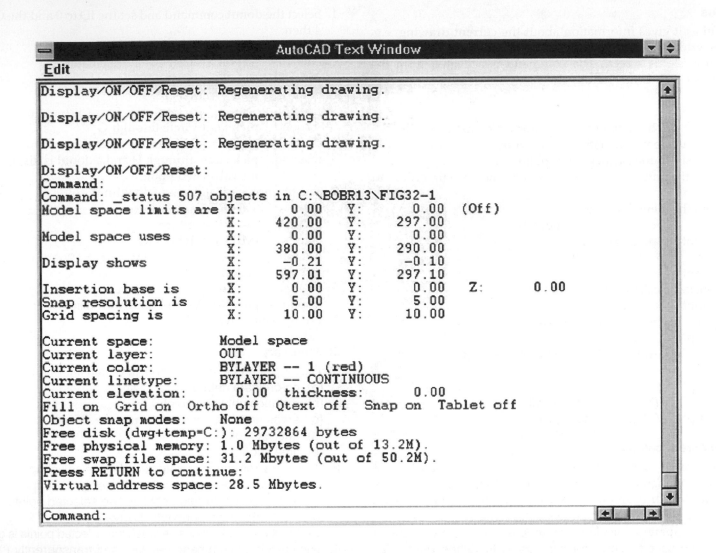

```
AutoCAD Text Window
Edit

Display/ON/OFF/Reset: Regenerating drawing.

Display/ON/OFF/Reset: Regenerating drawing.

Display/ON/OFF/Reset: Regenerating drawing.

Display/ON/OFF/Reset:
Command:
Command: _status 507 objects in C:\BOBR13\FIG32-1
Model space limits are X:        0.00   Y:        0.00   (Off)
                       X:      420.00   Y:      297.00
Model space uses       X:        0.00   Y:        0.00
                       X:      380.00   Y:      290.00
Display shows          X:       -0.21   Y:       -0.10
                       X:      597.01   Y:      297.10
Insertion base is      X:        0.00   Y:        0.00   Z:        0.00
Snap resolution is     X:        5.00   Y:        5.00
Grid spacing is        X:       10.00   Y:       10.00

Current space:         Model space
Current layer:         OUT
Current color:         BYLAYER -- 1 (red)
Current linetype:      BYLAYER -- CONTINUOUS
Current elevation:        0.00  thickness:        0.00
Fill on  Grid on  Ortho off  Qtext off  Snap on  Tablet off
Object snap modes:     None
Free disk (dwg+temp=C:): 29732864 bytes
Free physical memory: 1.0 Mbytes (out of 13.2M).
Free swap file space: 31.2 Mbytes (out of 50.2M).
Press RETURN to continue:
Virtual address space: 28.5 Mbytes.

Command:
```

Fig. 32.4. STATUS text screen.

33. Text fonts and styles

Text has been added to drawings without any consideration about 'appearance'. In this chapter we will investigate:
(a) text fonts and styles
(b) text control codes
(c) paragraph text.

The terms 'font' and 'style' are used extensively with text and they can be explained as:

Font: defines the pattern which is used to draw characters, i.e. it is basically an alphabet 'appearance'. Figure 33.1 shows some text fonts available with the standard font file as well as some additional fonts.

Style: defines the parameters used to draw the actual text characters, i.e. the obliquing angle, the width, whether backwards text, etc.

Notes

1. Text fonts are 'part of' AutoCAD R13.
2. Text styles are created by the user.
3. A text font can be used for many different styles.
4. A text style uses only one font.

Getting started

1. Open A:STDA3 standard sheet with toolbars as required and refer to Fig. 33.2.
2. At the command line enter **STYLE**<R>

prompt	Text style name (or ?)<STANDARD>
enter	**?**<R>
prompt	Text style(s) to list<*>
enter	**<RETURN>**
prompt	AutoCAD Text Window with:

Style name: STANDARD
Font   files: C:\ACADR13\COMMON\FONTS\
ISOCP.SHX
Height: 0.00 Width factor: 1.00 Obliquing
angle: 0
Generation: Normal

3. This is R13's 'default' text style with the name STANDARD. The text font used is ISOCP.SHX.
4. It is useful to note this STANDARD name for future reference.
5. F2 to flip back to drawing screen.
6. Using DTEXT with the default text style, add text at the 145,255 at height 8 and 0 rotation. The text item is **AutoCAD R13**.

Creating text styles

To create any text style, the user must:
(a) select a text font
(b) define the text style parameters.

We will create several new text styles using a variety of fonts and then save them for future work.

1. From the menu bar select **Data**
Text Style

prompt	Text style name (or ?)<STANDARD>
enter	**ST1**<R>
prompt	New style and Select Font File dialogue box
respond	1. scroll up until romans appears in list
	2. pick romans.shx
	(a) turns blue
	(b) romans.shx in File Name box
	3. pick OK
prompt	Height<0.00> and enter **0**<R>
prompt	Width factor<1.00> and right-click

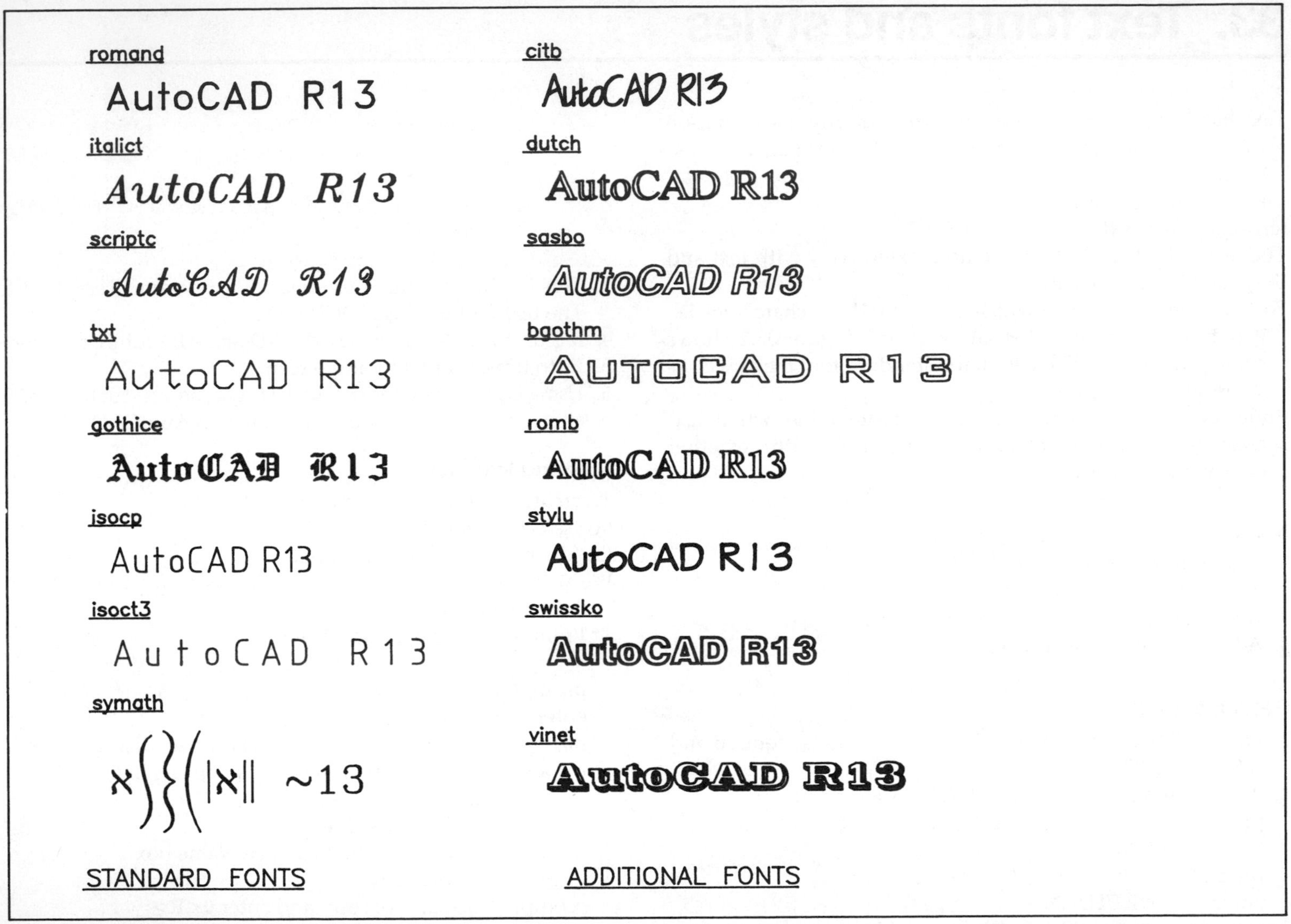

romand

AutoCAD R13

italict

AutoCAD R13

scriptc

AutoCAD R13

txt

AutoCAD R13

gothice

AutoCAD R13

isocp

AutoCAD R13

isoct3

AutoCAD R13

symath

$$x \int \left\{ \begin{array}{c} \\ \end{array} \right\} \left(\|x\| \sim 13 \right.$$

citb

AutoCAD R13

dutch

AutoCAD R13

sasbo

AutoCAD R13

bgothm

AutoCAD R13

romb

AutoCAD R13

stylu

AutoCAD R13

swissko

AutoCAD R13

vinet

AutoCAD R13

STANDARD FONTS

ADDITIONAL FONTS

Fig. 33.1. Some text fonts with AutoCAD R13 at height 8.

prompt	`Obliquing angle<0>` and right-click
prompt	`Backwards<N>` and right-click
prompt	`Upside-down<N>` and right-click
prompt	`Vertical<N>` and right-click
prompt	`ST1 is now the current style`

2. The height, width factor, obliquing angle, etc. are the parameters which must be defined for every text style created.
3. At present we will not use this text style, but continue to create the other required styles.
4. Using the Data–Text Style selection, create the text styles using the information given in Table 33.1.
5. When all text styles have been created, save the drawing as **A:TEXST** as it will be used in other exercises.

Table 33.1

Style name	ST2	ST3	ST4	ST5	ST6	ST7	ST8
Font name	gothice	syastro	italict	romant	scriptc	monotxt	symath
Height	12	6	5	10	4	15	5
Width factor	1	2	3	1	1	1	1
Obliquing angle	0	0	30	0	−30	0	0
Backwards	N	Y	N	N	N	N	Y
Upside-down	N	N	N	Y	N	N	Y
Vertical	N	–	N	N	N	Y	Y

Using created text styles

Text styles can be used with both single and dynamic text commands.

1. Select the dynamic text icon and

prompt	`Justify/Style/<Start point>`
enter	**S<R>** – the style option
prompt	`Style name (or ?)<ST8 probably>`
enter	**ST1<R>**
prompt	`Justify/Style/<Start point>`
enter	**15,255<R>**

prompt	`Height<0>` and enter **8<R>**
prompt	`Rotation angle<0>` and enter **0<R>**
prompt	`Text` and enter **AutoCAD R13**<R>

2. The text item will be displayed in the romans text font.
3. Repeat the dynamic text command, entering **AutoCAD R13** as the text item using the information below and referring to Fig. 33.2.

Style	Start point	Height	Rotation	
ST1	15,255	8	0	– already entered
ST2	55,220	NA	0	– not applicable
ST3	315,200	NA	0	
ST4	15,115	NA	30	
ST5	160,170	NA	0	
ST6	125,155	NA	−30	
ST7	355,250	NA	270(default?)	
ST8	315,25	NA	270(default?)	

4. When complete you should have nine AutoCAD R13's displayed (eight created styles and the default) at various points on the screen.

Notes

Text styles and fonts can be confusing to new AutoCAD users, and the following may be of some assistance.

1. Width factor is a parameter which 'stretches' the text characters – Fig. 33.2 displays text for factors of 1, 2 and 3.
2. Obliquing angle 'slopes' the text characters and Fig. 33.2 displays text with angles of 0, 5 and 10.
3. The text items displayed with styles ST4 and ST6 are interesting. The obliquing and the rotation angles are:
   ST4   30 obliquing,   30 rotation
   ST6   −30 obliquing,   −30 rotation
   These values give 'isometric' type text?
4. When the dynamic text command was used to insert the AutoCAD R13 text item, only one style prompted for a height. This was ST1. The reason for this is that the height

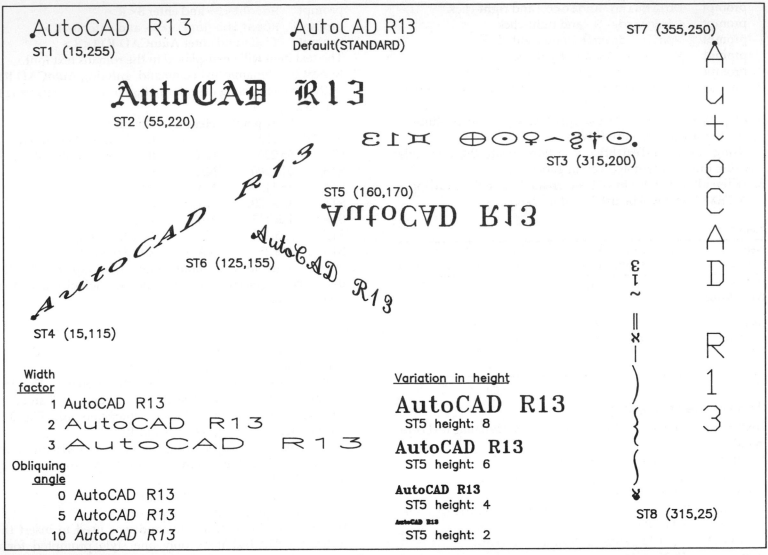

Fig. 33.2. Creating and using text styles.

entered when ST1 was being created was 0, while all the other created styles had a non-zero value entered, i.e. *if a created text style has a non-zero height value, there is no height prompt when that style is used for text.*

5. I recommend that when text styles are being created, the height is entered as 0. This allows the user to set the height when the text command is used. If a text height is entered when the style is created, then that style can only be used with the entered height. I have displayed the text style ST5 with differing heights.

Text control codes

When text is being added to a drawing it may be required to underline the text, or add the diameter/degree symbol. Auto-CAD has several control codes which when used with text will allow underlining, overscoring and symbol insertion. The codes which are available are:

%%O toggles the OVERSCORE on/off
%%U toggles the UNDERSCORE on/off
%%D draws the DEGREE symbol for angle or temperature (°)
%%C draws the DIAMETER symbol (Ø)
%%P draws the PLUS/MINUS symbol (±)
%%% draws the PERCENTAGE symbol (%)

1. Open the **A:TEXST** drawing with the created text styles and refer to Fig. 33.3. Toolbars and layer to suit.
2. Select the dynamic text icon and

prompt	`Justify/Style/<Start point>`
enter	**S<R>** – the style option
prompt	`Style name (or ?)<?>`
enter	**ST1<R>**
prompt	`Justify/Style...`
enter	**25,200<R>**
prompt	`Height` and enter **8<R>**
prompt	`Rotation` angle and enter **10<R>**
prompt	`Text`

enter   **%%UAutoCAD R13%%U<R>**

3. Select the dynamic text icon and enter
   (a) ST2 as the style
   (b) 155,235 as the start point
   (c) 0 as the rotation angle (no height?)
   (d) text: **123.45%%DF**
4. Repeat the dynamic text selection and enter
   (a) ST5 as the style
   (b) 35,135 as the start point
   (c) 0 as the rotation angle
   (d) text: **%%UUNDERLINE%%U and %%OOVERSCORE%%O**
   (e) interesting result?
5. Using dynamic text enter the following:

Style	ST4
Start point	225,35
Rotation	30
Text	**%%UAutoCAD%%U %%OR13%%O**
and	
Style	ST6
Start point	285,175
Rotation	−30
Text	**%%OAutoCAD%%O %%UR13%%U**

6. Refer to Fig. 33.3 and add the other items of text. These should all have ST1 as the text style. The height and start points are at your discretion.
7. Save the drawing if required.

Paragraph text

When text was being discussed in an earlier chapter, only the single-line and dynamic text commands were discussed. Auto-CAD R13 has another text command called paragraph text, which allows the user to add text to a defined rectangular area. I decided to leave paragraph text to this chapter on fonts and styles, as it allows us to investigate some new text concepts incorporated in R13. Paragraph text is called **MTEXT**.

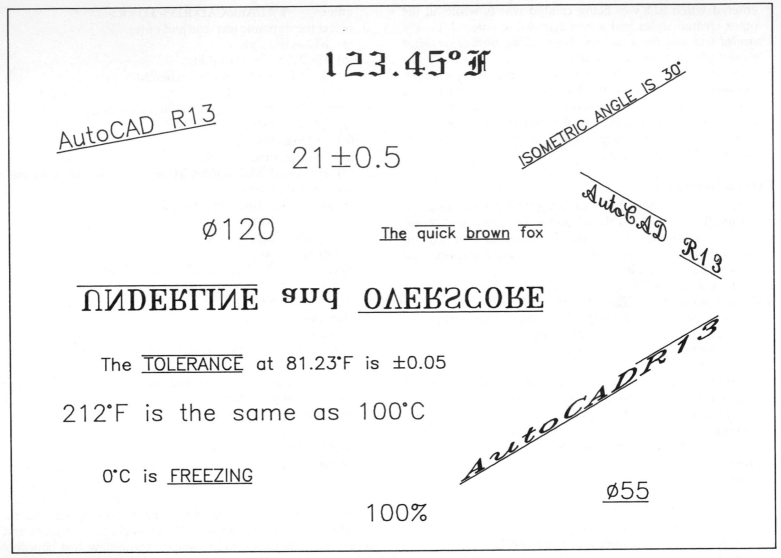

Fig. 33.3. Text control codes.

1. Open the **A:TEXST** drawing saved with the created text fonts.
2. Toolbars to suit, layer TEXT current.
3. From the menu bar select **Draw**

Text

Text

prompt   `Attach/Rotation/Style/Height/`
               `Direction/<Insertion point>`

enter   **S\<R>** then **ST1\<R>**

prompt   `Attach/...`

enter   **H\<R>** then **5\<R>**

prompt   `Attach/...`

enter   **10,260\<R>** – the insertion point

prompt   `Attach/...`

enter   **125,175\<R>** – the other corner

prompt   Edit MText dialogue box – Fig. 33.4

respond   type in the following lines of text without \<RETURN>. As you type, the text will 'wrap-around' the window width. Do not worry about the appearance of the text as it appears in the dialogue box 'white area'. There are several (seven) deliberate spelling mistakes (underlined) which you should type in as given. This is to allow us to 'test' the spellcheck:

CAD is a draughting <u>tol</u> with many benefits when compared to conventional draughting. Some of the <u>benefitds</u> include <u>incresed</u> productivity, shorter lead <u>tines</u>, standardisation, <u>acuracy</u> <u>amd</u> rapid <u>resonse</u> to change.

respond   when all text is typed in pick OK from the Edit MText dialogue box.
4. The types text will be fitted into the **'width'** of the selected area of the screen – *not into the full rectangular area* (as I thought it would!)
5. Fig. 33.5(a) displays this original 'error' text.

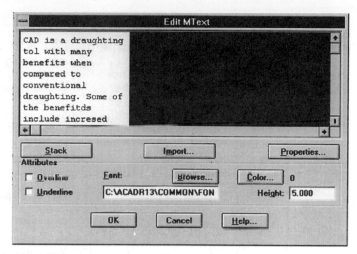

Fig. 33.4. Edit MText dialogue box.

Spellcheck

AutoCAD R13 has a built-in spellchecker, which can be activated:

   (a) from the menu bar with **Tools–Spelling...**
   (b) by icon selection from the Standard toolbar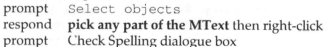

1. Activate the spell check command and

prompt   `Select objects`

respond **pick any part of the MText** then right-click

prompt   Check Spelling dialogue box

with   1. Current word – probably `draughting?`
          2. Suggestions – maybe `draughtiness?`
          3. Content – `CAD is a ...`

respond **pick Ignore** if draughting spelling correct

prompt   Check Spelling dialogue box

with   1. Current word – `tol?`
          2. Suggestions – `toll` and some other words

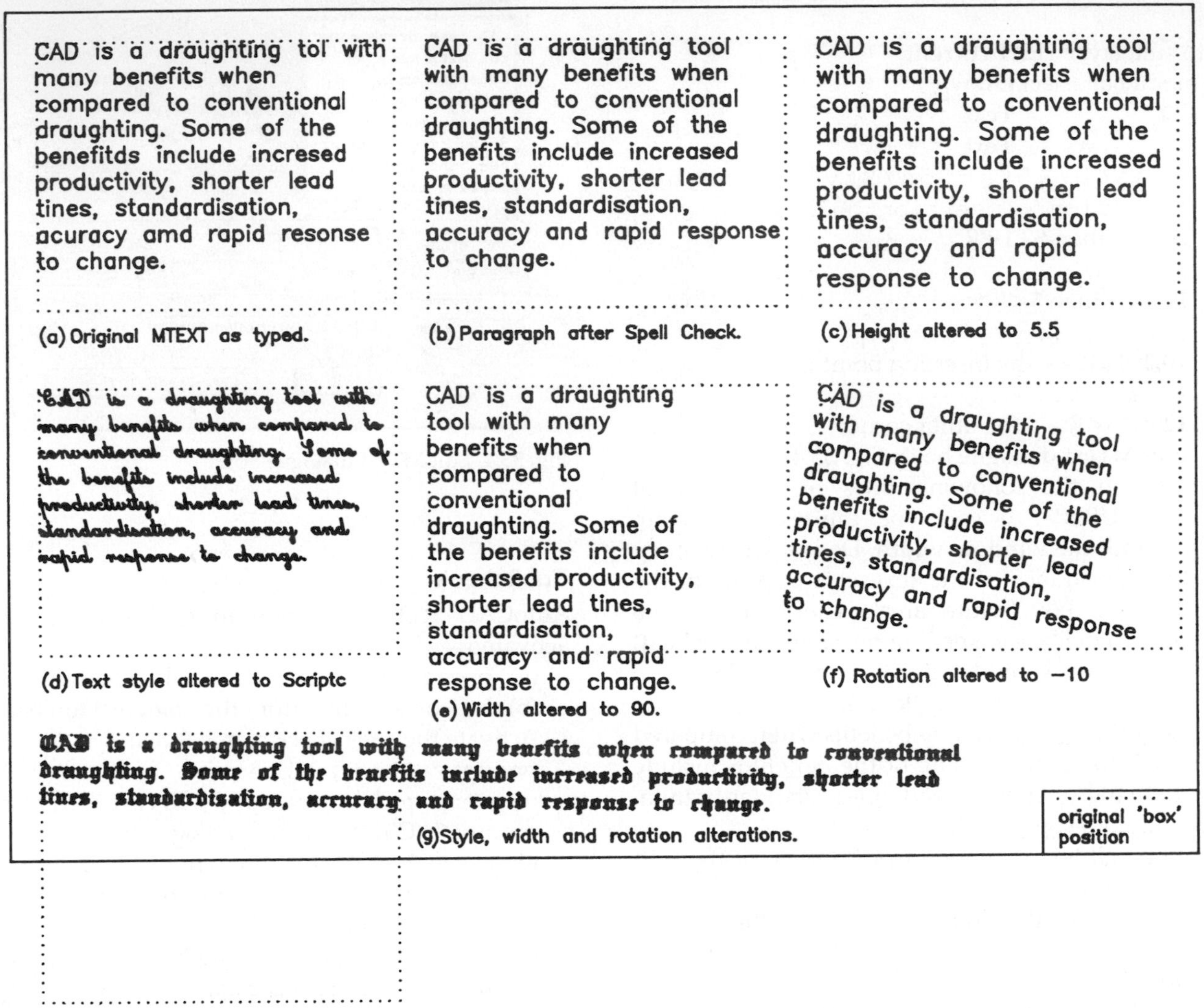

CAD is a draughting tol with many benefits when compared to conventional draughting. Some of the benefitds include incresed productivity, shorter lead tines, standardisation, acuracy amd rapid resonse to change.

(a) Original MTEXT as typed.

CAD is a draughting tool with many benefits when compared to conventional draughting. Some of the benefits include increased productivity, shorter lead tines, standardisation, accuracy and rapid response to change.

(b) Paragraph after Spell Check.

CAD is a draughting tool with many benefits when compared to conventional draughting. Some of the benefits include increased productivity, shorter lead tines, standardisation, accuracy and rapid response to change.

(c) Height altered to 5.5

CAD is a draughting tool with many benefits when compared to conventional draughting. Some of the benefits include increased productivity, shorter lead tines, standardisation, accuracy and rapid response to change.

(d) Text style altered to Scriptc

CAD is a draughting tool with many benefits when compared to conventional draughting. Some of the benefits include increased productivity, shorter lead tines, standardisation, accuracy and rapid response to change.

(e) Width altered to 90.

CAD is a draughting tool with many benefits when compared to conventional draughting. Some of the benefits include increased productivity, shorter lead tines, standardisation, accuracy and rapid response to change.

(f) Rotation altered to −10

CAD is a draughting tool with many benefits when compared to conventional draughting. Some of the benefits include increased productivity, shorter lead tines, standardisation, accuracy and rapid response to change.

(g) Style, width and rotation alterations.

original 'box' position

Fig. 33.5. Paragraph text.

respond	1. pick `tool` (turns blue)
	2. `tool` added to Suggestion box – Fig. 33.6
	3. pick **Change**
prompt with	Check Spelling dialogue box
	`next word not known`
respond	1. pick Ignore to: `draughting`
	`standardization` (note z!)
	2. pick Change to: `benefitdc` → `bcncfits`
	`incresed` → `increased`
	`acuracy` → `accuracy`
	`amd` → `and` (manually)
	`resonse` → `response`
prompt	AutoCAD message: `Spell check complete`
respond	**pick OK**

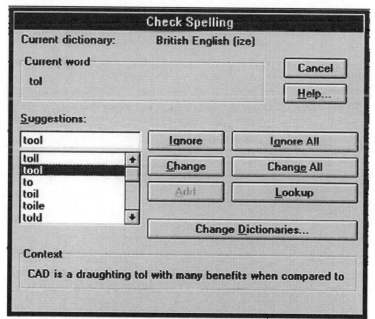

Fig. 33.6. Check Spelling dialogue box.

2. The paragraph text will be 'reprinted' with the correct spelling as shown in Fig. 33.5(b).
3. One of the original spelling mistakes was 'tines' (times) and this was not highlighted with the spellcheck. This means that 'tines' is a 'real word' as far as the AutoCAD spellcheck is concerned although it is wrong to us. This is a major problem with spellchecks – they check the spelling, not the sense of the word.
4. Multiple copy the corrected paragraph text to five other places on the screen, referring to Fig. 33.5 for the layout.

Editing paragraph text

1. From the menu bar select **Modify**

   Edit Text...

prompt	`<Select a TEXT or ATTDEF objcct>...`
respond	pick a paragraph text item
prompt	Edit MText dialogue box
respond	1. pick Properties...
	(MText Properties dialogue box displayed)
	2. change Text Height to 5.5
	3. pick OK from MText Properties dialogue box
	4. pick OK from Edit MText dialogue box
prompt	paragraph text displayed at new height – Fig. 33.5(c) then right-click to end command.

2. Repeat the Edit Text command, pick the next paragraph text item then:
   (a) pick Properties...
   (b) scroll and pick Text Style **ST6**
   (c) pick OK from MTExt Properties dialogue box
   (d) pick OK from Edit MText dialogue box
   (e) text alter to scriptc font – Fig. 33.5(d)
   (f) right-click

3. Using the Edit Text command, alter the remaining paragraph text as follows:
   (a) Properties: width to 90 – Fig. 33.5(e)
   (b) Properties: rotation to –10 – Fig. 33.5(f)
   (c) Properties: style to ST2, width to 300, rotation to –1 as Fig. 33.5(g).
4. This completes the paragraph text exercise and the chapter on fonts and styles.

❏ *Summary*

1. FONTS define the pattern of text characters.
2. A font can be considered as an alphabet.
3. STYLES define the parameters for drawing characters.
4. Text styles are created by the user.
5. Every text style must use a text font.
6. A text font can be used for several styles.
7. The AutoCAD R13 default text style is STANDARD.
8. MTEXT is paragraph text.
9. Paragraph text can be edited in dialogue box format.
10. R13 has a built-in spellcheck.

34. The array command

ARRAY is a command which allows multiple copying of objects in either a rectangular or polar (circular) pattern. It is one of the most powerful and useful of the AutoCAD commands, yet is one of the easiest to use. We will demonstrate the command by example so:

1. Open A:STDA3 standard sheet, layer OUT current with toolbars Draw, Modify and Object Snap.
2. Refer to Fig. 34.1 and draw the rectangular shape to the sizes given. Do not add the dimensions.
3. Multiple copy the rectangular shape from the mid-point indicated to the points A, B, C and D using the co-ordinates given. The donuts are for reference only.
4. Draw two circles, centre at 290,190 with radius 30 and centre at 205,65 with radius 15.
5. Erase the original shape when the copy command is complete.

Rectangular array

Select the RECTANGULAR ARRAY icon from the copy flyout of the Modify toolbar and

prompt Select objects
respond **window the shape at A** then right-click
prompt Number of rows (--)<1>
enter   **3<R>**
prompt Number of columns (||||)<1>
enter   **5<R>**
prompt Unit cell or distance between rows (--)
enter   **30<R>**
prompt Distance between columns (||||)
enter   **25<R>**

The shape at A will be copied 14 times into a three row and five column matrix pattern.

Polar array with rotation

Select the POLAR ARRAY icon from the Modify toolbar and

prompt Select objects
respond **window the shape at B** then right-click
prompt Center point of array
respond **CENter icon and pick circle below B**
prompt Number of items
enter   **10<R>**
prompt Angle to fill (+=ccw, -=cw)<360>
enter   **360<R>**
prompt Rotate objects as they are copied<Y>
enter   **Y<R>**

The shape at B is copied in a circular pattern about the selected centre point. The objects are 'rotated' about this point as they are copied.

Polar array without rotation

From the menu bar select **Construct–Array**
               Polar
prompt Select objects and window the shape at C then right-click
prompt Center point of array and pick small circle centre
prompt Number of items and enter 10
prompt Angle to fill and enter 360
prompt Rotate objects and enter **N<R>**

The shape at C is copied about the selected centre point, but is not rotated as it is copied.

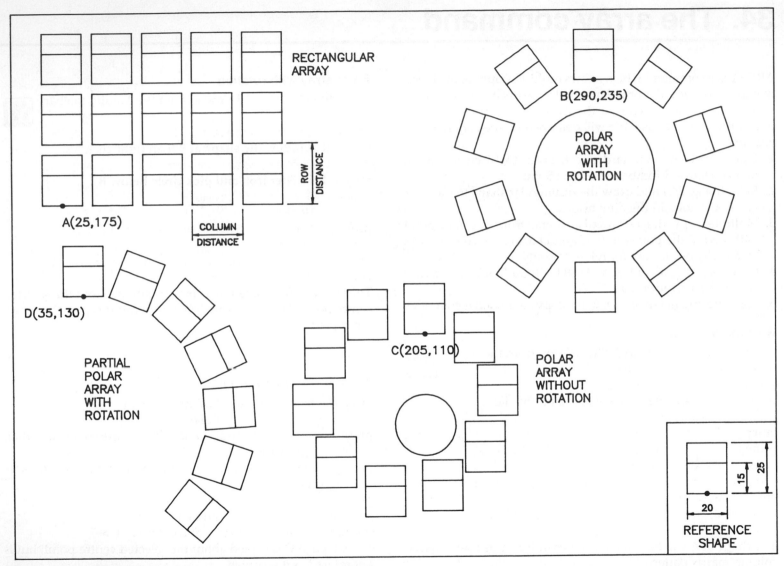

RECTANGULAR ARRAY

ROW DISTANCE

A(25,175)

COLUMN DISTANCE

B(290,235)

POLAR ARRAY WITH ROTATION

D(35,130)

PARTIAL POLAR ARRAY WITH ROTATION

C(205,110)

POLAR ARRAY WITHOUT ROTATION

REFERENCE SHAPE

20

15

25

Fig. 34.1. The ARRAY command 1.

Polar array with partial fill angle

Activate the polar array command then:
(a) Select objects: window the shape at D then right-click.
(b) Center point: enter 35,60<R>
(c) Number of items: enter 7<R>
(d) Angle to fill: enter –130<R>
(e) Rotate objects: enter Y<R>
Hopefully your drawing resembles Fig. 34.1 and can now be saved.

Using polar arrays

The polar array is a very useful command and will be further demonstrated by example, so:
1. Open A:STDA3 again with usual toolbars.
2. Refer to Fig. 34.2 and draw three concentric circles:
   (a) on layer OUT with radii 40 and 10.
   (b) on layer CL with radius 25.
3. Multiple copy these three circles to three other parts of the screen, using Fig. 34.2 for positioning.
4. Draw the line (CL) and circle (OUT) to the reference sizes given and then multiple copy the two entities to the centre of each circle. Use END → CEN icons.
5. Using the polar command, array the centre line and circle using the following data:
   (a) six items, angle 360
   (b) seven items, angle 360
   (c) eight items, angle 240
   (d) 10 items, angle –240.

Angular rectangular array

A rectangular array can be made 'angular' using the **snapangle**. Refer to Fig. 34.2 and
1. Draw the 20 × 25 rectangular shape from the previous exercise at the points A (265,145) and B (365,85).
2. Rotate the shape at A by 20° and the shape at B by –5.

3. From the menu bar select **Options–Drawing Aids...** and
   prompt   Drawing Aids dialogue box
   respond   1. set Snap Angle to 20
              2. pick OK
4. The grid and on-screen cursor are now 'rotated' by 20°.
5. Use the rectangular array command with
   (a) window the shape at A
   (b) 3 rows
   (c) 5 columns
   (d) row distance 35
   (e) column distance 25.
6. Set the snap angle to –5 using Options–Drawing Aids.
7. Rectangular array the shape at B for 3 rows, 5 columns, row distance –35, column distance –25.
8. Figure 34.2 is now complete.

User exercise 3

This exercise will involve both arrays and text styles.
1. Open A:STDA3 with toolbars displayed as required.
2. Refer to Fig. 34.3 and draw a 30-unit square at point A (15,15).
3. Multiple copy this square from point A to points B (85,230); C (205,90) and D (280,15).
4. Array the squares as follows:
   A – Rectangular with two rows; five columns; 35 row distance; 35 column distance
   B – Polar with centre at 100,180; 10 items; 360 angle; with rotation
   C – Rectangular with five rows; two columns; 35 row distance; 35 column distance
   D – Angular rectangular with snap angle –10; five rows; two columns; 35 row/column distance.
5. At this point save as **A:USEREX3**.
6. Create eight new text styles using the font names given in Fig. 34.3 with the style names as S1, S2, etc. Add the text

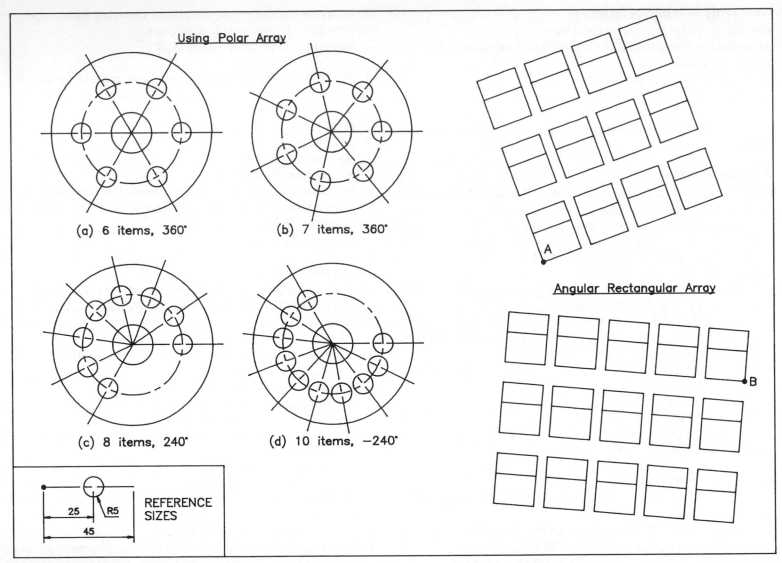

Fig. 34.2. The ARRAY command 2.

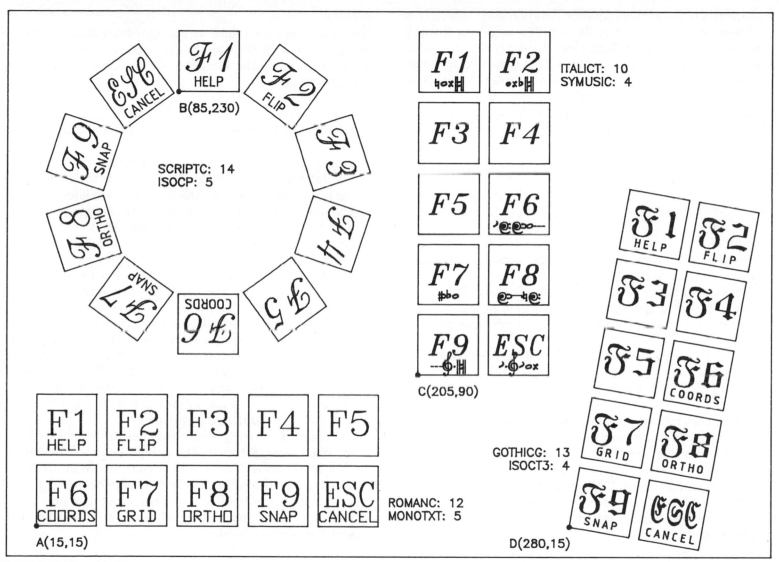

Fig. 34.3. Toolbox positions.

characters to the arrayed squares. Arrays A and C should not present any problem, but the rotation angle for array B requires some thought. Remember that array B had 10 items with a fill angle of 360°, so every item is rotated by about how many degrees?. The snap angle for array D was –10 so the text rotation angle is, what?

7. When all text is added, save your completed drawing.

❏ *Summary*

1. The ARRAY command allows multiple copying in a rectangular or circular (polar) pattern.
2. The command can be activated from the menu bar, in icon form or by entering ARRAY<R> at the prompt line.
3. Rectangular arrays must have at least one row and one column.
4. The rectangular row/column distance can be positive or negative.
5. Altering the snap angle will give an angular rectangular array.
6. Polar arrays require a centre point and this can be:
   (a) entered as co-ordinates
   (b) picked on the screen
   (c) referenced to existing entities.
7. Polar arrays can be full (360°) or partial.
8. The polar fill angle can be positive or negative.
9. The polar array objects can be rotated/not rotated about the centre point.

Activity

It has been some time since we attempted any activities, so I've included four with this chapter. I have tried to give a variety of drawings to show the versatility of the array command. As with all activities:

(a) start with your A:STDA3 standard sheet
(b) use layers correctly for outlines, centre lines, etc.
(c) think about dimensioning some of the drawings for practice.

1. Tutorial 20: two similar type components.
   The ratchet is fairly straightforward once the tooth shape has been drawn. Use the angled construction lines then trim. The saw blade tooth construction is interesting to draw, and may be more difficult than you would think. Perhaps not? Once arrayed, the trim command is needed with the circle.

2. Tutorial 21: typical engineering type application of array.
   The thread part is interesting as is the countersunk hole arrangement. The mirror command is helpful and use the pick point hatch option for the four areas.

3. Tutorial 22: one of my most popular tutorials.
   The bulb shape is harder than you would think especially the R10 arc. I've added a filament which is drawn from continuous arcs. The size does not matter. There are also two trimmed donuts on the base. The bulb is then copied, scaled and arrayed. This is a good drawing to dimension.

4. Tutorial 23: two different components.
   The bracket is fairly easy, the hexagonal object being inscribed in an R5 circle. The gauges is a nice drawing to complete. I drew a vertical line from the inside circle top quadrant, then arrayed this line twice. The arrays had 26 items with angles to fill of +160° and –160°. The smaller dial indicators were obtained by trimming to a smaller circle which was then erased.

35. Changing properties

All entities have properties, e.g. linetype, colour, layer, position, orientation, etc. Text has also height, style, width factor, etc. This chapter will demonstrate how properties can be changed with a serious of worked examples.

Several entities

1. Open A:STDA3 with layer OUT current and required toolbars.
2. Refer to Fig. 35.1 and draw a 30-unit square – Fig. 35.1(a). Multiple copy the square to four other places.
3. From the Objects Properties toolbar select the Properties icon and
   prompt   Select objects
   respond **window the second square** then right-click
   prompt   Change Properties dialogue box
   respond **pick Layer...**
   prompt   Select Layer dialogue box with OUT the current layer in blue
   respond **pick CL layer** then OK
   prompt   Change Properties dialogue box – Fig. 35.2
   respond   pick OK
4. The selected square is displayed with green centre lines – Fig. 35.1(b).
5. From the menu bar select **Edit**
   Properties...
   prompt   Select objects
   respond **window the third square** then right-click
   prompt   Change Properties dialogue box
   respond   pick Linetype...
   prompt   Select Linetype dialogue box
   respond **scroll and pick PHANTOM** then OK
   prompt   Change Properties dialogue box

respond   pick OK
6. The square is displayed with red phantom lines – Fig. 35.1(c).
7. Repeat the Properties icon selection and
   (a) window the fourth square then right-click
   (b) pick Color...
   (c) pick magenta then OK
   (d) pick OK from Change Properties dialogue box
   (e) square displayed as magenta – Fig. 35.1(d)
8. Finally repeat the Properties command and
   (a) window the fifth square then right-click
   (b) change colour to blue; layer to SECT; linetype to DOT
   (c) pick OK, OK
   (d) blue, dotted square – Fig. 35.1(e).
9. It is important to realise the changes made to the various figures:
   (b) layer changed to CL, i.e. green with center linetype
   (c) linetype changed to PHANTOM – current layer is OUT (continuous)
   (d) colour changed to magenta – current layer is OUT (red)
   (e) colour changed to blue, linetype to DOT, layer to SECT which is cyan and continuous.
10. The changes to Figs 35.1(c) and (d) have resulted in objects on layer OUT having a different colour and linetype to the 'default' layer settings. It is sometimes desirable to have different linetypes and colour on the one layer, but it is a practice I would not recommend until you are proficient at using (and understanding) layers.
11. Finally with layer 0 current, freeze layer OUT – only a green centre line square and a blue dotted line square displayed?
12. Undo this last entry.

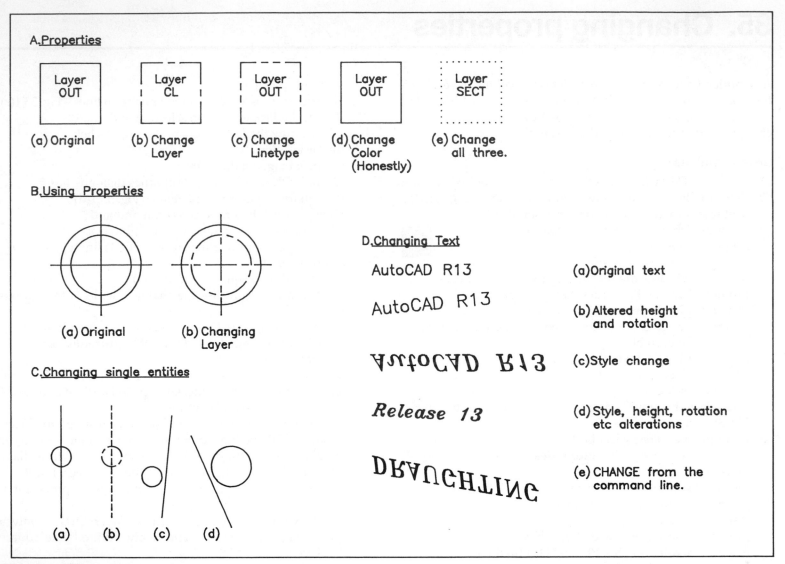

A. Properties

Layer OUT	Layer CL	Layer OUT	Layer OUT	Layer SECT
(a) Original	(b) Change Layer	(c) Change Linetype	(d) Change Color (Honestly)	(e) Change all three.

B. Using Properties

(a) Original (b) Changing Layer

C. Changing single entities

(a) (b) (c) (d)

D. Changing Text

AutoCAD R13 — (a) Original text

AutoCAD R13 — (b) Altered height and rotation

ΛⱯⱵⱢⱭⱯ ꓤƖƐ — (c) Style change

Release 13 — (d) Style, height, rotation etc alterations

DꓤⱯՈⱩⱵƖⱤⱩ — (e) CHANGE from the command line.

Fig. 35.1. Change properties exercise.

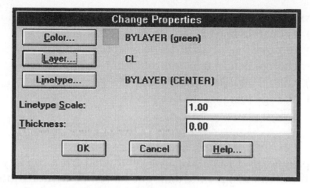

Fig. 35.2. Change Properties dialogue box.

Using properties

Changing properties is a very useful command for the user, and one of the most common requirements is to change layers:

1. With OUT the current layer, draw two circles and two lines as Fig. 35.1B(a).
2. Activate the Properties icon and
   (a) pick the two lines and small circle then right-click
   (b) from Change Properties dialogue box, pick Layer...
   (c) from Select Layer dialogue box, pick CL
   (d) pick OK then OK.
3. Lines and circle now green centre lines and on the required layer – Fig. 35.1B(b).

Single entity selection

1. Draw a line from 25,20 to 25,70 and a circle centre 25,50 with radius 5 – Fig. 35.1C(a).
2. Multiple copy the line and circle from a line endpoint by @25,0; @50,0 and@75,0
3. Select the Properties icon and
   prompt   Select objects
   respond   **pick the second line** then right-click
   prompt   Modify line dialogue box with

1. different layout from other dialogue box
2. more information given
3. top-left as before, i.e. Color, Layer...
4. start, end point of line given
5. length, angle of line given

respond   **alter layer to HID** to give Fig. 35.1C(b).

4. Repeat the properties command, pick the third line and alter:
   (a) To point X to 70
   (b) To point Y to 70 – Fig. 35.3
   (c) gives Fig. 35.1C(c).
5. Finally change the fourth line properties to:
   (a) line start point 110,15
   (b) line end point 90,60
   (c) Fig. 35.1C(d).
6. Using the properties command, change the circle as follows:
   (a) layer to CL
   (b) centre point to 70,40
   (c) centre point to 90,25 and radius to 10.

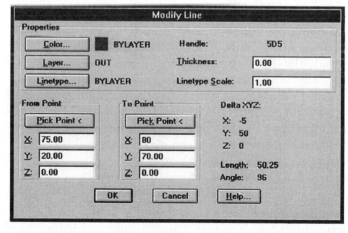

Fig. 35.3. Modify Line dialogue box.

Dialogue boxes

When the Properties command is activated by icon or from the menu bar there are two different types of dialogue box which can be displayed, this being dependent on the entities selected:
(a) several entities – Change Properties dialogue box as Fig. 35.2. The user can change the entity's colour, layer and linetype.
(b) single entity – Modify Line (or Circle, Text, etc.) dialogue box as Fig. 35.3. The user can change the colour, layer, linetype as well as the entity position, etc. The dialogue box also displays other useful information, this being dependent on the type of entity selected.

Changing text

Text has several properties that other entities do not, e.g. style, height, width factor, etc. as well as layer, colour, linetype. These can all be altered with the properties command so:
1. Create two new text styles

name:	ST1	ST2
font:	romans	italict
height:	0	8
width:	1	1
obliquing:	0	0
backwards:	N	N
upside-down:	N	Y
vertical:	N	N

2. With ST1 the current style, enter the text item AutoCAD R13 at a height of 5 and 0 rotation. Use layer OUT – Fig. 35.1D(a).
3. Multiple copy this text item to four other places.
4. Select the properties icon and pick the second text item:
   prompt   Modify Text dialogue box
   respond   1. study the information given
               2. alter height to 6, rotation to 5
               3. pick OK – Fig. 35.1D(b).
5. Repeat the icon selection with the third text item, and alter the text style to ST2 – Fig. 35.1D(c).

6. Properties icon again with the fourth item of text and
   (a) alter style to ST2
   (b) remove the UPSIDE-DOWN option
   (c) change height to 6 and rotation to –3
   (d) change obliquing angle to 5
   (e) change text item to Release 13
   (f) OK to give Fig. 35.1D(d).

Command line CHANGE

The properties command can be activated from the keyboard which will not display the dialogue boxes. To demonstrate this:
1. At the command line enter **CHANGE**<R>
   prompt   Select objects
   respond   **pick the fifth text item** the right-click
   prompt   Properties/<Change point>
   enter   **P**<R> – the properties option
   prompt   Change what properties...
   enter   **LA**<R> – layer option
   prompt   New layer<OUT>
   enter   **DIM**<R>
   prompt   Change what properties...
               i.e. any more changes?
   respond   right-click
2. The text item will be displayed in magenta? This is layer DIM's colour.
3. Select the UNDO icon or enter **U**<R> at the keyboard to return the text item to its original layer OUT (red).
4. Enter **CHANGE**<R> at the command line and
   prompt   Select objects
   respond   **pick the same text item as before** then right-click
   prompt   Properties/<Change point>
   respond   **right-click** – default change point option
   prompt   Enter text insertion point
               and text moves as mouse moved
   respond   **right-click** – no text movement

prompt	Text style: ST1
	New style or RETURN for no change
enter	**ST2**<R>
prompt	New rotation angle<0>
enter	**–10**<R>
prompt	New text<AutoCAD R13>
enter	**DRAUGHTING**<R>

5. The text item is altered – Fig. 35.1(e).
6. The command line CHANGE is the same as the dialogue box, but not as versatile. It is the user's preference as to what is used – the dialogue box is probably easier.

Combining ARRAY and PROPERTIES

The combination of the array command with the properties command can produce interesting results. Think back to User Exercise 3 when you were required to add text to a polar array. Remember the angle problems?

1. Open A:STDA3, layer OUT current and refer to Fig. 35.1.
2. Draw the two arc segments as trimmed circles using the start point and sizes given – fig. (a).
3. Draw the polyline and 0 text item using the reference information.
4. Using the polar array command (twice) array the polyline and 0 text item, using arc centre as the array centre:
   (a) for four items, angle to fill +30° with rotation
   (b) for seven items, angle to fill –60° with rotation
   (c) result is fig. (b).
5. Using the Properties icon, select each item of text and alter them
   (a) item 10 at height 10
   (b) item 20 at height 9
   (c) item 30 at height 8, etc.
6. Figure (c) shows the final drawing which can be saved.

❏ *Summary*

1. The Properties command is used to change the layer, linetype, colour, etc. of entities.
2. There are two dialogue boxes, dependent on whether one or several entities are selected.
3. The command is very useful for altering text items, especially if the text is in a polar array.
4. The command is activated by icon or menu bar.
5. The CHANGE command from the keyboard gives the same result as the other options, but does not use a dialogue box.

Activity

I have included two activities for this chapter which should give you a bit of light relief(?)

1. Tutorial 24: two everyday components?
   (a) Telephone dial – old style but easy to draw. The text is ROMANT at a height of 15, but where to start the array? Do you array with rotation or without rotation?
   (b) Flow gauge – a nice drawing to complete. No help given, but take care with the 'notches'.
2. Tutorial 25 – a dart board. Draw the circles then array the 'spokes'. The 'filled sections' are trimmed donuts. The text is middled, height 10 and ROMANT. Array then Properties?

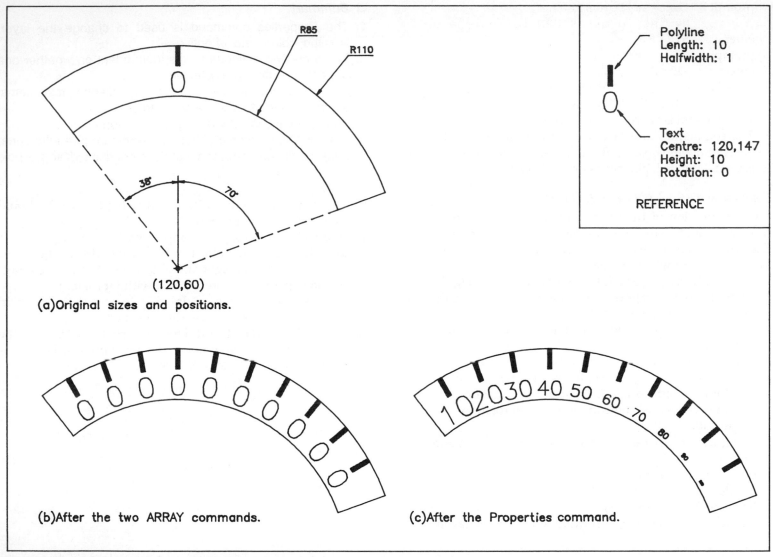

Fig. 35.4. The combined ARRAY and PROPERTIES commands.

36. Dimension styles 2

In Chapter 20 we investigated how dimensions could be customised to our own needs by setting and saving a dimension style in our A:STDA3 standard sheet. This style was named STDA3. In this chapter we will create several other dimension styles which will be used to dimension entities and will also investigate tolerances, limits and dimension 'families'. The process of creating dimension styles involves altering variables which control how the dimension is displayed on the screen.

Creating the new dimension styles

1. Open the A:STDA3 standard sheet.
2. Create two new text styles, accepting all defaults other than the font name, the styles being:
   (a) ST1 using romanc
   (b) ST2 using scripts
3. From the menu bar select **Data–Dimension Style...** and
   prompt   Dimension Style dialogue box with
             1. Current: STDA3
             2. Name: STDA3
   respond   1. alter Name: to **DIMST1**
             2. pick **Save**
             3. Create DIMST1 from STDA3 displayed
             4. pick OK.
4. What has been achieved? We have created a new dimension style called DIMST1 which has all the STDA3 settings. We will alter some of these settings shortly.
5. Repeat the Data–Dimension Style selection and create the styles DIMST2, DIMST3, DIMST4, DIMST5 and DIMST6 from STDA3 using step 3 as a guide.

Modifying the new styles

The six created dimension styles have the STDA3 style settings and some of these settings will now be altered to allow us to use different styles when dimensioning.

1. We will start with **DIMST1** so select Data–Dimension Style and
   (a) scroll and pick DIMST1 – current?
   (b) pick Geometry... and alter
      1. Center – None
      2. OK
   (c) pick Format... and alter
      1. Vertical – Centred
      2. OK
   (d) pick Annotation... and alter
      1. Tolerance – Method: Basic
      2. OK
   (e) pick Save – Saved to DIMST1 displayed
   (f) pick OK.
2. This is the basic procedure for 'customising' dimension styles, the steps being:
   (i) pick Data–Dimension Style
   (ii) pick required current name, e.g. DIMST1
   (iii) pick Geometry... and alter as required
   (iv) pick Format... and alter as required
   (v) pick Annotation... and alter as required
   (vi) pick Save – display Saved to ??????
   (vii) pick OK – ends dimension style command.

3. Using the procedure described, change the named dimension to include the following alterations:
   (a) **DIMST2**
      Geometry – Arrowheads: Closed; Size: 5
      Center: Line; Size: 3
      Format – Text: Outside Horizontal: Off (no X)
      Inside Horizontal: Off (no X)
      Annotation – Units: Trailing: Off (no X)
      Precision: 0.00
   (b) **DIMST3**
      Geometry – Arrowheads: Oblique; Size: 3
      Center: Mark; Size: 5
      Format – no change
      Annotation – Text: Height: 5
      Alternative Units: Enable (X in box)
   (c) **DIMST4**
      Geometry – Arrowheads: Dot; Size: 2
      Center: None
      Format – Text: Outside Horizontal: ON (X in box)
      Inside Horizontal: ON
      Vertical: Centred
      Annotation – Units: Linear Scale: 2
   (d) **DIMST5**
      Geometry – no change
      Format – no change
      Annotation – Text Style: ST1; Height: 5; Gap: 0
   (e) **DIMST6**
      Geometry – no change
      Format – no change
      Annotation – Text Style: ST2; Height: 6; Gap: 3
4. At this stage save your drawing as **A:DIMST**, i.e. we are saving the six created dimension styles on our standard A:STDA3 drawing.

Using the customised dimension styles

1. Using Fig. 36.1 as a guide, create seven horizontal lines; vertical lines, angled lines and circles.
2. Activate Data–Dimension Style and
   (a) scroll until STDA3 displayed
   (b) pick STDA3 – current?
   (c) pick OK.
3. This sets STDA3 as the current dimension style – remember this is the original style.
4. Dimension one of each entity using this style – fig. (a).
5. At the command line enter **DIMSTYLE**<R>
   prompt   Dimension Style Edit...
   enter   **R**<R> – the restore option
   prompt   ?/Enter dimension style name...
   enter   **DIMST1**<R>
6. DIMST1 is now the current dimension style. Dimension entities using this style – fig. (b).
7. Using the dialogue box or command line entry, set each new style as current and dimension one of each entity.
8. Note that when I used DIMST4 the circle would not dimension as I had expected it would. Same with you? The problem seems to be with the 2 scale.
9. Your completed drawing should now resemble Fig. 36.1 and can now be saved if required.

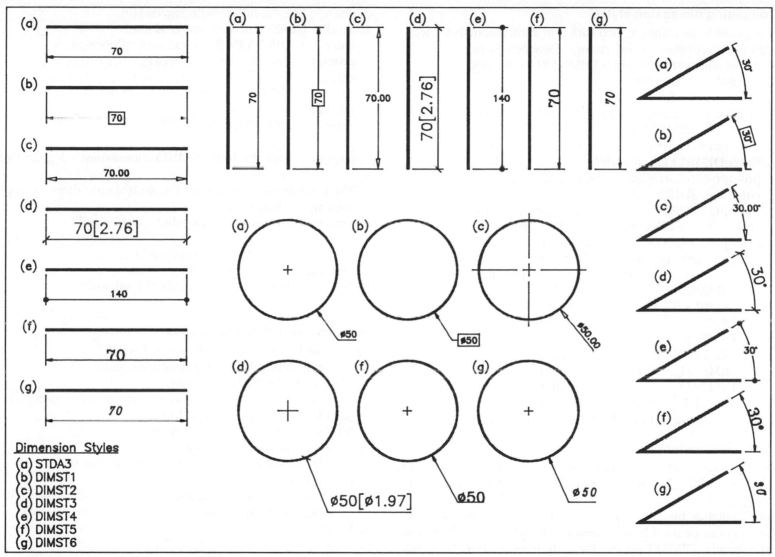

Fig. 36.1. Using different dimension styles.

Comparing dimension styles

It is possible to compare two different dimension styles with each other and observe any changes between them.

1. At the command line enter **DIMSTYLE**<R> and

   prompt   `Dimension Style Edit...`
   enter   **R**<R>
   prompt   `?/Enter dimension style name...`
   enter   **DIMST4**<R>
2. This makes DIMST4 the current dimension style.
3. Enter **DIMSTYLE**<R> and

   prompt   `Dimension Style Edit...`
   enter   **R**<R>
   prompt   `?/Enter dimension style name...`
   enter   **~STDA3**<R> – note the ~ symbol
   prompt   AutoCAD Text Window with:
   Difference between STDA3 and current settings

	STDA3	Current Setting
DIMASZ	3.00	2.00
DIMBLK1		_DOT
DIMBLK2		_DOT
DIMCEN	2.00	0.00
DIMLFAC	1.00	2.00
DIMSAH	Off	On
DIMTAD	1	0
DIMTIH	Off	On

4. Enter **ESC** the F2 to flip back to drawing screen.

Dimension variables

Pre-R13 users may recognise the above comparison as some of the AutoDESK dimension variables. While the dimension style dialogue box is useful for altering settings, all the dimvars are still available by keyboard entry. I will demonstrate how dimvars can be used to alter dimension styles with DIMST1 as an example. DIMST1 set the Basic dimension style, i.e. a box was placed around the dimension text. This box is above the

dimension line – compare with Fig. 36.1(b).

1. To alter DIMST1, at the command line:

   enter   **DIMTVP**<R> – text vertical position
   prompt   `New value for DIMTVP<1.0000>`
   enter   **0**<R>
   enter   **DIM**<R> – keyboard dimension command
   prompt   `Dim:`
   enter   **UPDATE**<R>
   prompt   `Select objects`
   respond   **pick the four DIMST1 dimensions** – Fig. 36.1(b) and right-click.
2. The basic dimension style for Fig. 36.1(b) now alters – except the angular dimension?
3. Activate the Dimension Style dialogue box and

   prompt   `the current style is` **+DIMST1**?, i.e. there has been an alteration to it
   respond   pick Save then OK
4. This saves DIMST1 with the DIMTVP alteration.

Problems with dimension styles

Before leaving the current drawing, I want to demonstrate a 'problem of sorts' when using dimension styles.

1. Make DIMST4 the current style.
2. Using the dimension style dialogue box, pick Geometry and
   (a) Dimension Line – Color: Blue
   (b) Extension Line – Color: Green
   (c) pick OK from Geometry
   (d) pick Save from Dimension Styles dialogue box
   (e) pick OK.
3. The dimensions which used DIMST4 will be displayed with green extension lines and blue dimension line – no circle?
4. Undo this with **U**<R>.

Tolerances and limits

AutoCAD R13 allows tolerances and limits to be added to saved dimension styles. The terms used are symmetrical, deviation, limits and basic – used already. To demonstrate how tolerances are used, we will create new dimension styles, so:

1. Open the **A:DIMST** with the six saved styles.
2. Create five new dimension styles called D1, D2, D3, D4 and D5 from the STDA3 style.
3. Save A:DIMST with these new styles for future work.
4. Refer to Fig. 36.2 and draw six of each entity as shown.
5. With STDA3 as the current dimension style, dimension one of the entities.
6. Data–Dimension Styles and
   (a) pick **D1** as the current style
   (b) pick Annotation and
      1. scroll Tolerance and pick Symmetrical
      2. set Upper Value to 0.05
      3. pick OK from Annotation dialogue box
   (c) pick Save then OK.
7. Now dimension an entity using the D1 current style.
8. Using the procedure in step 6, modify the other four new dimension styles using the following information then dimension one of each entity.
   D2: Annotation – Deviation: Upper Value 0.006
                                 Lower Value 0.003
   D3: Annotation – Limits: Upper Value 0.05
                            Lower Value 0.02
   D4: Annotation – Deviation: Upper Value 0.07
                                 Lower Value 0.01
                                 Justification: Top
   D5: Annotation – Deviation: Upper Value 0.1
                                 Lower Value 0.05
                                 Justification: Bottom
9. When all the entities are dimensioned, your drawing should resemble Fig. 36.2 and can be saved if required.

Dimension families

It is possible to allocate a particular dimension style to a family of dimensions, i.e. whether linear, diameter, angular, etc. At present the dimension styles are global (or applied to the parent), i.e. they are added to all dimensions whether linear, diameter or angular. To demonstrate how dimension families are created:

1. Open **A:DIMST** which has several dimension styles:
   (a) the STDA3 'standard' style
   (b) the styles DIMST1–DIMST6 used in the dimension style exercise
   (c) the five style D1–D5 used with the tolerance exercise
   (d) other R13 styles – which have not been investigated.
2. Refer to Fig. 36.3 and draw entities similar to those shown.

Linear family
1. Select the Dimension Style icon from the Dimensioning toolbar
2. Pick Linear family.
3. Pick D4 dimension style.
4. Pick Geometry and alter the arrowheads to Right-angled, size 10.
5. Pick OK from Geometry dialogue box.
6. Pick Save then OK from Dimension Style dialogue box.
7. Dimension a line, circle (diameter) and angle.
8. The linear dimension should be displayed with the modified D4 style, while the circle and angle should have the original D4 dimension style?

Diameter family

1. Dimension Style dialogue box.
2. Pick Diameter family.
3. Pick DIMST1 dimension style.
4. Pick Annotation and alter:
   (a) Text style to ST1
   (b) Tolerance to Symmetrical: Upper Value 0.05.
5. Pick OK, Save, OK
6. Dimension three entities with DIMST1.

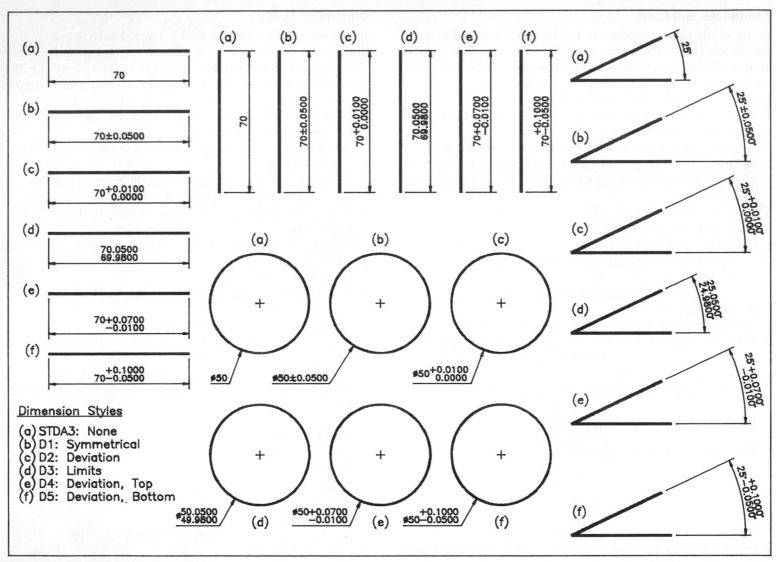

Fig. 36.2. Dimension style tolerances.

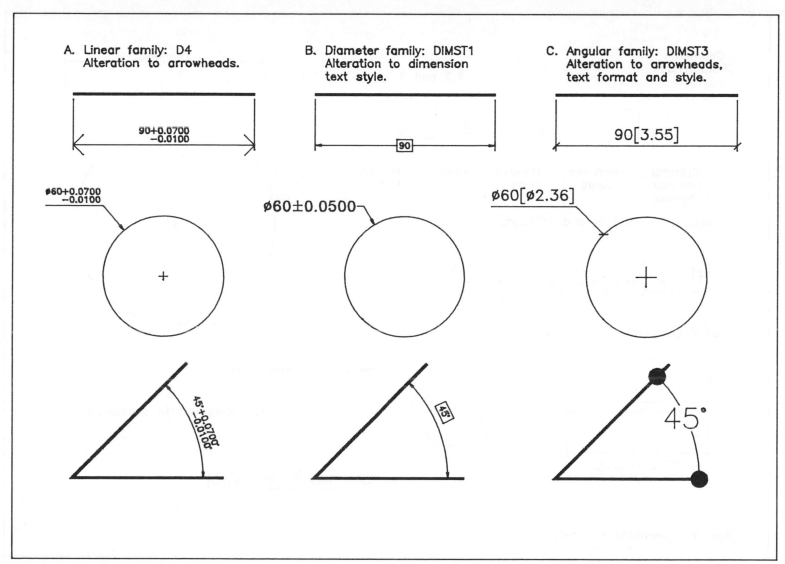

A. Linear family: D4
Alteration to arrowheads.

B. Diameter family: DIMST1
Alteration to dimension
text style.

C. Angular family: DIMST3
Alteration to arrowheads,
text format and style.

90+0.0700
−0.0100

90

90[3.55]

ø60+0.0700
−0.0100

ø60±0.0500

ø60[ø2.36]

45°+0.0700
−0.0100

45°

45°

Fig. 36.3. Dimension families.

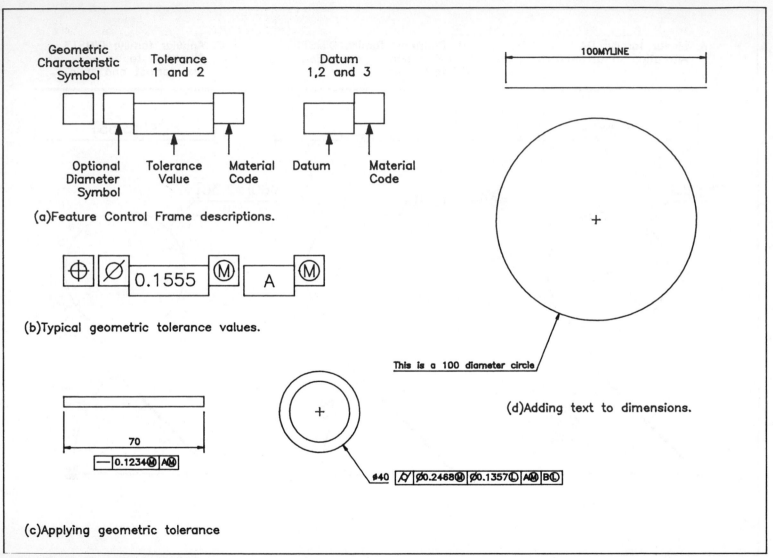

Fig. 36.4. Geometric tolerance application.

Angular family

1. Dimension Style dialogue box.
2. Pick Angular family.
3. Pick DIMST3 dimension style.
4. Pick Geometry and alter:
   (a) arrowheads: Dot, Size 8
   (b) pick OK.
5. Pick Format and alter:
   (a) Inside Horizontal ON, i.e. X
   (b) pick OK.
6. Pick Annotation and alter:
   (a) Text style: STANDARD, Height: 10
   (b) pick OK.
7. Pick Save then OK.
8. Dimension three entities.

Hopefully your drawing should resemble Fig. 36.3 with the various entities displaying the family dimension style set.

Geometric tolerancing

For the first time AutoCAD has geometric tolerancing facilities. It was not my intention to discuss geometric tolerancing in this book, but I then thought that a brief introduction would do no harm and perhaps encourage the user to further investigation.

1. Open your A:STDA3 standard sheet and refer to Fig. 36.4.
2. From the menu bar select **Draw**
   Dimensioning
   Tolerance...

prompt	Symbol dialogue box as Fig. 36.5
respond	**pick the symbol indicated** in Fig. 36.5 then OK
prompt	Geometric Tolerance dialogue box
respond	**pick Cancel** at present

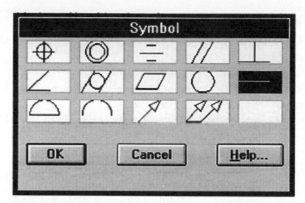

Fig. 36.5. Symbol dialogue box.

Tolerance frames

R13 has 14 tolerance symbols (Fig. 36.5) which cover straightness, roundness, cylindricity, etc. When the required symbol is selected from the Symbol dialogue box, the user has then to enter specific values in the **Feature Control Frames** of the Geometric Tolerancing dialogue box.

The feature control frame is divided into three distinct sections and these are shown in Fig. 36.4(a) and are:

1. the geometric character symbol area
2. the tolerancing area 1 and 2 for first and second tolerance values
3. the datum area 1, 2 and 3 for primary, secondary and tertiary datum reference letters
4. typical tolerance entries are shown in Fig. 36.4(b).

Applying tolerances

To use geometric tolerances, refer to Fig. 36.4(c) and draw a dimensioned line and circle, then:

1. Select the TOLERANCE icon from the Dimensioning toolbar and

    prompt   Symbol dialogue box
    respond   **pick Straightness symbol** (Fig. 36.5) then OK
    prompt   Geometric Tolerancing dialogue box
    respond   1. Sym symbol straightness?
               2. at Tolerance 1, enter value 0.1234
               3. at Tolerance 1, pick MC and

           prompt   Material Control dialogue box
           respond   pick M then OK
           4. at Datum 1, enter A
           5. at Datum 1, pick MC, pick M then OK
           6. result is Fig. 36.6
           7. pick OK to complete tolerancing
    prompt   Enter tolerance location
    respond   pick under linear dimension text.

2. Repeat the tolerance command and
   (a) select the Cylindricity symbol then OK – Help helps!
   (b) from the Geometric Tolerancing dialogue box:
        1. pick Dia at Tolerancing 1
        2. enter 0.2468 at Tolerancing 1
        3. pick M at Tolerancing 1 MC
        4. pick Dia at Tolerancing 2
        5. enter 0.1357 at Tolerancing 2
        6. enter A at Datum 1
        7. pick M at Datum 1 MC
        8. enter B at Datum 2
        9. pick L at Datum 2 MC
      10. pick OK
   (c) apply to side of diameter dimension
3. Figure 36.4(c) displays the two tolerances added.

Adding user text to dimensions

The last item for discussion in this long chapter is how user text can be added to dimension text. Refer to Fig. 36.4(d) and

1. Draw a line and a circle.
2. Select Linear dimension icon and
    prompt   First extension...
    respond   pick the endpoints of the line
    prompt   Dimension line location...
    enter   **T<R>** – the text option
    prompt   Edit MText dialogue displaying **< >**
    enter   **MYLINE then OK**
    prompt   Dimension line location...
    respond   pick required dimension position.
3. Select the Diameter dimension icon and
    prompt   Select arc or circle
    respond   pick the circle
    prompt   Dimension line location...
    enter   **T<R>**
    prompt   Edit MText dialogue box with **< >**
    enter   **This is a < > diameter circle** then OK
    prompt   Dimension line location...
    respond   pick position as required.

Finally

This completes the exercises in this chapter. It has been a long chapter and has introduced several new concepts to the user. Dimension styles, tolerancing, geometric tolerancing, etc., are not always easy to understand and it is only with continual practice that you will become proficient with them – so persevere.

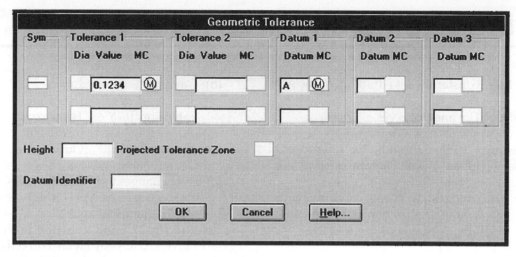

Fig. 36.6. Geometric Tolerance dialogue box.

❏ *Summary*

1. Dimension styles are created by the user.
2. Dimension styles can be customised to user/customer requirements.
3. There is no limit to the number of dimension styles which can be created and saved.
4. Dimension styles can be used for tolerance styles.
5. R13 allows different types of tolerance – symmetrical, deviation and limits. The tolerance values can be positioned at the top or bottom of the dimension text.
6. Geometric tolerancing is available with R13.
7. There are 14 possible geometric tolerancing 'types'.

Activity

Tutorial 26: a simple component to draw.

Use your **A:DIMST** drawing with the 11 saved dimension styles and add all the dimensions. Also use the text control codes to add the given text. I have listed the dimension styles used in the activity, but you can use any of the saved styles.

37. Drawing to different sizes

Two questions which I am constantly asked about AutoCAD are:

1. Can you draw in inches? The answer is yes.
2. How do you set a scale at the start of a drawing?

Generally all drawing work should be completed full-size, but it is possible to set a scale before starting the drawing.

In this chapter we will investigate these concepts with worked examples.

Drawing in inches

We will use our A:STDA3 for this investigation, but will have to modify several parameters as everything is 'set for metric'. The reason that A:STDA3 is being used is that it has layers, etc. customised to our requirements.

1. Open A:STDA3 and erase the black border – it is the wrong size.
2. Select Data–Units and
   (a) pick Engineering
   (b) precision 0'–0.00"
   (c) angle: Decimal with 0.0 precision.
3. Select Data–Drawing Limits and
   (a) accept 0'–0.00",0'–0.00" lower left corner
   (b) enter 16",11.5" as the upper right corner.
4. Set grid to 0.5 and snap to 0.25.
5. With layer 0 current, use the line command to draw the drawing area as a 15.5 × 11 rectangle.
6. Set LTSCALE to 0.4.
7. Select Data–Dimension Style and
   (a) Current style: STDA3

(b)

Geometry	Format	Annotation
Spacing: 0.76"	User Defined	Text: STANDARD
Extension: 0.18"	Text,Arrows	Ht: 0.18"
Offset: 0.18"	Inside Hor	Gap: 0.09"
Arrows: 0.18"	Outside Hor	Units: Engineering
Center: None		0'–0.00"

(c) Save changes to STDA3 then OK.
8. At this stage save as **A:STDIMP** – it may be useful to you, but we will not use it again.
9. Refer to Fig. 37.1 and draw the two components using the sizes given. Use your layers correctly and add all text and dimensions remembering to use your discretion for any sizes omitted. This is more of an activity than an exercise as I have no intention of telling you how to complete a drawing at this stage.
   Note: (a) Inches are entered with double primes ("), e.g. @3",4" and feet are entered with a single prime ('), e.g. @1'6.5",1'2.75". (b) All the fillets are 0.125". (c) Hatching is user-defined at 45°. The problem is with the spacing, which I have entered as 0.2".
10. When complete, save your completed drawing.

Large-scale drawing

This exercise will alter the original drawing scale to allow a very large-sized drawing to fit onto A3 paper.

1. Open A:STDA3 and erase the black border – it is too small for the limits we will enter.
2. Make layer 0 current, and toggle grid off.
3. At the command line enter **MVSETUP<R>**
   prompt Initializing... then Enable   paper
           space?(No/<Yes>)

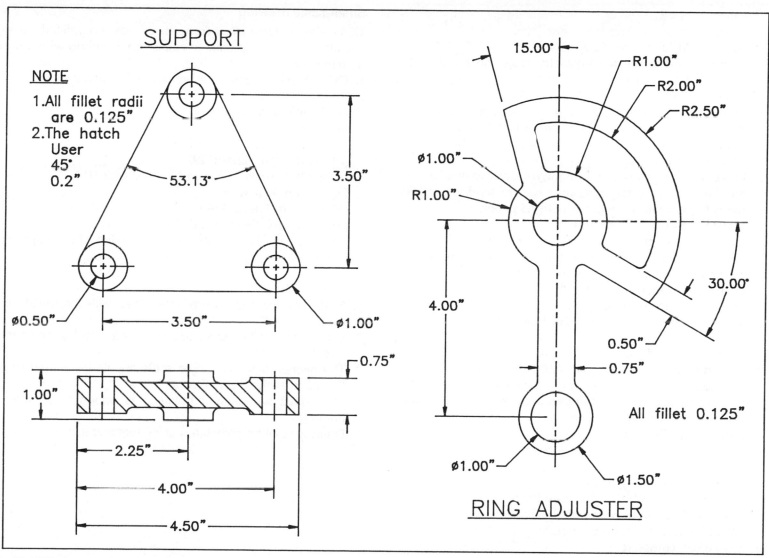

SUPPORT

NOTE

1. All fillet radii are 0.125″
2. The hatch User 45° 0.2″

53.13°

3.50″

3.50″

Ø0.50″

Ø1.00″

0.75″

1.00″

2.25″

4.00″

4.50″

RING ADJUSTER

15.00°

R1.00″

R2.00″

R2.50″

Ø1.00″

R1.00″

4.00″

30.00°

0.50″

0.75″

All fillet 0.125″

Ø1.00″

Ø1.50″

Fig. 37.1. Working with Imperial sizes.

```
enter    N<R>
prompt   Units type (Scientific...
enter    M<R> – metric option
prompt   Text Window with metric sizes and Enter the
         scale factor
enter    1000<R>, i.e. scale of 1:1000
prompt   Enter the paper width and enter 420<R>
prompt   Enter the paper height and enter 297<R>
```

4. A polyline black border will be displayed which is our drawing area.
5. Move the cross-hairs and note the co-ordinate display. The numbers are very large because we are working at **1000 times larger** than normal, but with A3 paper.
6. Make layer OUT current and:
   - (a) draw a line from 35000,35000 by @350000,150000
   - (b) linear dimension this line, horizontal and vertical
   - (c) cannot 'see' the dimension text?
7. With Date–Dimension Style:
   - (a) STDA3 current style
   - (b) Geometry: Overall Scale: **1000** the OK
   - (c) Save then OK
   - (d) Line dimensions now 'readable'?
8. The original drawing scale was 1000 and the overall dimension scale is also set to this value. This ensures that all the dimension variables are 'compensated' for the scale factor.
9. Erase the line and dimensions.
10. Refer to Fig. 37.2 and
    - (a) draw the house to the sizes given
    - (b) add the dimensions
    - (c) add the hatching using
       - (i) roof: AR-RSHKE with scale 1000
       - (ii) wall: AR-B816 with scale 1000
    - (d) add text, but what is the height?
11. Save when complete.

Small-scale drawing

This is the opposite effect from the exercise completed, i.e. we will alter the drawing scale to suit a very small drawing for an A3 paper size.

1. Open A:STDA3, erase border and make layer 0 current.
2. MVSETUP and
   - (a) Enable paper space: N
   - (b) Units: M
   - (c) Scale: 0.01, i.e. 1/100 full size
   - (d) Width: 420; Height: 297
3. Layer OUT current with grid 0.1 and snap 0.05.
4. Dimension Style with
   - (a) Current style: STDA3
   - (b) Geometry: Overall scale **0.01**
5. Refer to Fig. 37.3, draw and dimension the component given.

❏ *Summary*

1. Scale drawing factors are determined with the MVSETUP command.
2. Large and small drawing scales can be 'fitted' to any paper size.
3. The overall dimension style scale should be altered to be the same as the drawing scale factor.
4. Care must be taken if hatching is added to a 'scaled' drawing.
5. Drawings can be completed using feet and inches.

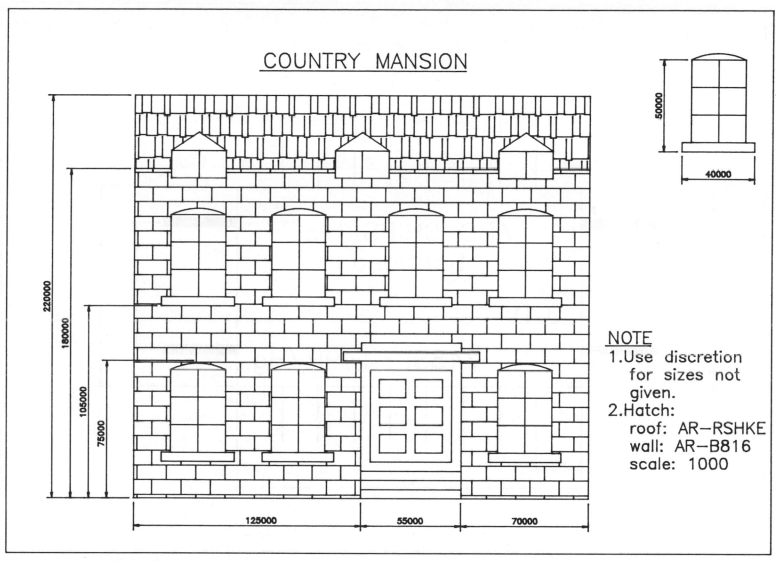

Fig. 37.2. Large scale drawing.

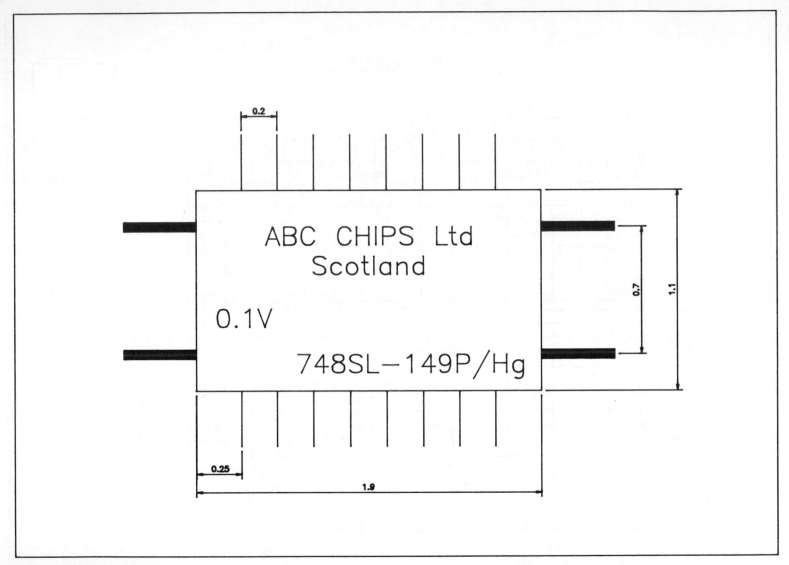

Fig. 37.3. Small scale drawing.

38. Groups and filters

AutoCAD is equipped with a very extensive selection set allowing ease at selecting objects. With large and complex drawings, selecting individual entities can be tedious and time consuming and AutoCAD R13 has two facilities to help overcome this problem. Groups and filters allow the user a degree of flexibility to the user when selecting objects.

Grouped objects

A *group* is a named collection of objects. Groups are stored with the drawing and group definitions can be external referenced (not discussed in this book). To demonstrate groups:
1. Open A:STDA3 and refer to Fig. 38.1.
2. Using the reference sizes draw the given shape – discretion for any size omitted. Position the component with its lower vertex at the point 210,125.
3. Select the Object Group icon from the Standard Toolbar and

    prompt   Object Grouping dialogue box
    respond   1. at Group Name enter **GR1**
                 2. at Description enter **First group**
                 3. Selectable ON, i.e. X in box – Fig. 38.2
                 4. pick New
    prompt   `Select objects`
    respond   **pick entities d1,d2 and d3** then right-click
    prompt   Object Grouping dialogue box again
    with   Group Name   `Selectable`
                 GR1   Yes
    respond   **pick OK**
4. From the menu bar select **Edit**
                             Group Object...

    prompt   Object Grouping dialogue box
    respond   1. at Group Name enter **GR2**
                 2. at Description enter **Second group**
                 3. pick New
    prompt   `Select objects`
    respond   pick entities **d4,d5,d6 and d7** then right-click
    prompt   Object Grouping dialogue box
    respond   pick OK
5. Select the polar array icon and
    prompt   `Select objects`
    respond   from the menu bar select **Edit**
                               Select Objects
                               Group

    prompt   `Enter group name`
    enter   **GR1<R>**
    prompt   `3 found` and `Select objects`
    respond   right-click
    prompt   `Center point` and enter 225,105
    prompt   `Number of items` and enter 4
    prompt   `Angle to fill` and enter 360
    prompt   Rotate... and enter Y – Fig. 38.1(a).
6. With the rectangular array icon:
    (a) pick Edit–Select Objects–Group
    (b) enter GR2<R><R>
    (c) enter 2 rows
    (d) enter 3 columns
    (e) enter the row distance as 55
    (f) enter the column distance as –70 – Fig. 38.1(b).
7. Activate the copy command and
    prompt   `Select objects`

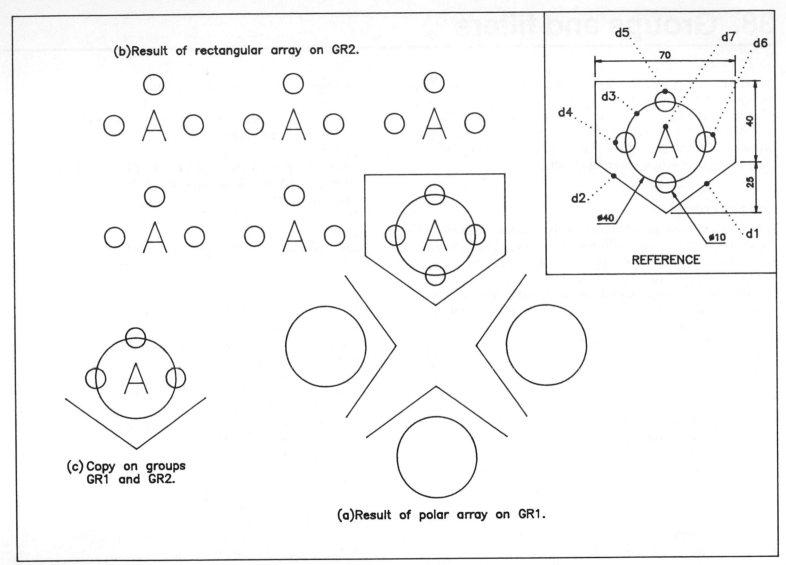

(b)Result of rectangular array on GR2.

d5   d7   d6

70

d3·

d4·····

d2·

⌀40   A   40

⌀10····d1

25

REFERENCE

(c) Copy on groups GR1 and GR2.

(a)Result of polar array on GR1.

Fig. 38.1. Grouped objects.

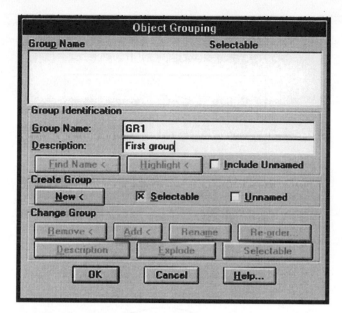

Fig. 38.2. Object Grouping dialogue box.

Object filters

Filters allow the user the facility to create a 'filter list' thereby only selecting entities which have been specified in the filter definition. Common filters include entity type, co-ordinate data, colour, etc. To prepare for the filter exercises:

1. Open A:STDA3 and refer to Fig. 38.3.
2. Draw the calculator – fig. (a) – as follows:
   (a) outline and buttons on layer OUT
   (b) text, middled on layer TEXT
   (c) the hatch display area on layer 0.

Filter example 1

1. From the menu bar select **Edit**

Select Objects
Selection Filters...

prompt	Object Selection Filters dialogue box
respond	1. scroll down at the Select Filter area where Arc is displayed
	2. pick Text – turns blue – and Text appears in the Select Filters box
	3. pick Add to List and selection appears in the white display area
	4. at Save As box enter **TEXTENT**
	5. pick Save As box and TEXTENT appears in Name Filter Current box – Fig. 38.4
	6. pick Apply
prompt	dialogue box disappears and drawing screen returned with Applying filter to selection
	`Select objects`
respond	**window the calculator**
prompt	`95 found`
	`76 were filtered out`
respond	**right-click**
prompt	`Exiting filtered command 19 found`

respond	pick the Group icon from the Select Objects toolbar
prompt	`Enter group name` and enter GR1
prompt	`3 found` and `Select objects`
respond	pick the Group icon again
prompt	`Enter group name` and enter GR2
prompt	`4 found` and `Select objects`
respond	<R><R>
prompt	`Base point...` and enter 210,125
prompt	`Second point...` and enter @–**150,–70** to give Fig. 38.1(c).

Note that grouped objects (groups) give the user an additional selection method, but (like grips) they do not have to be used.

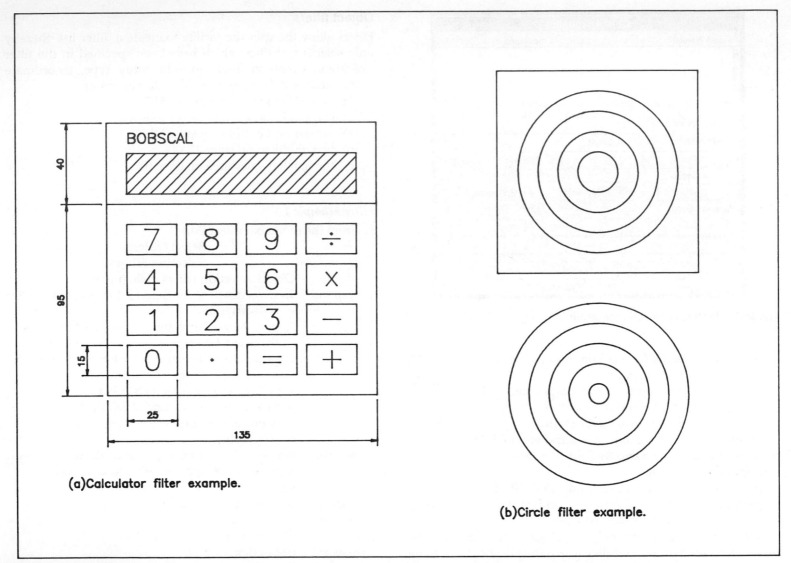

BOBSCAL

(a)Calculator filter example.

(b)Circle filter example.

Fig. 38.3. Object filter exercises.

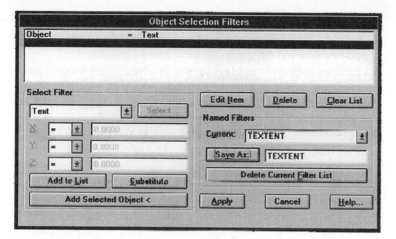

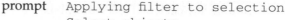

Fig. 38.4. Object Selection Filters dialogue box.

2. Select the ERASE icon and

prompt	`Select objects`
enter	**P**<R> – the previous selection
prompt	`19 found and Select objects`
respond	**right-click**

3. All text will be erased from the calculator. The previous entry selected the filter text list.
4. Pick the undo icon or enter **U**<R> to restore the text.

Filter example 2

1. At the command line enter **CHANGE**<R>

prompt	`Select objects`
respond	pick the FILTER icon from the windows flyout of the Standard toolbar
prompt	Object Selection Filters dialogue box
respond	1. pick Current arrow
	2. pick TEXTENT
	3. pick Apply

prompt	`Applying filter to selection`
	`Select objects`
respond	**window the calculator**
prompt	`95 found`
	`76 were filtered out`
then	`Select objects` **and right-click**
prompt	`Exiting filtered selection 19 found`
then	`Select objects` **and right-click**
prompt	`Properties/<Change point>`
enter	**P**<R> – the properties option
prompt	`Change what properties...`
enter	**LA**<R> – the layer option
prompt	`New layer<TEXT>`
enter	**OUT**<R>
prompt	`Change what properties...`
respond	right-click to end command

2. The filtered list (the text items) should be displayed in red as they are now on layer OUT.

Filter example 3

Filters allow conditional tests to be applied to the entities being selected and we will use circles as a demonstration. The filter entry procedure is rather long but is necessary, so:

1. Select a suitable clear space on the screen and draw nine concentric circles of radii 5,10,15,20, ..., 45. Draw a 50-unit square around the circles – Fig. 38.3(b).
2. Select the filters icon and

prompt	Object Selection Filters dialogue box
respond	1. select Clear List – removes text filters
	2. scroll down at Select Filters
	3. pick Circle
	4. pick Add to List
	5. scroll and pick **Begin OR
	6. pick Add to List
	7. scroll and pick Circle Radius

8. double left-click on 0.0000 at X: box
9. enter 5
10. pick Add to List
11. double left-click at 5, enter 15, Add to List
12. double left-click at 15, enter 25, Add to List
13. double left-click at 25, enter 35, Add to List
14. double left-click at 35, enter 45, Add to List
15. scroll and pick **End OR
16. at Save As box enter CIRCTEST
17. pick Save As and CIRCTEST current?
18. pick Apply

prompt   `Applying filters to selection`
           `Select objects`
respond **window the square and circles** then right-click
prompt   `13 found`
           `8 were filtered out`

3. Select the MOVE icon and
   prompt   `Select objects`
   respond **P<R>**
   prompt   `5 found` and `Select objects`
   respond right-click
   prompt   `Base point... pick CEN of a circle`
   prompt   `Second point...` and enter @0,–110
4. The filtered circles are moved.
5. The complete filter list definition for the example is:
Entity = Circle
**Begin OR
Circle Radius = 5.00
Circle Radius = 15.00
Circle Radius = 25.00
Circle Radius = 35.00
Circle Radius = 45.00
**End OR

❑ *Summary*
1. Groups and Filters are additional selection methods. They do not have to be used.
2. Entities with different layers and linetypes can be grouped if required.
3. Filters allow specific named entity types to the included in a defined list.
4. Filters allow conditions to be added to the definition list.
5. The normal commands can be used with groups and filters.

Activity

No formal activity, but spend some time on the concept of groups and filters until you are confident with their use.

39. Multilines

Multilines are parallel lines which can consist of up to 16 **elements** and are created by the user. The user defines the number of elements, the spacing between the element lines and the linetype and colour of the elements if this is required. Multilines have their own terminology and Fig. 39.1 explains some of this with:

(a) multilines of four and six elements showing the offset effect with various end caps – open, line, outer arc and inner arc
(b) an open-ended two-element multiline with two vertices
(c) a closed multiline with several vertices
(d) different scale effects on a two-element multiline
(e) a line cap multiline with the display joint option active
(f) a four-element open multiline with different linetypes.

Using the default multiline

R13 has a default multiline of two elements which we will use for comparison with our created styles.
1. Open A:STDA3 with layer OUT current and refer to Fig. 39.2.
2. From the menu bar select **Draw**
                    Multiline

prompt	Justification/Scale/STyle/<From point>
enter	**S**<R> – the scale option
prompt	Set Mline scale<1.00>
enter	**8**<R>
prompt	Justification...
enter	**20,250**<R>
prompt	To point and enter @60,0<R>
prompt	To point and enter @50<–90<R>
prompt	To point and enter @40,50<R><R> – fig. (a).

Multiline example 1
1. From the menu bar select **Data–Multiline Style...**

prompt	Multiline Styles dialogue box with
	1. STANDARD current – the default and
	2. a graphical description shown in the display area
respond	**pick Element Properties...**
prompt	Element Properties dialogue box
respond	1. pick 0.5 BYLAYER BYLAYER line
	2. at Offset 0.500, enter **0.0**
	3. pick 0.5 BYLAYER BYLAYER again
	4. at Offset, enter **–1.5**
	5. pick Add
	6. at Offset, enter **–2.5**
	7. pick Add – Fig. 39.3
	8. pick OK
prompt	Multiline Styles dialogue box with graphical description in the display area
respond	1. at Name, enter **ML1**
	2. at Description, enter **My first attempt**
	3. pick Add – Fig. 39.4
	4. pick OK

2. Select the MLINE icon from the Polyline flyout of the Draw toolbar and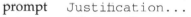

prompt	Justification...
enter	**ST**<R> – the style option
prompt	Mstyle name (or ?)
enter	**?**<R>
prompt	Text Window with:
	Name Description
	STANDARD
	ML1 My first attempt

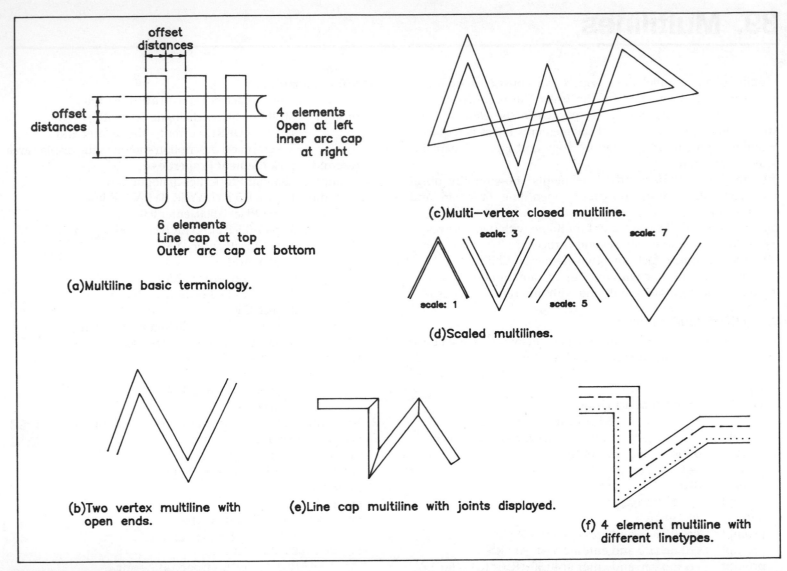

offset distances

offset distances

4 elements
Open at left
Inner arc cap
at right

6 elements
Line cap at top
Outer arc cap at bottom

(a)Multiline basic terminology.

(c)Multi—vertex closed multiline.

scale: 3   scale: 7

scale: 1   scale: 5

(d)Scaled multilines.

(b)Two vertex multiline with open ends.

(e)Line cap multiline with joints displayed.

(f) 4 element multiline with different linetypes.

Fig. 39.1. Basic multiline terminology.

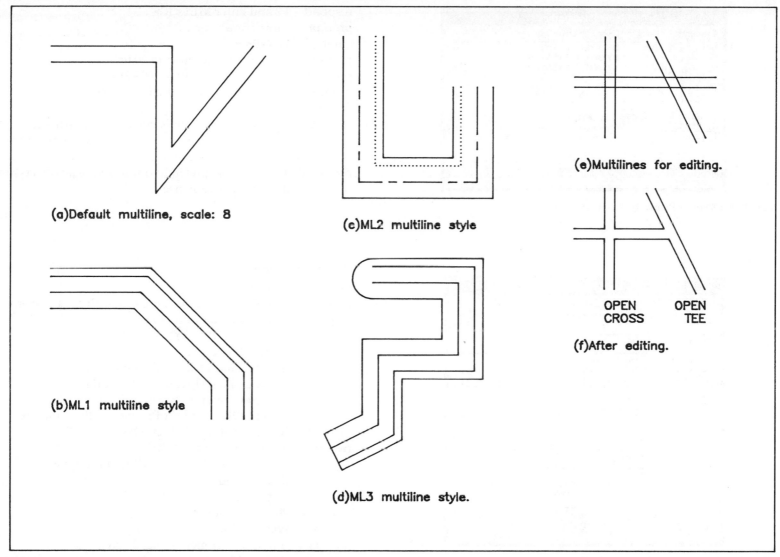

(a)Default multiline, scale: 8

(b)ML1 multiline style

(c)ML2 multiline style

(d)ML3 multiline style.

(e)Multilines for editing.

OPEN
CROSS

OPEN
TEE

(f)After editing.

Fig. 39.2. Using created multilines.

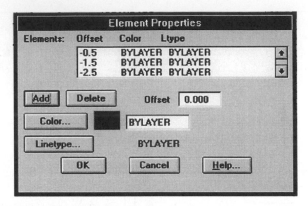

Fig. 39.3. Element Properties dialogue box.

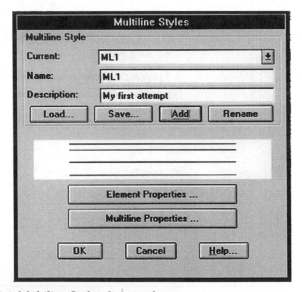

Fig. 39.4. Multiline Styles dialogue box.

respond   F2 and enter **ML1\<R\>**
prompt   `Justification...`
enter   **20,140\<R\>**
prompt   `To point` and enter **@50,0\<R\>**
prompt   `To point` and enter **@0,–25\<R\>**
prompt   `To point` and right-click – fig. (b).

3. The element offsets are either positive or negative and are relative to a datum line which is considered at 0.0 – not the screen origin but an imaginary line origin. A positive offset will draw a line above this datum line, while a negative offset will draw a line below it. In our example all offsets are negative purely for convenience.

Multiline example 2

1. Data–Multiline Style... and
   prompt   Multiline Styles dialogue box with ML1 current
   respond   1. pick Element Properties...
               2. pick –0.5 BYLAYER BYLAYER line
               3. pick Linetype...
               4. scroll and pick DOT then OK
               5. pick –1.5 BYLAYER BYLAYER line
               6. pick Linetype..., CENTER, OK
               7. pick OK from Edit Properties dialogue box
   prompt   Multiline Styles dialogue box
   respond   1. enter name as **ML2**
               2. enter description as **Altered linetypes**
               3. pick Add
               4. pick OK
2. Using the MLINE command
   (a) enter style as ML2
   (b) draw a multiline segment – Fig. 39.2(c).
3. Alter LTSCALE to 10 or 11 if necessary.

Multiline example 3

Activate the multiline style dialogue box and
1. make ML1 the current style
2. pick Multiline Properties...
3. pick Start: Outer arc, i.e. X
4. pick End: Inner arc
5. pick OK from Multiline Properties dialogue box
6. enter name as ML3
7. enter description as Capped ends
8. pick Add the OK
9. using the MLINE command, set the style to ML3 and draw Fig. 39.2(d).

Editing multilines

Multilines have their own extensive editing facility. It is not my intention to cover all the editing features which are available but:
1. Set STANDARD as the current multiline style.
2. Use the multiline command, set the scale to 5 and draw a series of three multilines as Fig. 39.2(e).
3. From the menu bar select **Modify**
   Edit Multiline...

prompt	Multiline Edit Tools dialogue box
respond	pick an icon, e.g. Open Cross
prompt	Select first mline and pick as required
prompt	Select second mline and pick as required
prompt	Select first mline and right-click to give Fig. 39.2(f).

Activity

Draw some other multiline segments and investigate the other editing tools which are available. Also investigate the justification option of the MLINE command which determines how the multiline is drawn.

40. Blocks

A block is part of a drawing which is 'stored away' for future recall *within the drawing in which it was created*. The block may be a nut, a diode, a tree, a house or even a complete drawing. Blocks are used when repetitive copying of entities is required but they have another very important feature – text can be attached to them. This text addition to blocks will be covered in a later chapter.

Creating a block

1. Open A:STDA3 with layer OUT current. Activate your toolbars and refer to Fig. 40.1.
2. Draw the house shape to the sizes given with:
   (a) the outlines on layer OUT
   (b) the circular windows on layer OUT but green
   (c) a text item on layer TEXT
   (d) four dimensions on layer DIM.
3. From the menu bar select **Construct**
                              Block

prompt	Block name (or ?)
enter	**HOUSE**<R>
prompt	Insertion base point
respond	**INTersection icon and pick lower left corner**
prompt	Select objects
respond	**window the house and dimensions**
prompt	14(?) found
respond	**right-click**

4. The house shape will disappear from the screen. It is now stored as a block within the current drawing, which has not yet been saved.

Inserting a block

Created blocks can be inserted into the current drawing using two methods:
(a) by direct keyboard entry
(b) with a dialogue box.
Both methods will be demonstrated.

Keyboard insertion

1. At the command line enter **INSERT**<R>

prompt	Block name (or ?)
enter	**HOUSE**<R>
prompt	Insertion point
enter	**35,180**<R>
prompt	X scale factor<1>/Corner/XYZ
enter	**1**<R>
prompt	Y scale factor (default=X)
enter	**1**<R> – i.e. full size, X = Y = 1
prompt	Rotation angle<0>
enter	**0**<R>

2. The house block is positioned as Fig. 40.1(a).
3. Repeat the keyboard INSERT command and

prompt	Block name and enter HOUSE
prompt	Insertion point and enter 145,190
prompt	X scale factor and enter 1.5
prompt	Y scale factor and enter 0.75
prompt	Rotation angle and enter 0 – Fig. 40.1(b).

Dialogue box insertion

1. From the menu bar select **Draw**
                              Insert
                              Block...

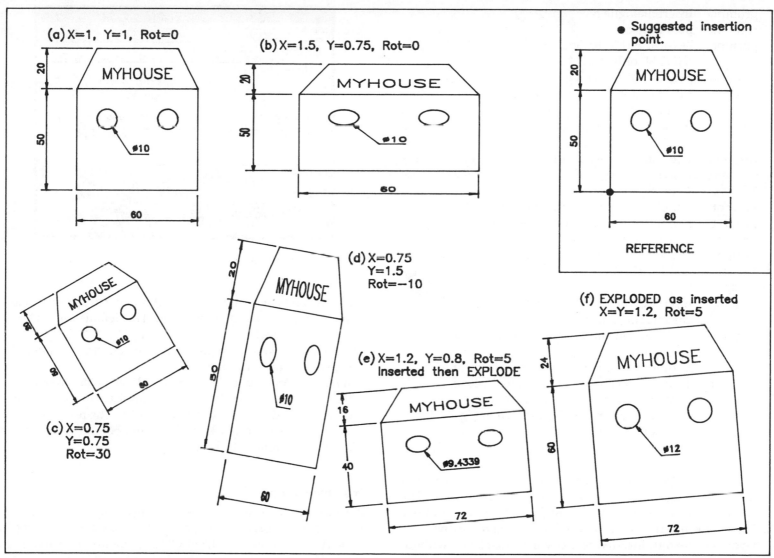

Fig. 40.1. Block exercise.

prompt	Insert dialogue box
respond	**pick Block...**
prompt	Defined Block dialogue box (HOUSE only?)
respond	**pick HOUSE** then OK
prompt	Insert dialogue box with HOUSE as block name (this was probably not needed as HOUSE was the block name from the previous exercise, still it was good practice for you)
respond	1. ensure Specify Parameters on Screen is active (X) 2. pick OK
prompt	`Insertion point` and enter 45,85
prompt	`X scale factor` and enter 0.75
prompt	`Y scale factor` and enter 0.75
prompt	`Rotation angle` and enter 30 – Fig. 40.1(c).

2. Select the INSERT BLOCK icon from the Draw toolbar and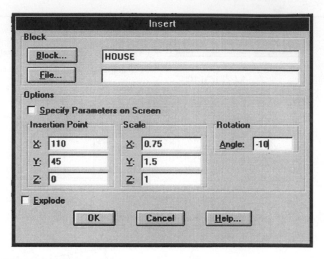

prompt	Insert dialogue box with HOUSE as current block name
respond	1. deactivate the Specify Parameters on Screen, i.e. no X 2. other parameters now available (in BLACK) 3. alter Insertion Point to X: 110; Y: 45; Z: 0 4. alter Scale to X: 0.75; Y: 1.5; Z: 1 5. alter Rotation to −10 as shown in Fig. 40.2 6. pick OK – Fig. 40.1(d).

Notes

1. An inserted block is a *single entity*. Select the erase icon and pick any point on one of the blocks the right-click. The complete block is erased with a single pick. Undo this erase.
2. Blocks are inserted with layers 'as used'. Freeze the DIM layer and the four inserted blocks will be displayed without dimensions. Now thaw layer DIM.

Fig. 40.2. Insert dialogue box.

3. Blocks can be inserted at different X and Y scales and at any angle of rotation as demonstrated. The default scale is X = Y = 1, i.e. the block is inserted full size.
4. Dimensions which are attached to blocks are not altered if the scale factors are changed.
5. A named block can be redefined and will be discussed later.
6. Blocks defined in a drawing can be listed by using the **?** option from the BLOCK keyboard entry. The text screen will display the named blocks and the number of unnamed and external reference blocks (later).

Exploding a block

The fact that a block is a single entity may not always be suitable to the user, i.e. you may want to copy certain parts of a block. AutoCAD uses the EXPLODE command to 'convert' an inserted block back into its individual entities.

The command can be used:

(a) after a block has been inserted
(b) during the insertion process

1. At the command line enter **INSERT**<R> and

   prompt   `Block name` and enter HOUSE
   prompt   `Insertion point` and enter 190,25
   prompt   `X scale factor` and enter 1.2
   prompt   `Y scale factor` and enter 0.8
   prompt   `Rotation` and enter 5

2. Select the EXPLODE icon from the Modify toolbar

   prompt   `Select objects`
   respond   **pick the inserted just inserted** then right-click

3. The block is restored to individual entities and the dimensions are **scaled to the factors entered** – Fig. 40.1(e). Individual entities of this exploded block can now be erased, etc. Note the dimension style of this exploded block.

4. Using the Insert block icon with the Insert dialogue box:

   (a) Block: HOUSE
   (b) Insertion Point X: 295; Y: 25; Z: 0
   (c) Scale X: 1.2; Y: 0.8; Z: 1
   (d) Rotation Angle: 5
   (e) Explode ON, i.e. X in box and *note scale factor alterations when explode is on!*
   (f) pick OK

5. The block is exploded as it is inserted but at a scale of X = Y = 1.2 and the dimensions display this – Fig. 40.1(f)

6. *Note*: (a) a block exploded after insertion will retain the original X and Y scale factors. (b) A block exploded as it is inserted has X = Y scale factors.

Block example

1. Open A:STDA3 with layer OUT current and toolbars as required. Refer to Fig. 40.3.
2. Draw the two components using the sixes given. Do *not* dimension.

3. Using **Construct–Block**:

   (a) enter CAM as the block name
   (b) pick CENter of large circle as insertion point
   (c) window the cam shape.

4. Repeat the block command for the FOL shape, picking the point apex as the insertion point and windowing the shape.

5. Enter **INSERT** <R> at the command line with:

   (a) Block name: CAM
   (b) Insertion point: 30,95
   (c) X scale: 0.8
   (d) Y scale: 0.8
   (e) Rotation: 0.

6. Repeat the INSERT command with the block CAM at 0.8 X and Y scales with the following insertion points and rotation angles:

   Insertion: 70,95   10,95   150,95   190,95   230,95   270,95 310,95 330,95
   Rotation: −20   −40   −60   −80   −100   −120   −140 −160

7. Using the Insert Block icon with the Insert dialogue box:

   (a) pick Block..., FOL then OK
   (b) enter coordinates as X: 30; Y: 125; Z: 0
   (c) X scale: 0.75
   (d) Y scale: 0.75
   (e) Z scale: 1
   (f) Rotation: 0,

8. Repeat the FOL insertion at 0.75 X and Y scales, the insertion points being 70,125; 110,125; 150,125; 190,125; 230,125; 270,125; 310,125; 330,125.

9. Now move the followers until they just touch the cam body – should give you no problem.

10. Draw a polyline (width 1) between the intersections of the cam and follower.

11. Finally find the vertical distance between the first and last cam/follower intersection. I got 14.64?

12. Save your work?

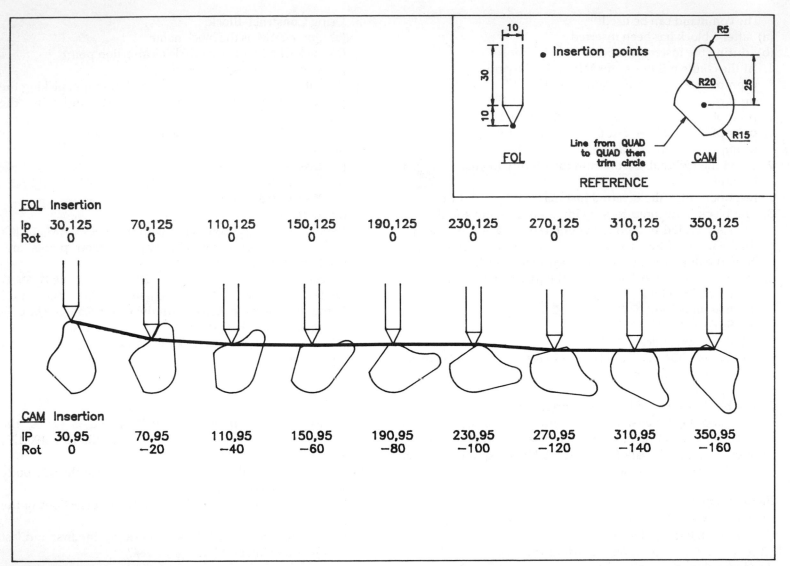

Fig. 40.3. Block worked example.

Block options

There are several options available to the user when working with blocks, these being:

1. to specify parameters on the screen or via the dialogue box
2. to explode the block after insertion or during insertion
3. the ? from the keyboard entry
4. Block... from the Insert dialogue box
5. File... from the Insert dialogue box
6. using Blocks
7. redefining blocks.

(a) Parameters: it's the user's preference whether parameters are entered with the dialogue box or not. I prefer to specify the parameters on the screen as I have 'more control' over the insertion point.

(b) Explode: I would recommend that blocks are inserted before they are exploded (if they need to be exploded). This maintains the original X and Y scale factors.

(c) ? option: allows the user to 'see' the blocks which have been defined in the current drawing. At the command line enter BLOCK or INSERT and

prompt   `Block name (or ?)`
enter   `?<R>`
prompt   `Block(s) to list<*>`
enter   `*<R>` – wildcard for all
prompt   Text screen with:

INSERT entry		BLOCK entry			
Defined blocks		Defined blocks			
CAM		CAM			
FOL		FOL			
User Blocks	Unnamed Blocks	User Blocks	External References	Dependent Blocks	Unnamed Blocks
2	abc	2	0	0	abc

(d) Block...: this option from the Insert dialogue box lists the Defined blocks in the current drawing, and allows them to be selected for insertion. It is similar to the ? command line option.

(e) File...: this option from the Insert dialogue box will be discussed in the next chapter on WBLOCKS.

(f) Using blocks is not just about creation and insertion.

Blocks have several interesting 'properties' which we will now investigate with a new drawing.

Using blocks

1. Open A:STDA3, layer OUT current with toolbars.
2. Refer to Fig. 40.4 and draw the two reference shapes to the sizes given, with:
   (a) shape BL1 on layer OUT but coloured green
   (b) shape BL2 on layer OUT but coloured blue
3. Create two blocks for these shapes using the names BL1 and BL2. The insertion points should be as shown, i.e. at the centre of the 'square' and the circle.
4. Draw the following entities, using Fig. 40.4 as a guide for size and position:
   (a) an inclined line
   (b) a circle
   (c) a polyshape with line and arc segments
   (d) a spline curve
5. Divide
   (a) From the menu bar select **Draw–Point–Divide** and
   prompt   `Select object to divide`
   respond   **pick the line**
   prompt   `<Number of segments>/Block`
   enter   **B**<R> – the block option
   prompt   `Block name to insert`
   enter   **BL1**<R>
   prompt   `Align block with object<Y>`
   enter   **Y**<R>
   prompt   `Number of segments`
   enter   **3**<R> – fig. (a).

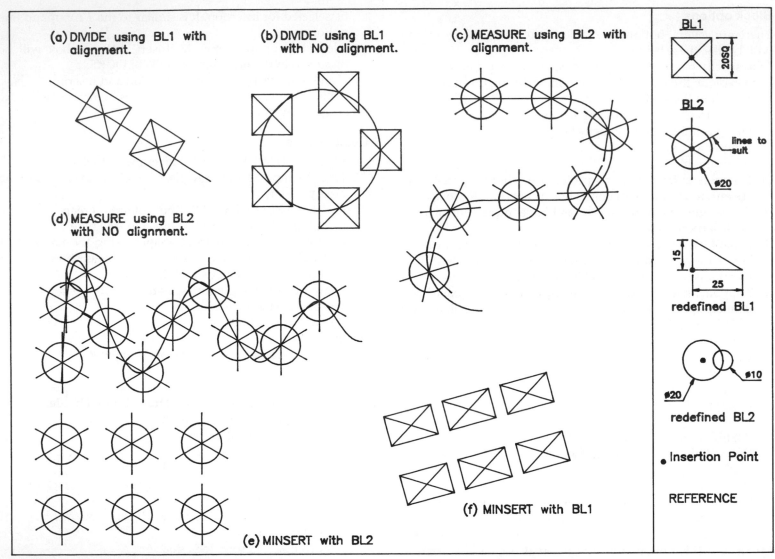

Fig. 40.4. Original drawing using blocks.

(b) Now divide the circle with:
  (i) block BL1
  (ii) no alignment
  (iii) 5 segments – fig. (b).

6. Measure
  (a) From the menu bar select **Draw–Point–Measure** and
      prompt Select object to measure
      respond **pick the polyshape**
      prompt <Segment length>/Block
      enter   **B**<R>
      prompt Block name to insert
      enter   **BL2**<R>
      prompt Align block with object<Y>
      enter   **Y**<R>
      prompt Segment length
      enter   **35**<R> – fig. (c).
  (b) Measure the spline using:
      (i) block BL2
      (ii) no alignment
      (iii) 30 segment length – fig. (d).

7. Multiple insert
  Blocks can be inserted into a drawing in a rectangular array
  with the MINSERT command. The command can be activated
  from the keyboard or an icon in the Miscellaneous toolbar.
  (a) At the command line enter **MINSERT**<R>
      prompt Block name and enter **BL2**<R>
      prompt Insertion point and enter **25,20**<R>
      prompt X scale and enter **1**<R>
      prompt Y scale and enter **1**<R>
      prompt Rotation angle and enter **0**<R>
      prompt Number of rows and enter **2**<R>
      prompt Number of columns and enter **3**<R>
      prompt Unit cell... and enter **35**<R>
      prompt Distance between... and enter **35**<R>
              –fig. (e).

(b) Select the Insert Multiple Block icon
    from the Miscellaneous toolbar with
    1. block name: BL1
    2. insertion point: 265,50
    3. X scale: 1.2
    4. Y scale: 0.75
    5. rotation: 15
    6. number of rows: 2
    7. number of columns: 3
    8. row distance: 30
    9. column distance: –30 – fig. (f).

8. Try and explode a multiple inserted block – you cannot.

9. At this stage your drawing should resemble Fig. 40.4. and
   may be saved if required.

10. Redefining blocks. Blocks which have been used in a
    drawing can be redefined, i.e. the same block name can be
    re-used with interesting results.
  (a) Refer to Fig. 40.4 and draw using the given sizes:
      1. the triangle – colour magenta
      2. the two circles – colour cyan.
  (b) At the command line enter **INSERT**<R>
      prompt Block name
      enter   **BL1**<R>
      prompt Block BL1 already exists
              Redefine it?<N>
      enter   **Y**<R>
      prompt Insertion point
      respond **pick corner point as indicated**
      prompt Select object
      respond **pick the three lines then right-click**
  (c) The green BL1 square blocks will change to the
      magenta triangle with:
      1. aligned on the line
      2. non-aligned on the circle
      3. minserted at the entered scales.

(d) Now redefine block BL2 for the two cyan circles and
   1. aligned on the polyshape
   2. non-aligned on the spline
   3. minserted at X = Y = 1.

Oops

When a block has been created it disappears from the screen. While the block can then be inserted back into the drawing it is a 'bit if a nuisance' to have 'lost' the block in the first place. The **OOPS** command overcomes this.

1. Erase your block insertions – save?
2. Draw a circle – any size.
3. Enter **BLOCK<R>** at the command line and
   prompt   Block name and enter CIR<R>
   prompt   Insertion point and pick any point
   prompt   Select objects and pick the circle
4. The circle disappears.
5. Before doing anything else enter **OOPS** at the command line.
6. The circle is re-displayed, **but is still a block**.
7. This is a very useful command.
8. The OOPS command can be selected in icon form from the Miscellaneous toolbar.

Layer 0 and blocks

So far all blocks have been created with the entities on their correct layers. Layer 0 is the AutoCAD R13 default layer and can be used for block creation with interesting results.

1. Erase all entities from the screen and draw:
   (a) a 50-unit square on layer 0 – black
   (b) a 20 radius circle inside the square on layer OUT – red
   (c) two centre lines on layer CL – green.
2. Block all entities with block name TRY, using the circle centre as the insertion point.
3. Make layer OUT current, and insert block TRY at 55,210 full size. The square is inserted with red continuous lines.
4. Make layer CL current, and insert the block at 135,210. The square has green centre lines.
5. With HID the current layer, insert the block at 215,210 and the square will have yellow hidden lines.
6. Make layer 0 current and insert at 295,210 – square is black.
7. Freeze layer OUT and
   (a) no red circles
   (b) no red square from the first insertion when layer OUT was current.
8. Thaw layer OUT and make it current then insert block TRY using the Insert dialogue box with the Explode option activated (X in box). The insertion point is 175,115. The square is black, i.e. it is on layer 0.
9. Explode the first three inserted blocks and the square should be black in each case, i.e. it has been 'transferred' back to layer 0.
10. Finally freeze layer 0 – no black squares?
11. Exit AutoCAD.

❏ *Summary*

1. Blocks are entities created and 'stored for recall' within the current drawing.
2. Blocks are used for insertion of frequently used 'shapes'.
3. An inserted block is a single entity.
4. Blocks can be inserted from the keyboard or from a dialogue box.
5. Blocks can be inserted at different X and Y scale factors with varying rotation angle.
6. The explode command will 'return' a block to its individual entities.
7. The explode command can be used:
   (a) after insertion
   (b) during insertion from the dialogue box.
8. Blocks which are exploded as inserted, can only have the same X and Y scale factor.
9. The block insertion point can be entered from the keyboard or using the dialogue box.
10. Blocks are inserted with layers 'intact'
11. Blocks can be inserted with the Divide and Measure commands.
12. Multiple insertion in a rectangular array is possible with blocks.
13. Blocks can be redefined. This will 'update' the current drawing to display the new block definition.
14. Blocks which are created on layer 0 are inserted into the current layer. It is recommended that blocks *are not* created on layer 0.
15. Unused blocks can be purged from the current drawing.

Activity

The activity I have included with blocks is not an engineering example, but is still interesting. The idea was used in my *Starting LT* book and was well received by the users. The activity is in two parts:

Tutorial 27(a): Shapes for a playground. Draw the shapes using the sizes as a rough guide. Make blocks using the names given, the insertion points being at your discretion. The only help I will give is with the hatch pattern for the sandpit and the pool. I used AR_SAND (scale 2.5) and SWAMP (scale 5).

Tutorial 27(b): Use the created blocks to design a playground for AutoCAD R13 users – we need it! Make the playground boundary a polyline and insert at varying X and Y scales.

41. WBLOCKS

Blocks are useful when frequently used shapes are required in a drawing, but they are **drawing-specific**, i.e. they can only be used with the drawing in which they were created. Blocks can however, be created for access by all AutoCAD users, i.e. they are **global** and these are called **WBLOCKS** or world blocks. WBLOCKS are used in the same manner as blocks with the exception that they are stored and recalled from a named directory. In our worked example, we will use our floppy disk as the named directory.

Creating WBLOCKS

1. Open A:STDA3 with layer OUT current with toolbars as required and refer to Fig. 41.1.
2. Draw a rectangular polyline shape – fig. (a) – starting at the point 2,2. The length is to be 376, the breadth 266 and the polyline is to have a constant width of 4. Close the rectangle with the close option. The sizes used will become apparent in the exercise.
3. At the command line enter **WBLOCK**<R>

prompt	Create Drawing File dialogue box
respond	1. pick Drive scroll arrow then **a:**
	2. enter **BORDER** as File Name
	3. pick OK
prompt	Block name
enter	**<RETURN>**
prompt	Insertion base point
enter	**0,0**<R>
prompt	Select objects
respond	**pick any point on the polyline** then right-click

4. The border disappears, but remember OOPS?
5. Construct the title box to the overall sizes in fig. (b). The detail can be of your own design. Note that the donut and two dotted lines are for reference only and should not be drawn. Having the snap on will assist.
6. At the command line enter **WBLOCK**<R>

prompt	Create Drawing File dialogue box
respond	1. pick a: drive
	2. enter **TITLE** as File Name
	3. pick OK
prompt	Block name and enter <RETURN>
prompt	Insertion point
respond	pick point indicated by donut (snap on)
prompt	Select objects
respond	window the title box then right-click.

7. Draw the parts list table to the sizes given – fig. (c).
8. At the command line enter WBLOCK<R> and

prompt	Create Drawing File dialogue box
respond	**pick Type it...**
prompt	File name
enter	**A:PLIST**<R>
prompt	Block name and <RETURN>
prompt	Insertion point
respond	pick point indicated by donut
prompt	Select objects
respond	window the parts list then right-click.

9. Now exit AutoCAD.

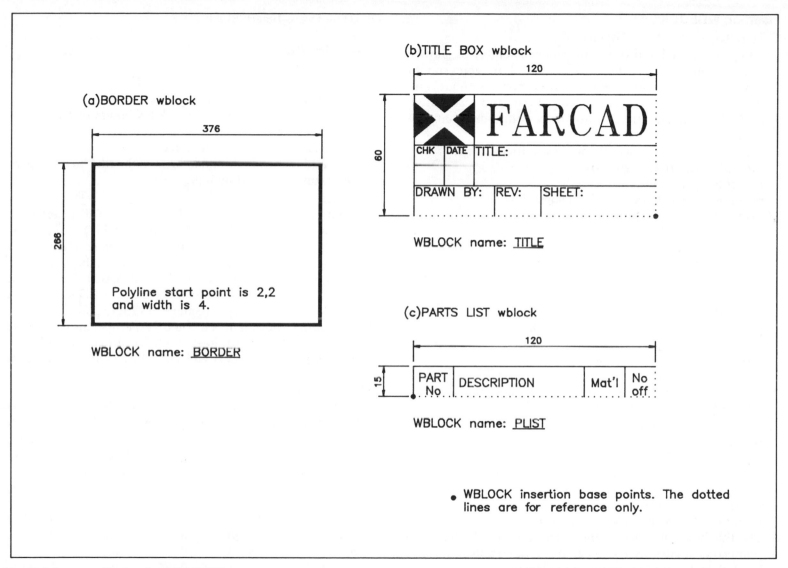

(a)BORDER wblock

376

268

Polyline start point is 2,2
and width is 4.

WBLOCK name: BORDER

(b)TITLE BOX wblock

120

60

FARCAD

| CHK | DATE | TITLE: |
| | | |

| DRAWN BY: | REV: | SHEET: |

WBLOCK name: TITLE

(c)PARTS LIST wblock

120

15

| PART No | DESCRIPTION | Mat'l | No off |

WBLOCK name: PLIST

• WBLOCK insertion base points. The dotted
lines are for reference only.

Fig. 41.1. Layout and sizes for WBLOCKS.

Inserting WBLOCKS

1. Start AutoCAD R13 and open A:STDA3.
2. Refer to Fig. 41.2 and draw the pulley assembly as shown. I have only given the main sizes, but you should have the ability to draw the assembly without any problems. I have added the hatch patterns and scales used. Add the balloon effect using donuts–line–circle–middle text.
3. From the menu bar select **Draw–Insert–Block...** and

prompt	Insert dialogue box
respond	**pick File...**
prompt	Select Drawing File dialogue box
respond	1. pick a: drive
	2. pick border.dwg – turns blue
	3. pick OK
prompt	Insert dialogue box with:
	(a) Block... BORDER
	(b) File... A:\BORDER.DWG
respond	pick OK
prompt	`Insertion point` and enter 0,0
prompt	`X scale...` and enter 1
prompt	`Y scale...` and enter 1
prompt	Rotation angle and enter 0

4. The polyline border should be inserted within the border of the A:STDA3 standard sheet.
5. At the command line enter **INSERT**<R>

prompt	`Block name`
enter	**A:TITLE**<R>
prompt	`Insertion point` and enter **376,4**<R>
prompt	`X scale...` and enter 1
prompt	`Y scale...` and enter 1
prompt	Rotation angle and enter 0

6. The title box is inserted at the entered point. The insertion point co-ordinates are relative to the border to allow the title box to just 'fit into the corner' of the border.

7. Using **Draw–Insert–Block**:
   (a) pick File...
   (b) pick a: drive
   (c) pick **plist.dwg**
   (d) pick OK from Select Drawing dialogue box
   (e) pick OK from Insert dialogue box
   (f) `Insertion point` and pick ENDpoint of top left line of title box
   (g) X scale 1; Y scale 1; Rotation 0.
8. Now add text and additional lines to the title box and parts list to complete the drawing.

Notes

1. What we have achieved in this exercise is to insert three drawings (A:BORDER; A:TITLE and A:PLIST) into another drawing A:STDA3. In the example we used our floppy disk to 'store' the drawings, but if the floppy had been a named directory, then anyone could have accessed the drawing files at any time. This is especially true if CAD systems are networked. This is the advantage of WBLOCKS.
2. The border and title block could be permanently added to the A:STDA3 standard sheet, but this is for you to decide.
3. We will refer to the PLIST wblock in the chapter on attributes.

About WBLOCKS

Every drawing is a WBLOCK and every WBLOCK is a drawing

The above statement is true. Think about it! To demonstrate the statement:

1. Open A:STDA3 with layer OUT current and refer to Fig. 41.3 which displays four drawings inserted at different scales.
2. The inserted drawings are:

Drawing file	IP	X	Y	Rot
A:TUT-1	5,5	0.5	0.5	0
A:TUT-14	5,150	0.75	0.4	0
A:TUT-20	205,5	0.25	0.5	0
A:TUT-7	305,5	0.175	0.9	0

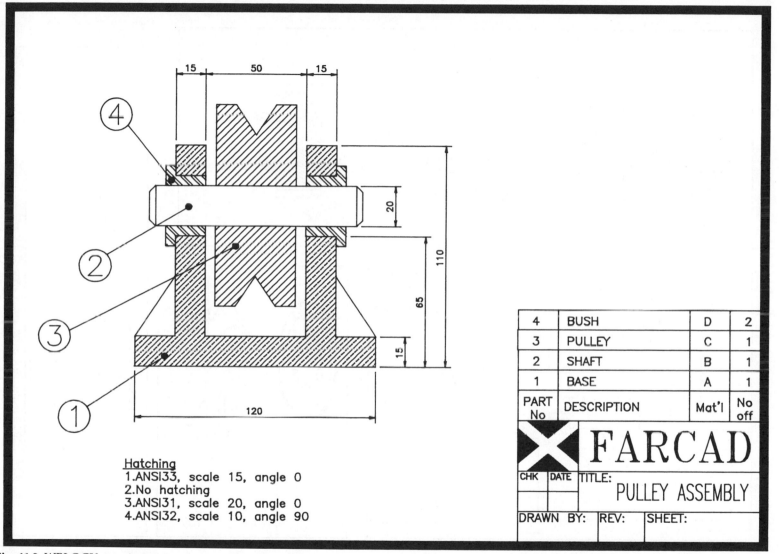

Hatching
1.ANSI33, scale 15, angle 0
2.No hatching
3.ANSI31, scale 20, angle 0
4.ANSI32, scale 10, angle 90

4	BUSH	D	2
3	PULLEY	C	1
2	SHAFT	B	1
1	BASE	A	1
PART No	DESCRIPTION	Mat'l	No off

FARCAD

CHK	DATE	TITLE: PULLEY ASSEMBLY
DRAWN BY:	REV:	SHEET:

Fig. 41.2. WBLOCK exercises.

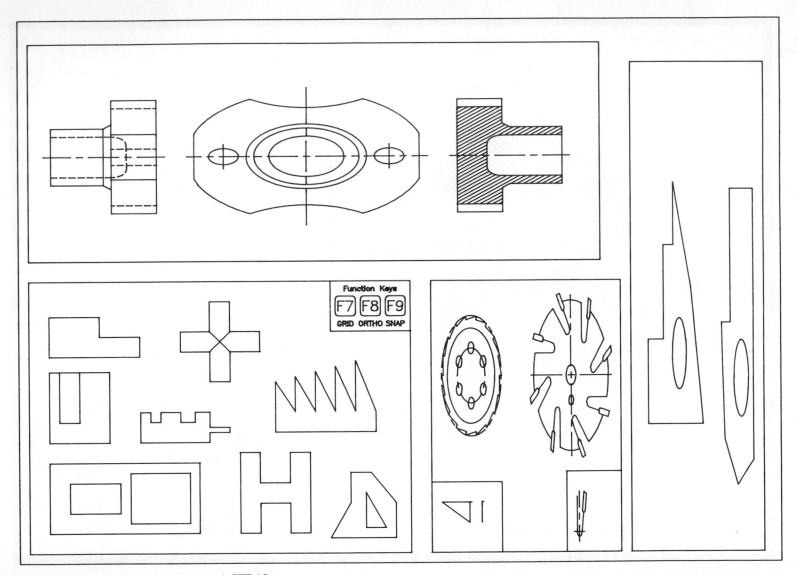

Fig. 41.3. Inserting four drawings into A:STDA3.

3. Try some wblock insertions for yourself, but remember any drawing with hatching usually uses a lot of memory.
4. If a wblock already exists with an entered name, the user is prompted with the message:
   ```
   A drawing with this name already exists
   Do you want to replace it?<N>
   ```
5. During the WBLOCK creation process, there was a prompt at which we always entered <RETURN> This was the **Block name** prompt. This prompt allows the user to convert an existing block into a wblock, and as we did not want to do this we entered <RETURN>.

❏ *Summary*
1. Wblocks are global and can be accessed by all users. They are usually saved to a named directory.
2. Wblocks are created with WBLOCK at the command line.
3. Wblocks are inserted into a drawing in a similar manner to blocks. This can be:
   (a) from the Insert dialogue box
   (b) by keyboard INSERT
4. Wblocks can be exploded when/as inserted.

Activity

No activity is given, but the three created wblocks can now be added to all future drawings if required.

42. Attributes

An attribute is an item of text which can be attached to a block or a wblock. This allows the user to add repetitive type text to frequently used drawing blocks which could be:

(a) weld symbols containing appropriate information
(b) electrical components with values
(c) parts lists containing codes, numbers off, etc.

Attributes can be edited, but their main advantage is that they can be *extracted* from the drawing and stored in an attribute extraction file. The extracted data can then be used as input to other computer packages, e.g. databases, spreadsheets, word-processors, CNC systems, etc. The editing and extraction features of attributes are beyond the scope of this book, and I will concentrate on how attributes are attached to blocks and inserted into drawings.

Getting started

Our first attribute example will consist of a small housing estate, each house being represented by a symbol (a block). On each symbol we want to add the following information in the form of attributes:

(a) the street number of the house
(b) the owner of the house
(c) the value of the house
(d) the number of rooms in the house.

1. Either (a) open A:STDA3 and draw the house to the sizes given in Fig. 42.1(a) or (b) open A:HOUSE saved during the chapter on blocks. Erase the text item and the two windows.
2. It is important that the lower left corner is at the point (150,100) as this will help us with text insertions.
3. Display the Attribute toolbar.

Defining the attributes

1. Select the DEFINE ATTRIBUTE icon from the attribute toolbar and
   prompt   Attribute Definition dialogue box
2. This dialogue box is in four parts:
   (a) the Mode options – all blank
   (b) the attribute Tag, Prompt and Value
   (c) the Insertion Point
   (d) the Text options.
3. Using the dialogue box:
   respond   1. enter **NUMBER** at the Tag box
              2. enter **House number?** at the Prompt box
              3. enter **999** at the Value box
              4. pick **Pick Point<**
                 prompt `Start point`
                 enter   **180,155**<R>
              5. set Text Justification to **Center**
              6. set Text Height to 10
              7. dialogue box as Fig. 42.2
              8. pick OK
4. The word NUMBER will appear in the roof area of the house – fig. (b).
5. Using the Attribute Definition dialogue box three more times, enter the following attribute information:

(a) Tag	OWNER
Prompt	Who owns the house?
Value	ABC
Insertion Point	X: 180, Y: 135
Justification	Center
Height, Rotation	8, 0

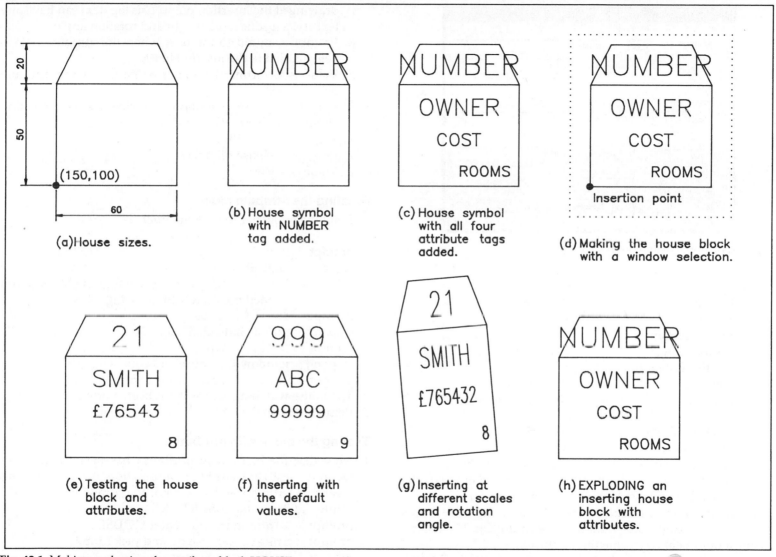

Fig. 42.1. Making and using the attribute block HOUSE.

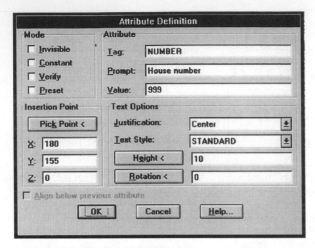

Fig. 42.2. Attribute definition dialogue box.

(b) Tag   COST
      Prompt   Price of house?
      Value   99999
      Insertion Point   X: 180, Y: 120
      Justification   Center
      Height, Rotation   6, 0
(c) Tag   ROOMS
      Prompt   Number of rooms?
      Value   9
      Insertion Point   205,105
      Justification   Right
      Height, Rotation   5, 0

6. When all the attribute information has been entered, the house symbol will display the four tags as fig. (c).
7. When attributes are used for the first time, the three words Tag, Prompt and Value tend to cause confusion. The following should help overcome this confusion:
    1. Tag is the actual attribute 'label' which is attached to the drawing at the insertion point. This tag item can have any text style, justification, height and rotation angle.
    2. Prompt is an aid to the user when the attribute data is being added to the inserted block.
    3. Value is an artificial number or name for the attribute being added.
8. In our first attribute definition sequence, we were creating the house number and entered the following:
    1. Tag   NUMBER
    2. Prompt   House number?
    3. Value   999

Creating the attribute block

1. From the menu bar select **Construct**
                                 Block
    prompt   Block name (or ?)
    enter   **HOUSE\<R\>**
                 Note you may have to redefine the block if you opened the A:HOUSE drawing – OK?
    prompt   Insertion base point
    respond   **pick as indicated** – fig. (d)
    prompt   Select objects
    respond   **window the house and tags** as fig. (d)
    prompt   11(?) found then right-click
2. The house will disappear as it has been made into a block.
3. Remember oops?

Testing the block with attributes

1. Now that the block with attributes has been created, we want to 'test' the attribute information it contains. This means inserting the block into the drawing so at the command line enter **INSERT\<R\>**
    prompt   Block name and enter HOUSE
    prompt   Insertion point and pick to suit
    prompt   X scale and enter 1

prompt   `Y scale` and enter 1
prompt   `Rotation angle` and enter 0
prompt   `Price    of    house?<99999>` and enter £76543`<R>`
prompt   `Who   owns   the   house?<ABC>` and enter SMITH`<R>`
prompt   `Number of rooms?<9>` and enter 8`<R>`
prompt   `House number?<999>` and enter 21`<R>`

2. Question: do you recognise the prompts and values?
3. The house symbol is displayed with the attribute information entered in response to the prompts – fig. (e).
4. Inserting blocks with attribute information is interesting when it is new. Figure 42.1 illustrates the following points:
   (f) it is possible to insert a block with the default values by simply pressing <RETURN> at the prompt lines
   (g) a block can be inserted at different X and Y scale factors and at varying rotation angles. This affects the attributes
   (h) if a block containing attribute information is exploded, the block is displayed with the attribute tags.
5. You may want to try some of these variations for yourself, then erase all entities from the screen.

Attribute information

Table 42.1. Attribute data

Tag	Number	Owner	Cost (£)	Rooms
Data	1	BROWN	60000	6
	2	GREEN	75000	7
	3	BLUE	120000	8
	4	GREY	92000	8
	5	JONES	85000	7
	6	BLOGGS	150000	10
	7	REID	30000	4
	8	McFARLANE	250000	15

1. The housing estate is to consist of eight houses, each house being represented by the house symbol with the appropriate attribute information added. This information is listed in Table 42.1
2. Attributes can be added to an inserted block:
   (a) from the keyboard
   (b) using a dialogue box We will investigate both methods with this example.
3. Open A:STDA3 standard sheet and refer to Fig. 42.3.
4. Insert the wblock A:BORDER full size with zero rotation at the point 0,0.
5. Draw a road layout to your own design using Fig. 42.3 as a guide.
6. From the menu bar select **Draw**
                       Insert
                       Block...
prompt   Insert dialogue box
respond   1. pick Block...
          2. pick HOUSE defined block then OK
          3. pick OK from the Insert dialogue box
prompt   `Insertion point`
respond   pick point to suit using the ghost image as a guide
prompt   `X scale` and enter 1`<R>`
prompt   `Y scale` and enter 1`<R>`
prompt   `Rotation` and enter 0`<R>`
prompt   `Price of house?` and enter £60000`<R>`
prompt   `Who owns house?` and enter **BROWN**`<R>`
prompt   `Number of rooms?` and enter **6**`<R>`
prompt   `House number` and enter **1**`<R>`
7. The house block is inserted with the entered attribute information.
8. At the command line enter **ATTDIA**`<R>`
prompt   `New value for ATTDIA<0>`
enter   **1**`<R>`

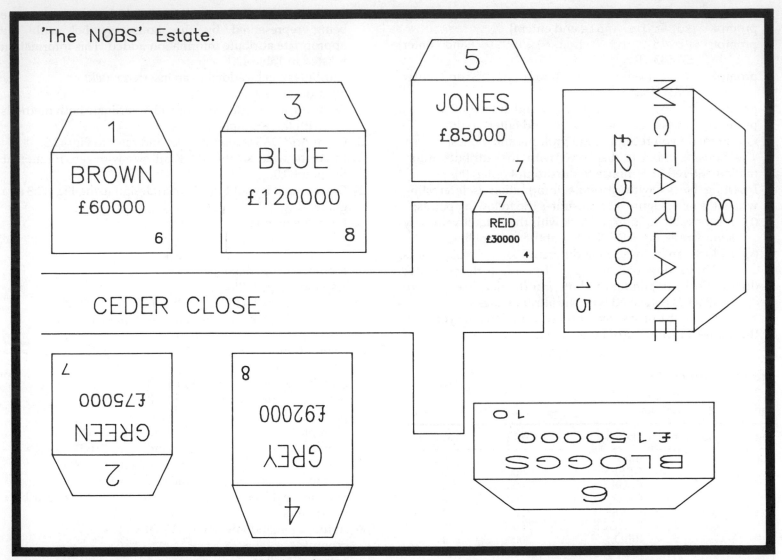

Fig. 42.3. Estate layout with inserted house and block attributes.

Note: (a) the variable ATTDIA (Attribute Dialogue box) controls whether a dialogue box will be used when inserting attributes, and ATTDIA 0 – no dialogue box, i.e. attributes entered from the keyboard as our example. ATTDIA 1 – dialogue box will be used; (b) the default ATTDIA value is 0, i.e. no dialogue box.

9. At the command line enter **INSERT**<R>

   prompt   Block name<HOUSE> and right-click
   prompt   Insertion point and pick to suit
   prompt   X scale and enter 1.2<R>
   prompt   Y scale and enter 1.2<R>
   prompt   Rotation and enter 0
   prompt   Enter Attributes dialogue box with default attribute values – Fig. 42.4(a)

   respond 1. alter price to £120000
            2. alter owner to BLUE
            3. alter rooms to 8
            4. alter number to 3
            5. Fig. 42.4(b) then pick OK

10. House number 3 is inserted at a slightly larger scale.
11. Now complete the housing estate using the HOUSE block and the attribute information in Table.42.1. You have to:
    (a) use the keyboard INSERT or the INSERT dialogue box
    (b) have ATTDIA at 0 (no dialogue box) or 1 (dialogue box)
    (c) use your discretion for the insertion point and the scale, but try and be logical with the layout
    (d) take care with the rotation angle?
12. Your completed housing estate can be saved.

Attribute example 2

The first attribute example was with a block created for use in a particular drawing. This second example will investigate how attributes can be added to a wblock, for access by everyone. We will use the wblock PLIST created earlier and modify it for use with attributes.

(a)

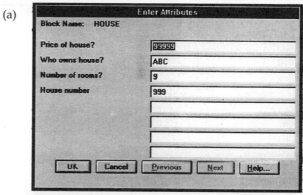

(b)

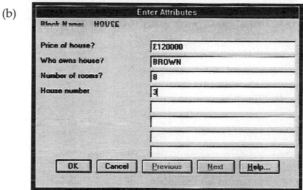

Fig. 42.4. Enter Attributes dialogue box. (a) Default and (b) entered values.

1. Open A:STDA3 standard sheet with toolbars and refer to Fig. 42.5.
2. Snap ON and set to 2.5 will help.
3. From the menu bar select **Draw**
   InsertBlock...
   prompt   Insert dialogue box
   respond 1. pick File...
            2. pick a: drive

PART No	DESCRIPTION	Mat'l	No off

(a) Inserted PLIST wblock.

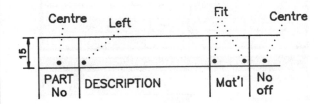

PART No	DESCRIPTION	Mat'l	No off

Centre   Left   Fit   Centre

15

(b) Additional lines and points to assist with attribute tag positioning

P.NO DESC		MATL N O F	
PART No	DESCRIPTION	Mat'l	No off

(c) Attribute tags added at the required points.

PART No	DESCRIPTION	Mat'l	No off

• Insertion point
.... Crossing window

(d) Insertion point and crossing window for the wblock PLIST_2

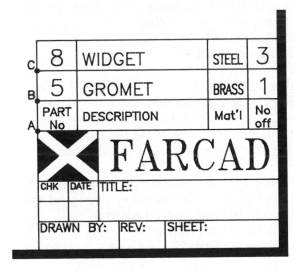

C 8	WIDGET	STEEL	3
B 5	GROMET	BRASS	1
A PART No	DESCRIPTION	Mat'l	No off

FARCAD

CHK	DATE	TITLE:

DRAWN BY:	REV:	SHEET:

(e) Insertion of wblocks BORDER, TITLE, PLIST and PLIST_2. PLIST_2 has attributes added.

Fig. 42.5. Attribute example 2.

3. scroll and pick **plist.dwg**
4. pick OK
5. pick OK from Insert dialogue box

prompt `Insertion point` and pick a point to suit

prompt `X scale` and insert full size with no rotation – fig. (a).

4. Zoom in on an area around the inserted wblock.
5. Draw five additional lines 'on top of' the inserted block as fig. (b). Also shown are donut points for attribute reference. Do not draw these donuts.
6. From the menu bar select **Construct-Attribute...**

prompt Attribute Definition dialogue box

respond 1. enter PNO as the Tag
      2. enter Part number? as the Prompt
      3. enter A1 as the Value
      4. pick Pick Point<

prompt `Start point`

respond pick point indicated by the left Centre donut

prompt Attribute Definition dialogue box

respond 1. pick Text Justification as Centre
      2. alter Text Height to 8
      3. pick OK

7. The attribute tag PNO will be added at the point selected – fig. (c).
8. Now add the other attribute information using the donuts in Fig. 42.5(b) as a guide for the justification. The required data are as follows:

Tag	DESC	MATL	NOF
Prompt	Description?	Material?	Number off?
Value	ABC123	ZY6	9
InsPt	as shown	as shown	as shown
Just'n	Left	Fit	Center
Height	6	5	8
Rot'n	0	0	0

9. At the command line enter **WBLOCK**<R>

prompt Create Drawing File dialogue box

respond **pick Type it...**

prompt `File name`

enter **A:PLIST_2**<R>

prompt `Block name` and <RETURN>

prompt `Insertion point`

respond **pick point indicated** in fig. (d)

prompt `Select objects`

respond **crossing option and window** as fig. (d) then right-click.

10. The new wblock disappears to leave the original inserted PLIST wblock.
11. Before proceeding think of the wblocks (drawings) which we have created. We have made four, these being:
   (a) BORDER – the polyline
   (b) TITLE – our designed title box
   (c) PLIST – the parts list headings
   (d) PLIST_2 – the attribute parts list.
12. Open A:STDA3 and insert the following drawings:
   (a) A:BORDER, full size at the point 0,0
   (b) A:TITLE, full size at the point 376,4
   (c) A:PLIST, full size at ENDpoint and pick point A – fig. (e).
13. Insert A:PLIST_2, full size at ENDpoint of B and:

prompt `Number off?<9>` and enter **1**<R>

prompt `Material?<ZY6>` and enter **BRASS**<R>

prompt `Description?<ABC123>` and enter **GROMET**<R>

prompt `Part number?<A1>` and enter **5**<R>

14. The attribute information will be added to the inserted wblock.

15. Repeat the A:PLIST_2 insertion and ENDpoint of C with the following attribute information:
    (a) Number off – 3
    (b) Material – STEEL
    (c) Description – WIDGET
    (d) Part number – 8.
16. The completed drawing is now as Fig. 42.1(e) and has used our four wblocks.
17. Save if required. This completes the chapter on attributes.

❏ *Summary*
1. Attributes are text items added to BLOCKS and WBLOCKS.
2. Attributes must be created by the user using the Define Attribute dialogue box.
3. Attributes are added by the user during the INSERT command.
4. Attributes can be added via the keyboard or by a dialogue box.
5. The variable ATTDIA controls the dialogue box and:
   ATTDIA 0 – no dialogue box
   ATTDIA 1 – dialogue box used.
6. Attributes can be edited and extracted from a drawing. These two topics have not been considered in this book.

43. Toolbox customisation

The toolbars supplied with R13 are more than adequate for the user's draughting requirements. It is possible to create a new toolbar and customise it to include any icons of your choice. As an exercise, we will create a new toolbar with three icons – LINE, ERASE and LINEAR dimensioning. The example will include several new dialogue boxes, which should not give you any problems.

1. Open A:STDA3 standard sheet.
2. From the menu bar select **Tools**
   Customize Toolbars...
   prompt   Toolbars dialogue box
   respond **pick New...**
   prompt   New Toolbar dialogue box
   respond 1. enter **MYOWN** as Toolbar name
            2. pick OK – Fig. 43.1
   prompt   Toolbars dialogue box with ACAD.MYOWN added to list in blue
   respond **pick Close**
3. Now refer to Fig. 43.2.
4. The new toolbar will be displayed on the screen, and can be moved as required. This toolbar is quite small and empty, i.e. it has no icons in it – Fig. 43.2(a). Note, I would advise that the new toolbar is moved to the left or right side of the screen. We want to be able to 'see it' when the Toolbars dialogue box is displayed.
5. Select **Tools–Customize Toolbars...** and
   prompt   Toolbars dialogue box
   respond **pick Customize...**
   prompt   Customize Toolbars dialogue box
   respond 1. scroll at Categories
            2. **pick Draw**

Fig. 43.1. New Toolbar dialogue box.

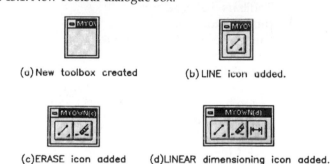

(a) New toolbox created   (b) LINE icon added.

(c) ERASE icon added   (d) LINEAR dimensioning icon added.

Fig. 43.2. Toolbar customisation example.

prompt   the Draw icons
respond 1. left-click on the LINE icon and hold down the left button
         2. drag the line icon 'into' the new toolbar
         3. release the left button – Fig. 43.2(b)
         4. pick Close
prompt   Toolbars dialogue box
respond **pick Customize...**
prompt   Customize Toolbars dialogue box

respond	1. scroll at Categories
	2. **pick Modify**
prompt	the Modify icons
respond	1. left-click on the ERASE icon and hold the button down
	2. drag the icon 'into' the new toolbar and place it next to the LINE icon
	3. release the button
	4. the new toolbar is increased in size to include the new icon – Fig. 43.2(c)
	5. pick Close
prompt	Toolbars dialogue box
respond	**pick Customize...**
prompt	Customize Toolbars dialogue box
respond	1. scroll at Categories
	2. pick Dimensioning
	3. pick the LINEAR icon and drag it into the new toolbar
	4. pick Close
prompt	Toolbars dialogue box
respond	**pick Close**

6. You now have a customized toolbar with three icons – Fig. 43.2(d). These icons can be used in the normal way, and the toolbar can be positioned anywhere on the screen. You can customize any number of toolbars to your requirements.

Displaying a new toolbar

A new customised toolbar will always be displayed when R13 is started, unless you have 'cancelled' it with the close icon in the top-left corner. This new toolbar is not included in the list of toolbar names displayed when Tools–Toolbars is selected from the menu bar. How then do we display new toolbars?

1. Cancel your new toolbar with a left-click on the close icon in the top-left corner of the toolbar.
2. From the menu bar select **Tools**
   Customize Toolbars...

prompt	Toolbars dialogue box
respond	scroll and pick toolbar name ACAD.MYOWN then pick Properties...
prompt	Toolbar Properties dialogue box
respond	1. remove the X from the Hide box
	2. pick Apply
	3. pick Close
prompt	Toolbars dialogue box
respond	pick Close

3. Your customized toolbar will be displayed.

❏ *Summary*

This has been a brief introduction into toolbar customisation, but I am sure you will agree that the procedure is very simply. I will let you decide if you need customised toolbars?

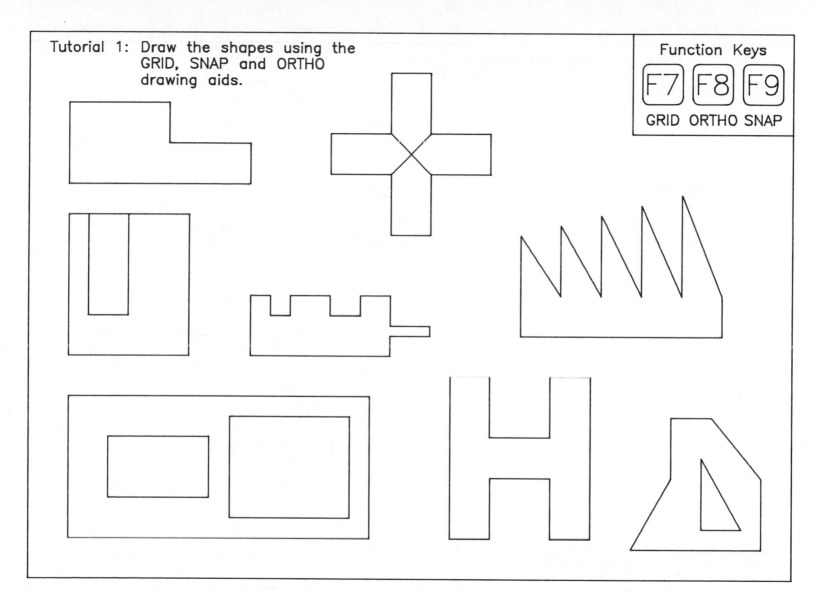

Tutorial 1: Draw the shapes using the GRID, SNAP and ORTHO drawing aids.

Function Keys

F7 F8 F9

GRID ORTHO SNAP

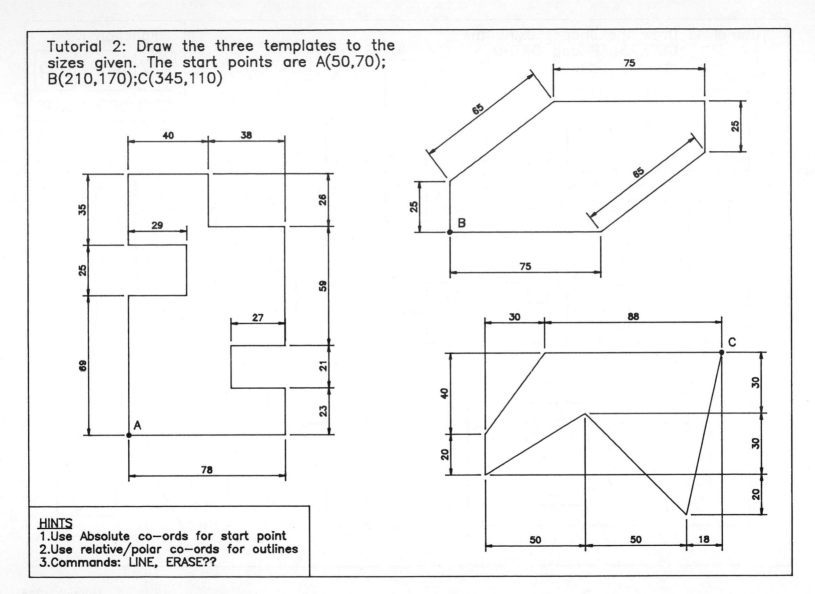

Tutorial 2: Draw the three templates to the sizes given. The start points are A(50,70); B(210,170);C(345,110)

HINTS
1.Use Absolute co-ords for start point
2.Use relative/polar co-ords for outlines
3.Commands: LINE, ERASE??

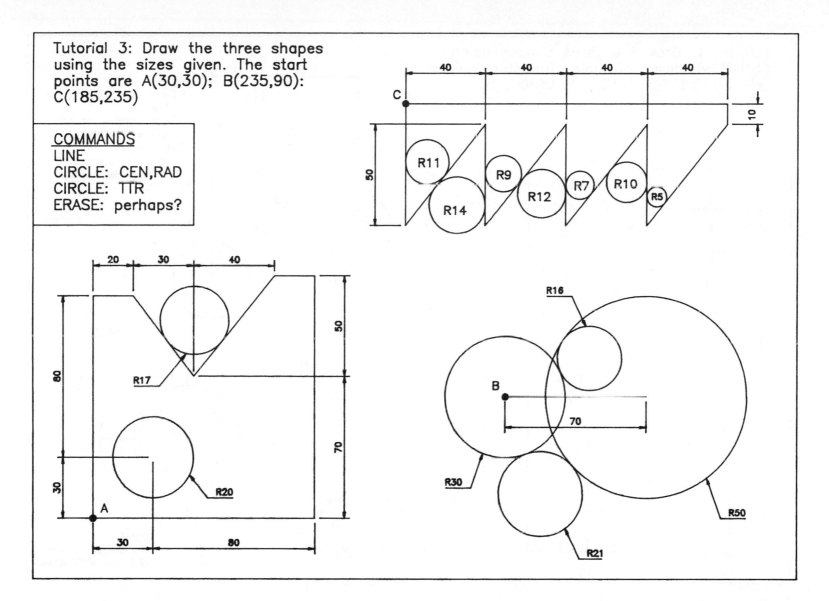

Tutorial 3: Draw the three shapes using the sizes given. The start points are A(30,30); B(235,90): C(185,235)

COMMANDS
LINE
CIRCLE: CEN,RAD
CIRCLE: TTR
ERASE: perhaps?

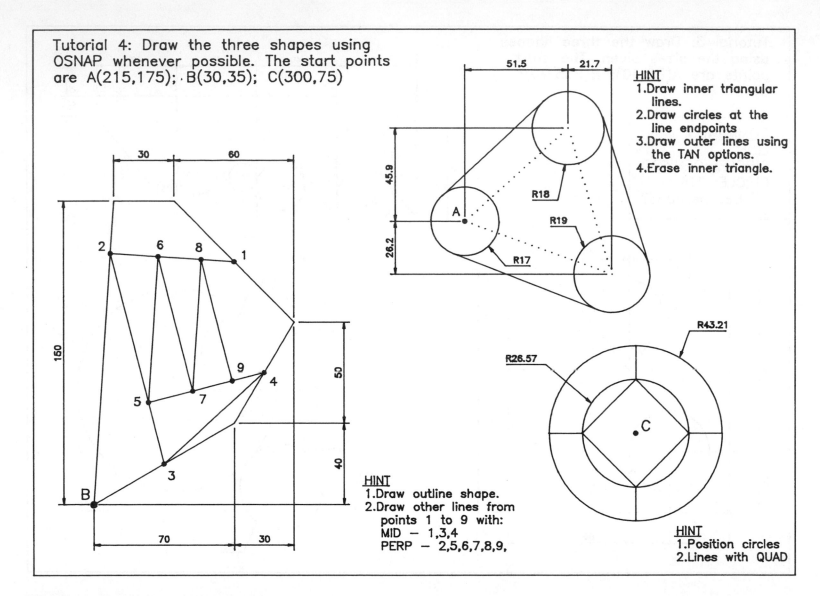

Tutorial 4: Draw the three shapes using OSNAP whenever possible. The start points are A(215,175); B(30,35); C(300,75)

HINT
1. Draw inner triangular lines.
2. Draw circles at the line endpoints
3. Draw outer lines using the TAN options.
4. Erase inner triangle.

R18
R19
R17

51.5 21.7
45.9
26.2
A

30 60
150
50
40
70 30

2 6 8 1
5 7 9 4
3
B

HINT
1. Draw outline shape.
2. Draw other lines from points 1 to 9 with:
   MID — 1,3,4
   PERP — 2,5,6,7,8,9,

R43.21
R26.57
C

HINT
1. Position circles
2. Lines with QUAD

Tutorial 5. Draw the two templates full size.
Suggested start points are A(90,170); B(340,85).

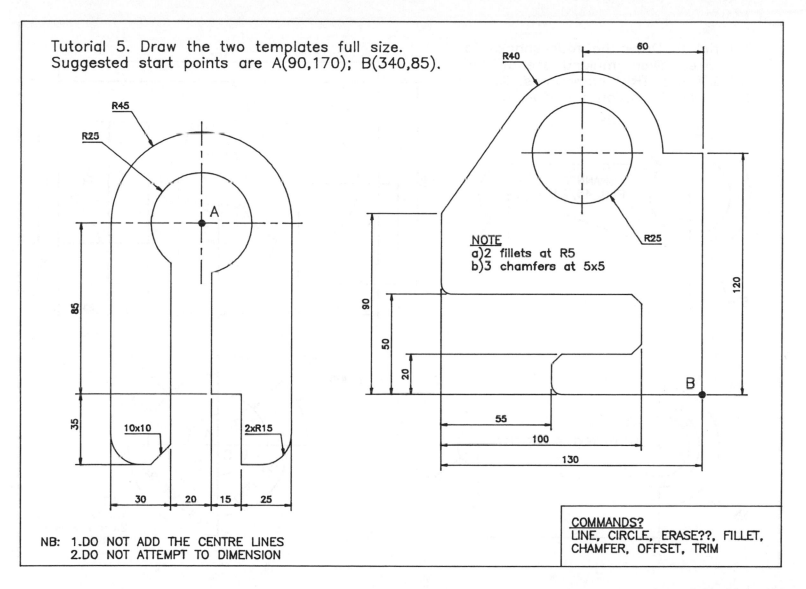

R45

R25

A

85

35

10x10

2xR15

30   20   15   25

R40

60

R25

NOTE
a)2 fillets at R5
b)3 chamfers at 5x5

90

50

20

55

100

130

120

B

NB: 1.DO NOT ADD THE CENTRE LINES
      2.DO NOT ATTEMPT TO DIMENSION

COMMANDS?
LINE, CIRCLE, ERASE??, FILLET,
CHAMFER, OFFSET, TRIM

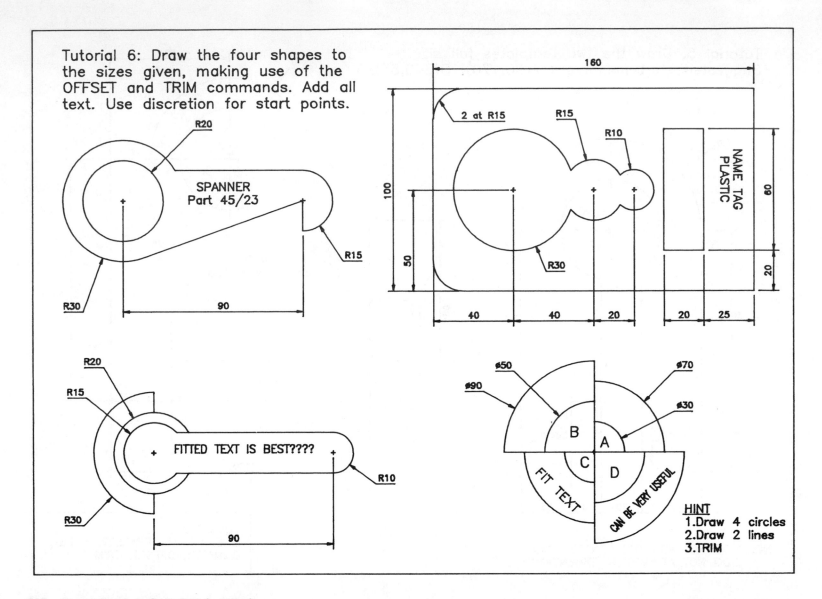

Tutorial 6: Draw the four shapes to the sizes given, making use of the OFFSET and TRIM commands. Add all text. Use discretion for start points.

R20

SPANNER
Part 45/23

R15

R30   90

160

2 at R15   R15   R10

100   50   R30

NAME TAG
PLASTIC

60   20

40   40   20   20   25

R20
R15
R30   FITTED TEXT IS BEST????   R10

90

ø50   ø70
ø90   ø30

B   A
C   D

FIT TEXT   CAN BE VERY USEFUL

HINT
1.Draw 4 circles
2.Draw 2 lines
3.TRIM

Tutorial 7: Draw the two components full size, adding all text and dimensions. Use your layers correctly. Suggested start points are A(50,70) and B(350,200)

COPPER LINER
0.15mm thick

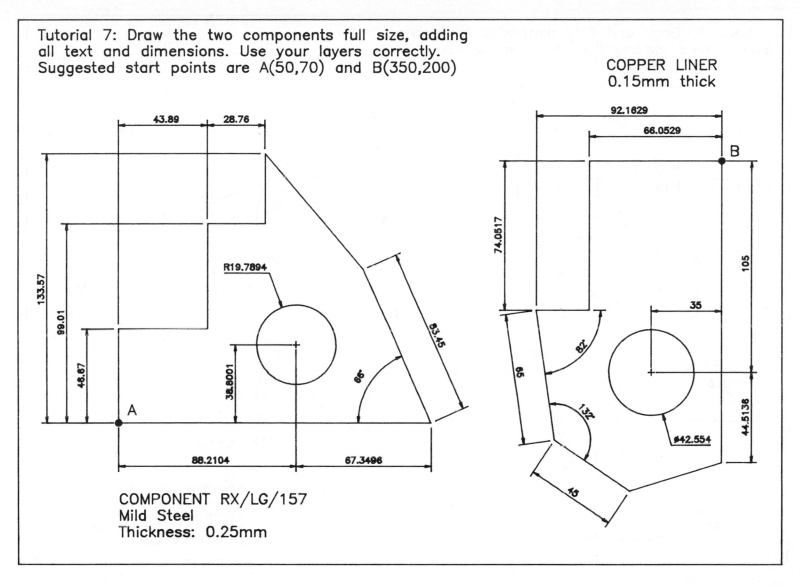

COMPONENT RX/LG/157
Mild Steel
Thickness: 0.25mm

Tutorial 8: Draw and fully dimension the two components, adding the text. Use layers.

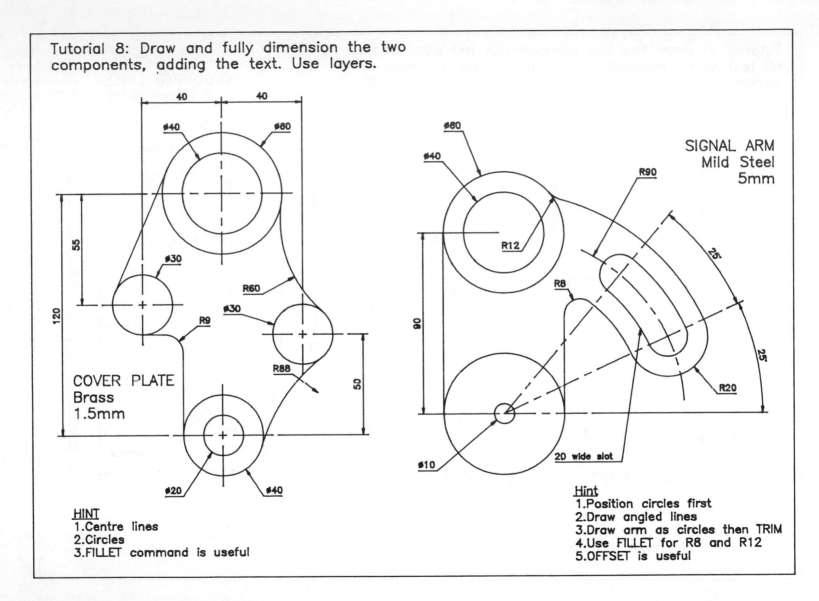

SIGNAL ARM
Mild Steel
5mm

COVER PLATE
Brass
1.5mm

HINT
1.Centre lines
2.Circles
3.FILLET command is useful

Hint
1.Position circles first
2.Draw angled lines
3.Draw arm as circles then TRIM
4.Use FILLET for R8 and R12
5.OFFSET is useful

20 wide slot

Tutorial 9: Draw the given component, adding all text and dimensions. Use layers correctly.

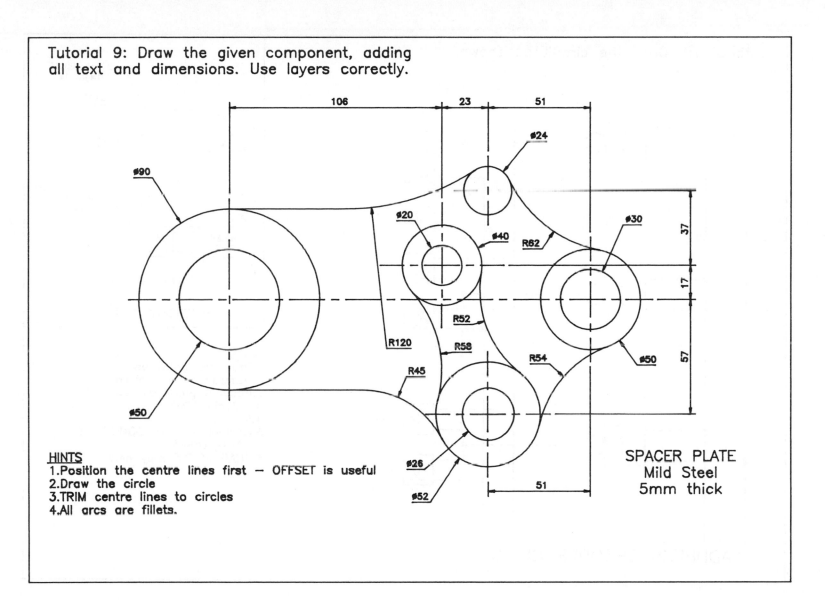

106   23   51

ø24

ø90

ø20

ø40   R62

ø30

37

R120

R52

R58

R54

17

R45

ø50

ø50

57

ø26

ø52

51

SPACER PLATE
Mild Steel
5mm thick

<u>HINTS</u>
1. Position the centre lines first — OFFSET is useful
2. Draw the circle
3. TRIM centre lines to circles
4. All arcs are fillets.

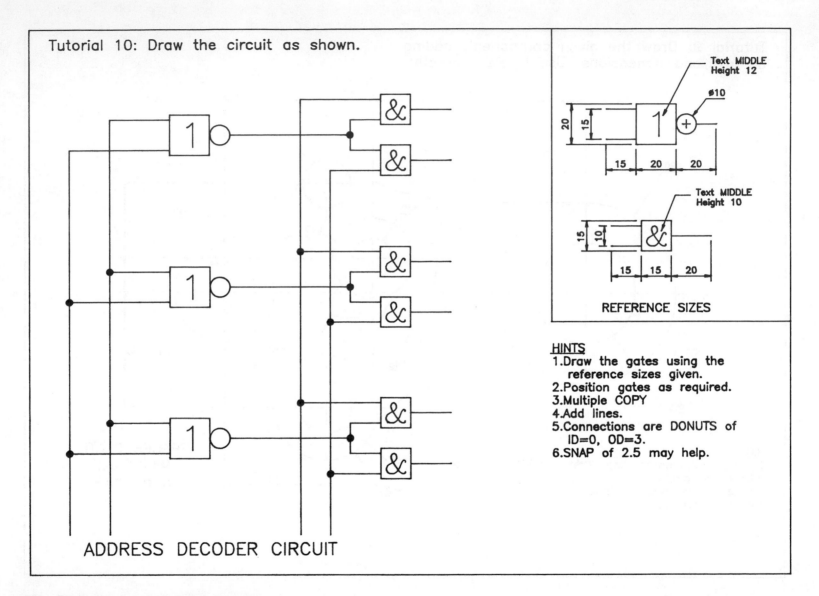

Tutorial 10: Draw the circuit as shown.

Text MIDDLE Height 12

⌀10

20
15
15 20 20

Text MIDDLE Height 10

15
10
15 15 20

REFERENCE SIZES

ADDRESS DECODER CIRCUIT

HINTS
1. Draw the gates using the reference sizes given.
2. Position gates as required.
3. Multiple COPY
4. Add lines.
5. Connections are DONUTS of ID=0, OD=3.
6. SNAP of 2.5 may help.

Tutorial 11: Draw the template full size using the reference sizes given.

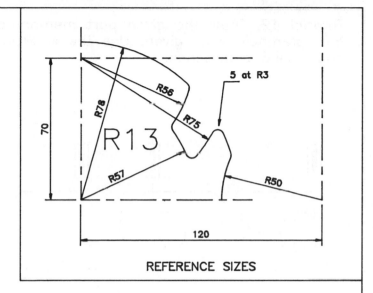

REFERENCE SIZES

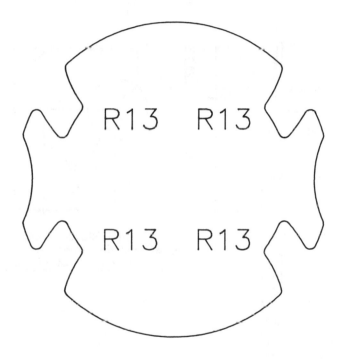

RUBBER TEMPLATE

<u>HINTS</u>
1. Position centre lines
2. Draw 5 circles using radii given.
3. TRIM circles to centre lines and to each other as required.
4. Add the 5 R3 fillets.
5. Add R13 text, centred to suit.
6. MIRROR command twice.
7. MIRRTEXT value?

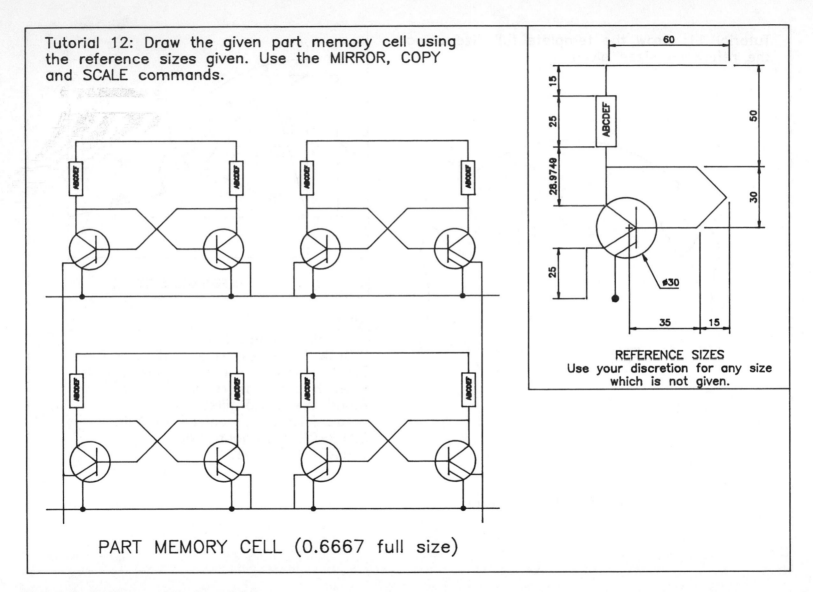

Tutorial 12: Draw the given part memory cell using the reference sizes given. Use the MIRROR, COPY and SCALE commands.

PART MEMORY CELL (0.6667 full size)

REFERENCE SIZES
Use your discretion for any size which is not given.

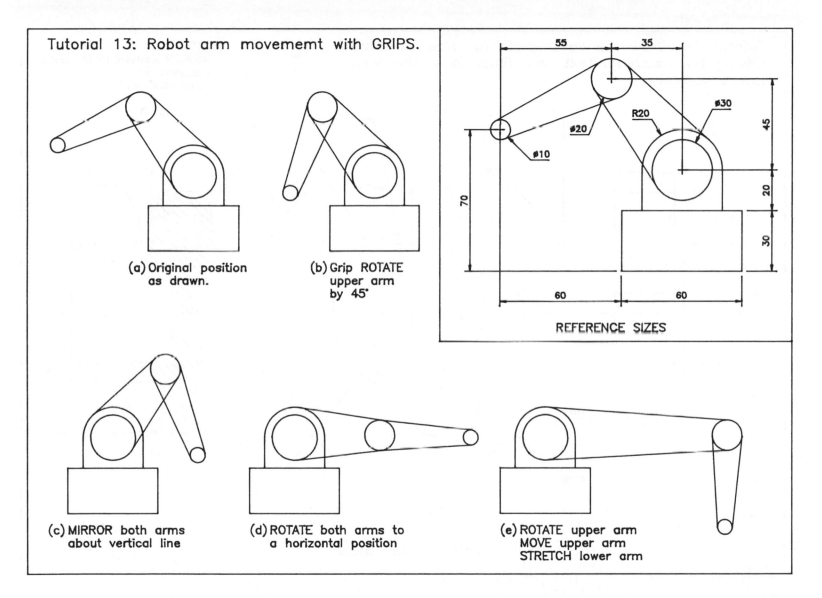

Tutorial 13: Robot arm movememt with GRIPS.

(a) Original position as drawn.

(b) Grip ROTATE upper arm by 45°

REFERENCE SIZES

(c) MIRROR both arms about vertical line

(d) ROTATE both arms to a horizontal position

(e) ROTATE upper arm MOVE upper arm STRETCH lower arm

Tutorial 14: Draw the cover plate full size as shown, adding the hatching, text and dimensions. Use your layers correctly.

HINTS
1.MIRROR command is useful.
2.Hatching is:
   User—defined
   Angle: 45
   Spacing: 3

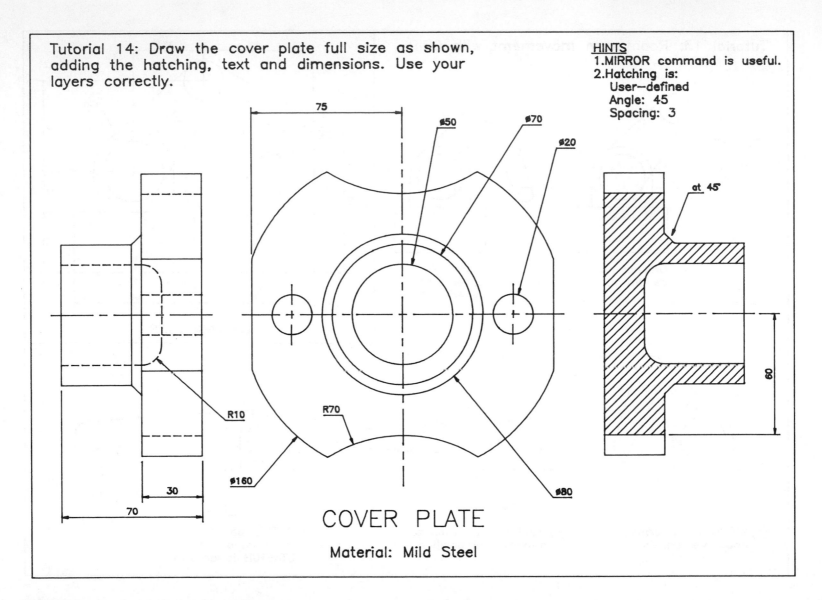

COVER PLATE

Material: Mild Steel

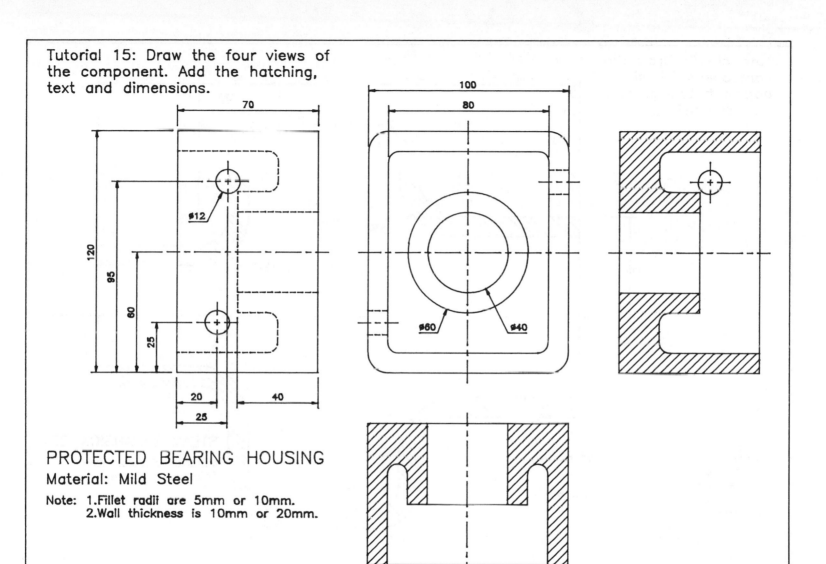

Tutorial 15: Draw the four views of the component. Add the hatching, text and dimensions.

PROTECTED BEARING HOUSING

Material: Mild Steel

Note: 1.Fillet radii are 5mm or 10mm.
2.Wall thickness is 10mm or 20mm.

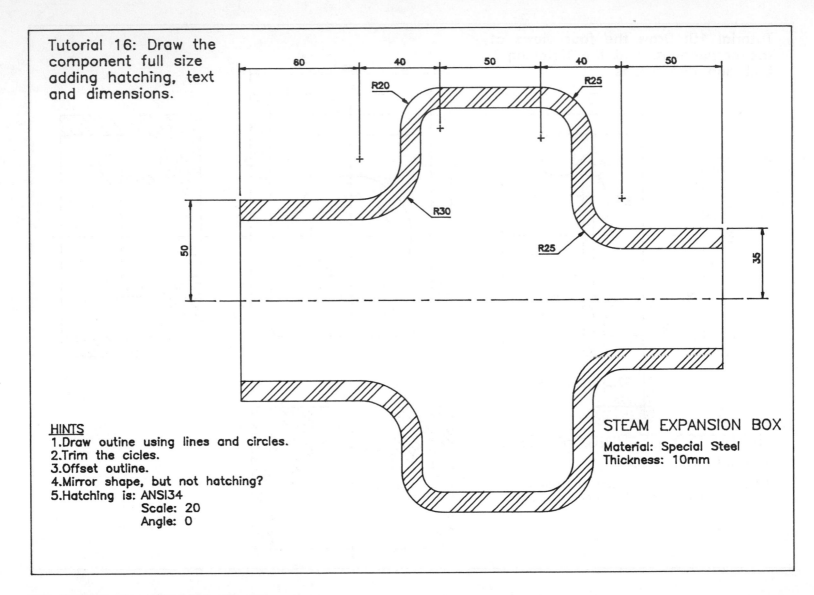

Tutorial 16: Draw the component full size adding hatching, text and dimensions.

R20

R25

R30

R25

60 40 50 40 50

50

35

STEAM EXPANSION BOX

Material: Special Steel
Thickness: 10mm

HINTS
1.Draw outine using lines and circles.
2.Trim the cicles.
3.Offset outline.
4.Mirror shape, but not hatching?
5.Hatching is: ANSI34
              Scale: 20
              Angle: 0

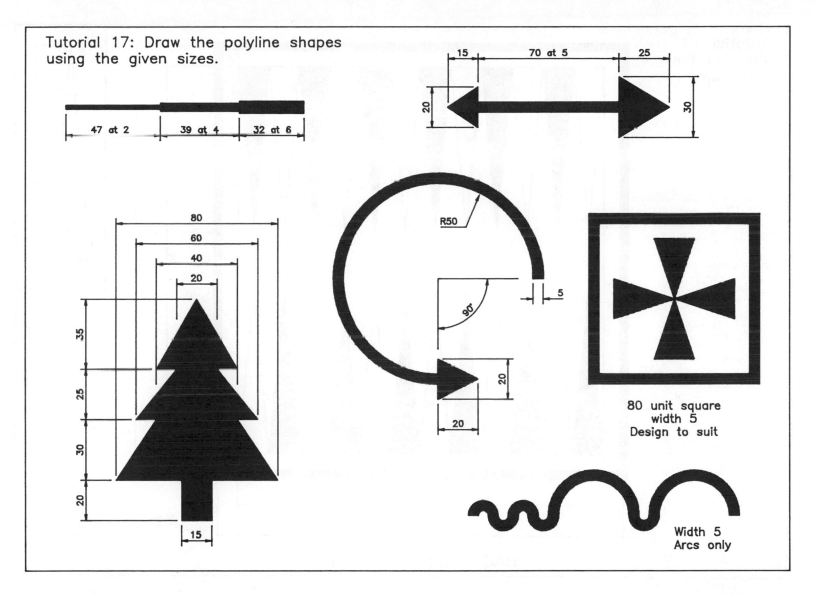

Tutorial 17: Draw the polyline shapes using the given sizes.

47 at 2 39 at 4 32 at 6

15 70 at 5 25
20 30

80
60
40
20
35
25
30
20
15

R50
90°
5
20
20

80 unit square
width 5
Design to suit

Width 5
Arcs only

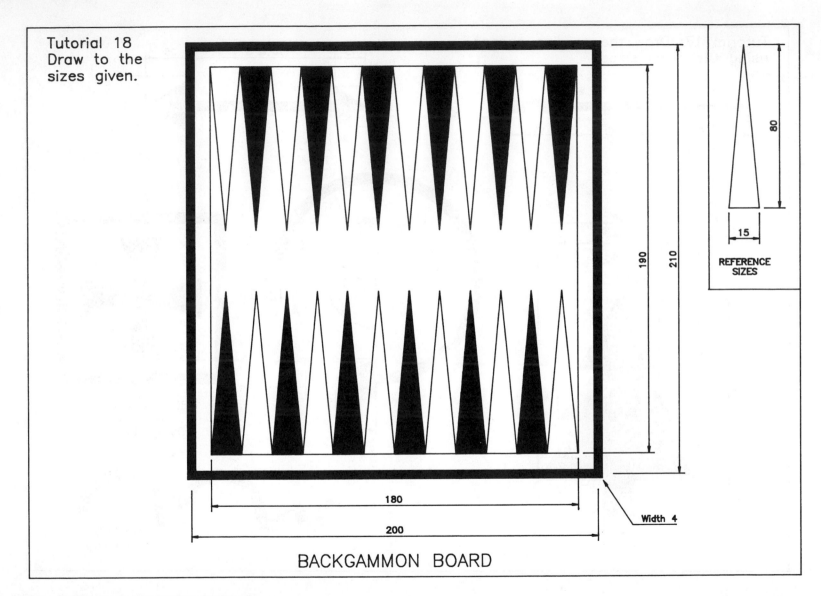

Tutorial 18
Draw to the
sizes given.

REFERENCE SIZES

80

15

190

210

180

200

Width 4

BACKGAMMON BOARD

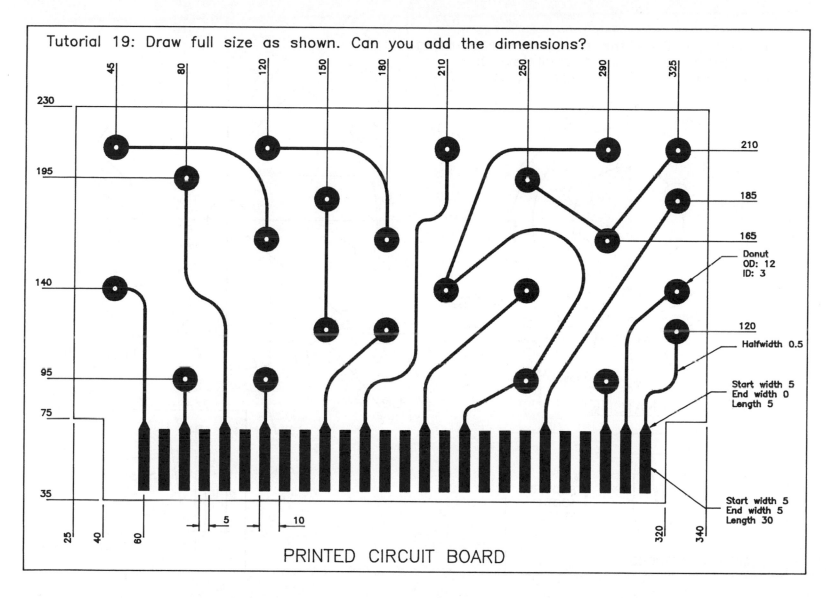

Tutorial 19: Draw full size as shown. Can you add the dimensions?

PRINTED CIRCUIT BOARD

Tutorial 20: Draw the two components using the ARRAY command. Add all text and dimensions.

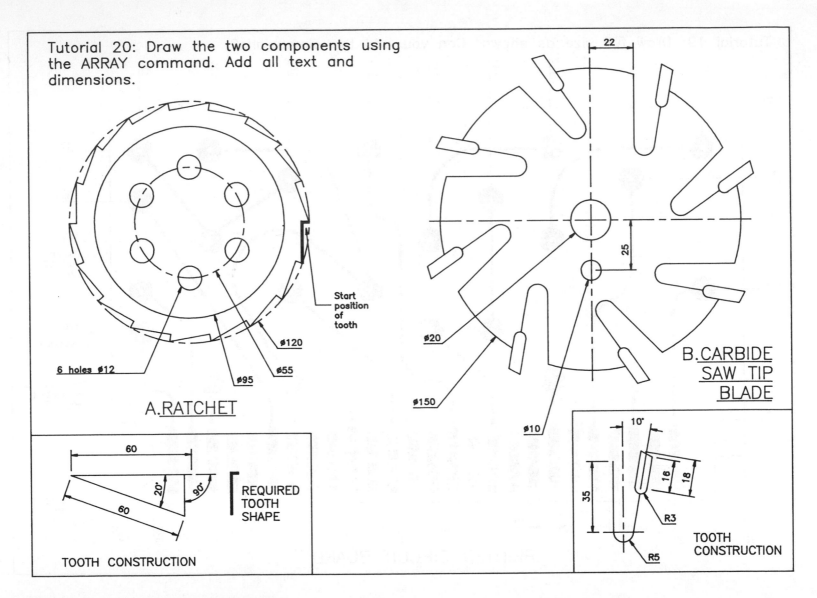

Start position of tooth

6 holes ⌀12

⌀120

⌀55

⌀95

A.RATCHET

B.CARBIDE SAW TIP BLADE

⌀20

⌀150

⌀10

25

22

60

20°

90°

60

REQUIRED TOOTH SHAPE

TOOTH CONSTRUCTION

10°

35

16

18

R3

R5

TOOTH CONSTRUCTION

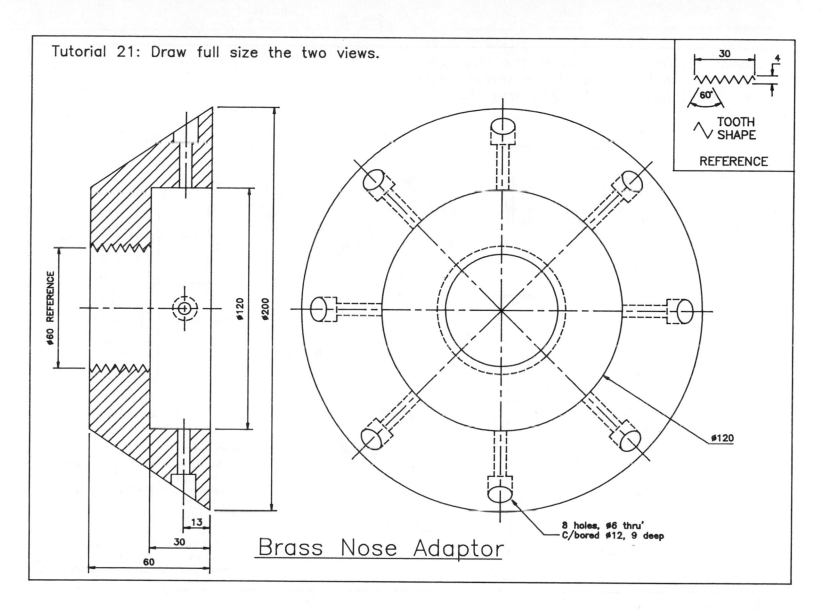

Tutorial 21: Draw full size the two views.

30

4

60°

TOOTH
SHAPE

REFERENCE

∅60 REFERENCE

∅120

∅200

13

30

60

∅120

8 holes, ∅6 thru'
C/bored ∅12, 9 deep

Brass Nose Adaptor

Tutorial 22: Draw the bulb to the sizes given.
Copy it to another part of the screen, then
scale the copied bulb by 0.5, Array to suit.

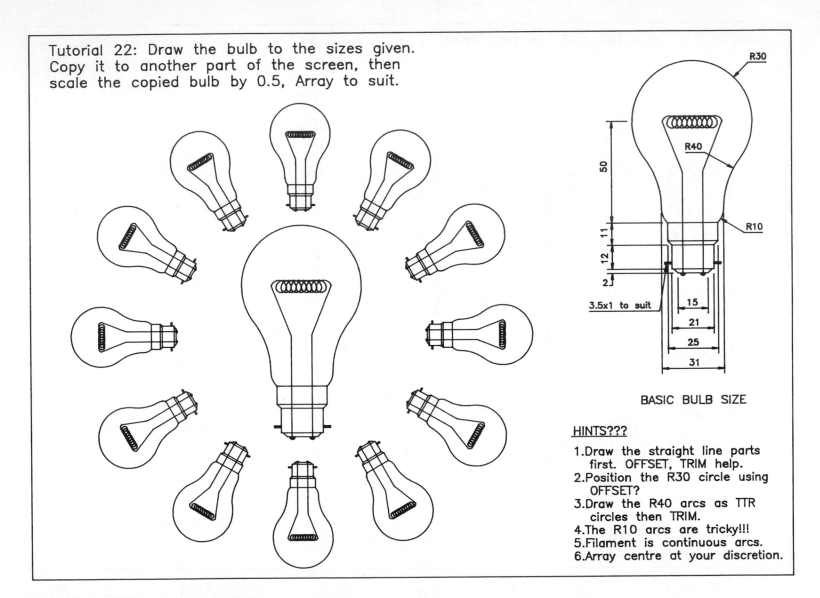

BASIC BULB SIZE

HINTS???

1. Draw the straight line parts
   first. OFFSET, TRIM help.
2. Position the R30 circle using
   OFFSET?
3. Draw the R40 arcs as TTR
   circles then TRIM.
4. The R10 arcs are tricky!!!
5. Filament is continuous arcs.
6. Array centre at your discretion.

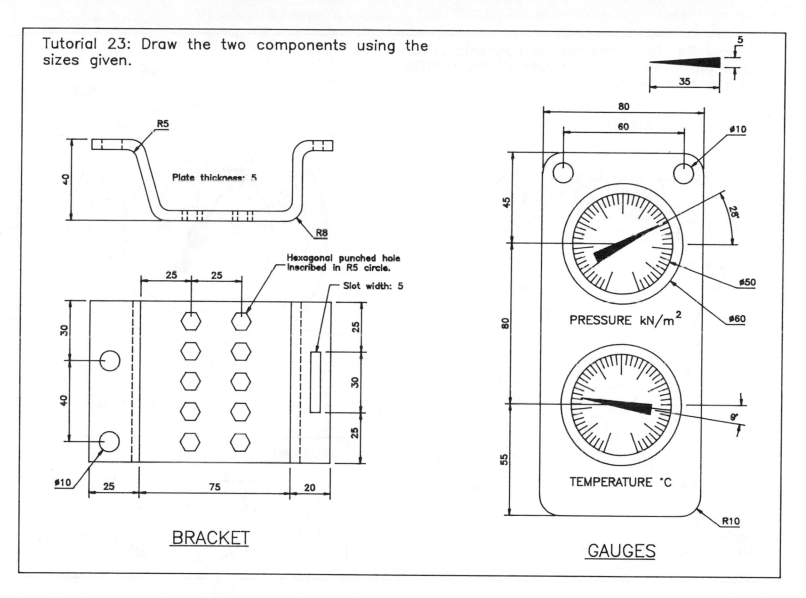

Tutorial 23: Draw the two components using the sizes given.

R5

Plate thickness: 5

40

R8

Hexagonal punched hole
inscribed in R5 circle.

Slot width: 5

25   25

30

40

25

30

25

ⵁ10

25   75   20

BRACKET

5

35

80

60

ⵁ10

45

28°

ⵁ50

80

ⵁ60

PRESSURE kN/m²

9°

55

TEMPERATURE °C

R10

GAUGES

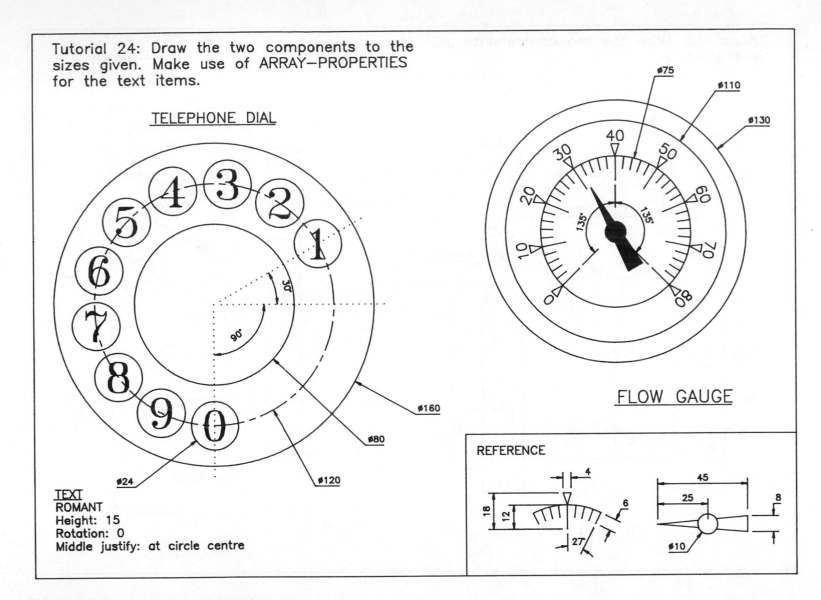

Tutorial 24: Draw the two components to the sizes given. Make use of ARRAY–PROPERTIES for the text items.

TELEPHONE DIAL

ø160

ø80

ø120

ø24

30°

90°

TEXT
ROMANT
Height: 15
Rotation: 0
Middle justify: at circle centre

FLOW GAUGE

ø75
ø110
ø130

135°   135°

REFERENCE

4
18   12
27

45
25
6
8
ø10

Tutorial 25: Draw the dart board with
the information given.

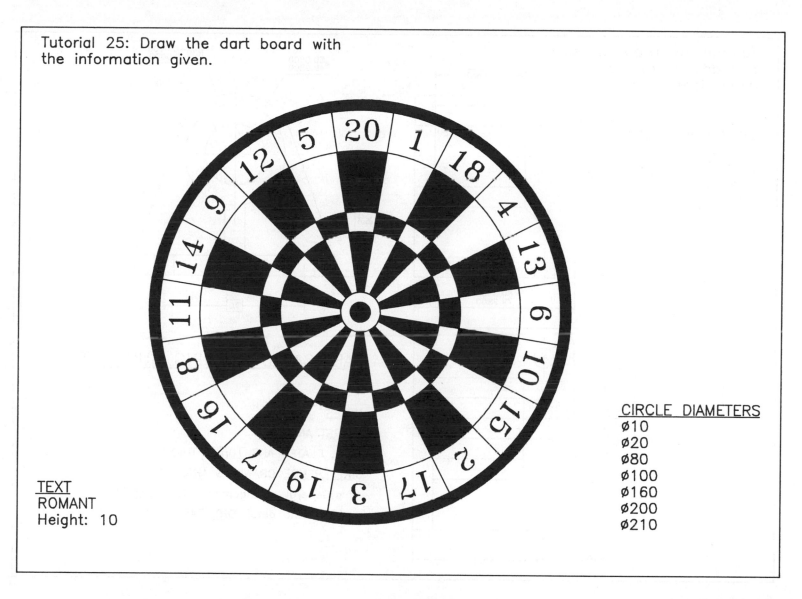

TEXT
ROMANT
Height: 10

CIRCLE DIAMETERS
ø10
ø20
ø80
ø100
ø160
ø200
ø210

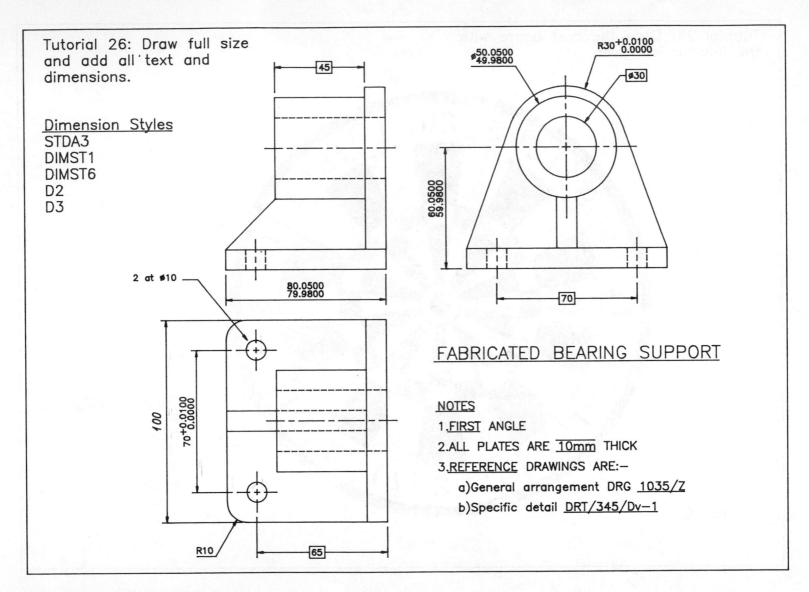

Tutorial 26: Draw full size and add all text and dimensions.

Dimension Styles
STDA3
DIMST1
DIMST6
D2
D3

45

Ø50.0500
49.9800

R30 +0.0100
0.0000

Ø30

60.0500
59.9800

70

80.0500
79.9800

2 at Ø10

100

70 +0.0100
0.0000

R10

65

FABRICATED BEARING SUPPORT

NOTES
1.FIRST ANGLE
2.ALL PLATES ARE 10mm THICK
3.REFERENCE DRAWINGS ARE:—
   a)General arrangement DRG 1035/Z
   b)Specific detail DRT/345/Dv—1

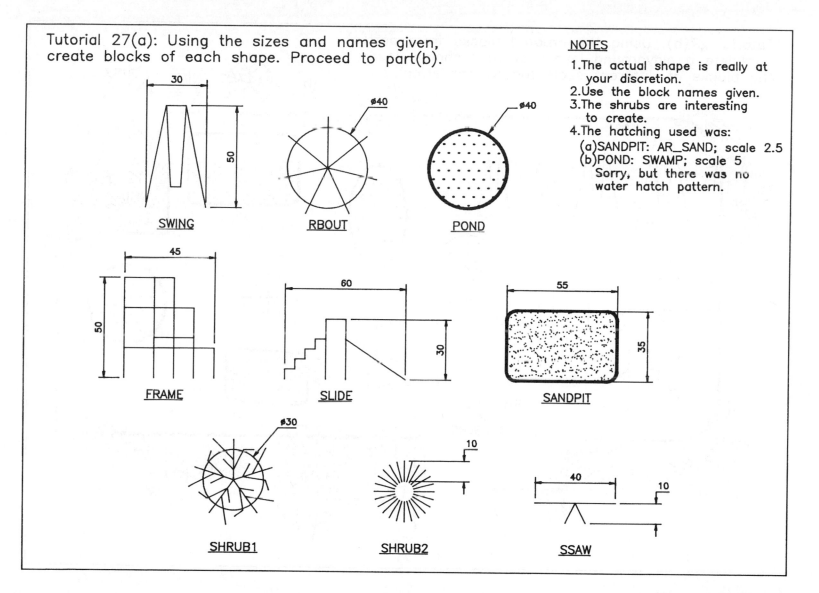

Tutorial 27(a): Using the sizes and names given, create blocks of each shape. Proceed to part(b).

Proceed to part(b).

SWING

RBOUT Ø40

POND Ø40

FRAME

SLIDE

SANDPIT

SHRUB1 Ø30

SHRUB2

SSAW

NOTES
1. The actual shape is really at your discretion.
2. Use the block names given.
3. The shrubs are interesting to create.
4. The hatching used was:
   (a) SANDPIT: AR_SAND; scale 2.5
   (b) POND: SWAMP; scale 5
   Sorry, but there was no water hatch pattern.

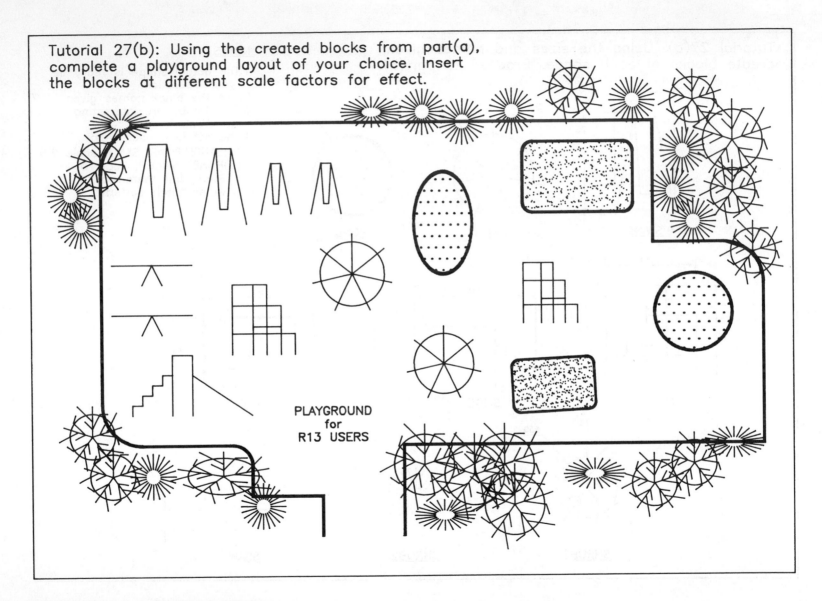

Tutorial 27(b): Using the created blocks from part(a), complete a playground layout of your choice. Insert the blocks at different scale factors for effect.

PLAYGROUND
for
R13 USERS

Index

Absolute coordinates 27, 29, 32
acadfull.mnu 5
acadisc.dwg 42, 44
Angle convention 31
Angular rectangular array 181
Applying tolerances 200
Associative dimensions 75
Associative hatching 119, 128
ATTDIA 242
Attribute block 236
Automatic dimensions 78

Blips 14, 63
Blocks 155, 218, 242
Block options 223

Cascade menu 9
Colour 61
Command 9
Command area 4, 8
Continuous arcs 45
Coordinate icon 4, 8
Coordinate system 30
Created text styles 171
Current layer 59, 63
Cursor 4, 8

Default 9
Dialogue boxes 10
    Aerial View 117
    Attribute Definition 236
    Boundary Hatch 121
    Change Properties 187
    Check Spelling 177

Create New Drawing 42
Dimension Annotation 84
Dimension Format 83
Dimension Geometry 83
Dimension Styles 82
Direction Control 26
Drawing Aids 10
Edit Text 71
Edit MText 175
Element Properties 216
Geometric Tolerances 201
Grips 102
Insert 226
Layer Control 59, 63
Load/Reload Linetypes 61
Modify Line 187
Multiline Styles 216
Object Grouping 209
Object Selection Filters 211
Point Style 136
Replace File 35
Running Object Snap 41
Save Changes 22
Save Drawing As 23
Select File 23, 27
Select Linetype 60
Select Menu File 5
Symbol 199
Toolbar 243
Units Control 26
Diameter families 195
Dimension families 192
Dimension styles 82, 191, 192
Dimension variables 194

DIMTVP 194
Distance 161
Docked toolbars 11, 12
Drawing files 13
Drawing in inches 202
Dynamic text 171

Edit vertex 148
Editing multilines 217
Entities 9, 42
Escape (ESC) 9
Exploding a block 220

Filter list 209, 211, 212
Floating toolbars 11, 12
Flyout menus 12
Frozen layers 64
Function keys 13

Geometric tolerancing 199
Global blocks 228
Graphics screen 4, 11, 12, 13
Grid 20, 21
Grip box 4, 9
GRIPS 25, 29
Groups 207

Hardware requirements 2
Hatch editing 131
Hatch scale factor 133
Hatch style 123
Hatching 1, 59

Icon 9, 26

Icons
   2D solid 136
   .X 107
   .YZ 107
   Aerial view 116
   Add 87
   Align 158
   Aligned dimension 77
   Angular dimension 77
   Arc, Start, End, Radius 45
   Arc, continuous 46
   Break 155
   Calculator 167
   Chamfer 51
   Circle, 3 point 35
   Circle, Cen, Rad 33
   Circle, Tan Tan Rad 38
   Colour 65
   Construction line 109
   Continuous dimension 77
   Copy 87
   Crossing 87
   Crossing polygon 19
   Define attribute 234
   Dimension style 195
   Divide 153
   Donut 48
   Dynamic text 69
   Edit polyline 140
   Edit spline 151
   Ellipse 46
   Ellipse arc 46
   Enter attribute 239
   Erase 15
   Explode 221
   Extend 58
   Fence 17
   Fillet 49

   Filter 211
   Hatch 119
   Home dimension 80, 160
   Insert 220
   Layer 65
   Lengthen 156
   Line 14, 27
   Linear dimension 78
   Linetype 68
   List 164
   Measure 153
   Mirror 95
   Move 90
   Multiline 213
   Multiple insert 228
   New 42
   Node 134
   None 41
   Object group 207, 209
   Offset 53
   Open 37
   Pan point 113
   Polar array 179
   Point 134
   Polygon 134
   Polyline 138
   Previous 96
   Properties 185
   Radius dimension 77
   Ray line 111
   Rectangle 29
   Rectangular array 179
   Redraw 14
   Remove 93
   Rotate 93
   Running object snap 41
   Save 42
   Scale 93

   Snap points 40
   Spellcheck 175
   Spline 144
   Stretch 160
   Text 69
   Tolerance 200
   Trim 55
   Undo 32
   Window 15, 90
   Window polygon 93
   X datum 86
   Y datum 86
   Zoom 113
Inserting blocks 218
Inserting wblocks 230
Installation 2
Interoperability 1
ISOCP.SHX 169

Large scale drawings 202
Layer 0 (zero) 226
Layer status 64, 65, 66
Limits 20, 111
Linetype scale 61
Linetypes 59, 60
Locate point 161
Locked layers 64
LTSCALE 63, 66

Measure 225
Menu 9
MENU 5
Menu bar 4, 5
MIRRTEXT 95, 98
MTEXT 173
Multiline elements 213
Multiple insert 225

NURBS 142

Object filter 209
Object properties toolbar 4, 7, 8, 65
Object snap 33, 37, 42
Oops 15
Ortho 20, 21
OSNAP pick points 41

Paragraph text 169, 173, 176, 177
PDMODE 137
PDSIZE 137
Pick arrow 5
Pickbox 19, 25
PICKADD 9
PICKFIRST 9
Polar array 179, 181
Polar coordinates 27, 30, 32
Polyline: return versus close 142
Polygon editing 150
Preferences 12, 25
Properties 185, 187
Prototype drawing 25, 42, 44
Purging layers 65

qsave 42

Rectangular array 179
Redraw 19
Regen 46
Renaming layers 65
Relative coordinates 27, 29, 32
Rendering 1
Rubberband 14

Screen menu 12
Scroll bars 8
Selection set 17
Set Ltype 61
Small entity dimensions 86
Small scale drawing 204
Snap 20, 21, 29
Snap angle 181
Software requirements 2
Solid fill 48
Solid modelling 1
Spellcheck 175
Spline curve 142
Spline editing 151
Standard sheet 25, 63, 82
Standard toolbar 4, 7
Status line 8

Text control codes 173
Text fonts 169, 171
Text justification 71
Text screen 165, 166, 168
Text style 74, 169, 171
Text with hatching 131
Title bar 4, 5
Toggle 13, 20, 21, 37, 46
Tolerance frames 199
Tolerances 195
Toolbars 11, 26
    Customised 243
    Object snap 38
    Object properties 8
    Standard 7
Tools 26, 243
Transparency 90
True ellipses 46
TTR 35

Units 25
Usability 1

Wblocks 223, 228, 230, 233, 242